ARCHAEOLOGY, HERITAGE, AND REACTIONARY POPULISM

Cultural Heritage Studies

UNIVERSITY PRESS OF FLORIDA

Florida A&M University, Tallahassee
Florida Atlantic University, Boca Raton
Florida Gulf Coast University, Ft. Myers
Florida International University, Miami
Florida State University, Tallahassee
New College of Florida, Sarasota
University of Central Florida, Orlando
University of Florida, Gainesville
University of North Florida, Jacksonville
University of South Florida, Tampa
University of West Florida, Pensacola

Archaeology, Heritage, and Reactionary Populism

Edited by Randall H. McGuire
and Alfredo González-Ruibal

Series Foreword by Katherine Hayes

Foreword by Felipe Criado-Boado

UNIVERSITY PRESS OF FLORIDA

Gainesville/Tallahassee/Tampa/Boca Raton
Pensacola/Orlando/Miami/Jacksonville/Ft. Myers/Sarasota

This book will be made open access within three years of publication thanks to Path to Open, a program developed in partnership between JSTOR, the American Council of Learned Societies (ACLS), University of Michigan Press, and The University of North Carolina Press to bring about equitable access and impact for the entire scholarly community, including authors, researchers, libraries, and university presses around the world. Learn more at https://about.jstor.org/path-to-open/

Cover: Archaeological excavation of a shanty town of the 1950s–1970s in Madrid. The project, focusing on working-class people, offers a counternarrative to imperialist, reactionary accounts of the Spanish past. Courtesy of Enrique Flores.

30 29 28 27 26 25   6 5 4 3 2 1

https://doi.org/10.5744/9780813079332

Library of Congress Cataloging-in-Publication Data
Names: Hayes, Katherine, author of series foreword. | Criado Boado, Felipe, author of foreword. | McGuire, Randall H., editor. | González Ruibal, Alfredo, editor.
Title: Archaeology, heritage, and reactionary populism / edited by Randall H. McGuire and Alfredo González-Ruibal ; series foreword by Katherine Hayes ; foreword by Felipe Criado-Boado.
Description: 1. | Gainesville : University Press of Florida, 2025. | Series: Cultural heritage studies | Includes bibliographical references and index.
Identifiers: LCCN 2024047965 (print) | LCCN 2024047966 (ebook) | ISBN 9780813079332 (cloth) | ISBN 9780813080994 (paperback) | ISBN 9780813074016 (pdf) | ISBN 9780813073767 (ebook)
Subjects: LCSH: Populism—United States—History. | Social movements—United States—History. | United States—Politics and government. | BISAC: SOCIAL SCIENCE / Archaeology | SOCIAL SCIENCE / Anthropology / Cultural & Social
Classification: LCC E661 .A698 2025 (print) | LCC E661 (ebook) | DDC 973—dc23/eng/20250113
LC record available at https://lccn.loc.gov/2024047965
LC ebook record available at https://lccn.loc.gov/2024047966

The University Press of Florida is the scholarly publishing agency for the State University System of Florida, comprising Florida A&M University, Florida Atlantic University, Florida Gulf Coast University, Florida International University, Florida State University, New College of Florida, University of Central Florida, University of Florida, University of North Florida, University of South Florida, and University of West Florida.

University Press of Florida
2046 NE Waldo Road
Suite 2100
Gainesville, FL 32609
http://upress.ufl.edu

GPSR EU Authorized Representative: Mare Nostrum Group B.V., Mauritskade 21D, 1091 GC Amsterdam, The Netherlands, gpsr@mare-nostrum.co.uk

CONTENTS

FIGURES

SERIES FOREWORD

In an election year it is almost a cliché to say that we must pay closer attention to the voices of "the people." It is unfortunately, and dangerously, also a common occurrence to see such attention evaporate once the election is over. This has parallels in how community or public archaeology is frequently pursued: researchers' commitments to communities evaporate upon conclusion of a project. In both the political and archaeological versions of this story, it is also the case that communities had needs, concerns, and historical narratives long before and long after the campaigns and projects. As scholars and professionals whose work focuses on historical narratives large and small, we must take note of the fact that, as Alfredo González-Ruibal notes, "nonacademic visions of the past are often more popular and can have more political influence and wider outreach than scholarly research." In the hands of reactionary populists, the consequences can be deadly.

The editors and authors in this volume want us to approach history and heritage more globally and inclusively while also remaining embedded in the local. If that sounds too difficult, perhaps instead think of it as practicing the craft of archaeology (per Randall McGuire) *relationally*. That is, be situated in a place but also understand how *this place* has reverberations and connections more broadly and at multiple scales. The authors and editors call for engaging with multiple audiences but without claims to neutrality or objectivity. Moreover, this call to engage with and especially to *speak back to* reactionary populism—which relies heavily on the appropriation of historical narratives—is our responsibility. The chapters within this volume document in ugly detail the interaction and impacts of reactionary populism framed as the will of "the people" with respect to heritage sites and archaeological remains and the people left out of that possessive claim. The case studies represent a global perspective and are inclusive of many different professional relations, from contract cultural resource management and tribal co-management to academic practice, commemorative monuments and heritage site interpretation, and a variety of community engagement or participatory projects. Speaking back can and must happen in all these fields.

How are we to speak back? The authors of these case studies provide remarkable, inspiring examples that arise from situating themselves in their works and moving pragmatically from scholarly critique to political and narrative intervention. For some, this means turning the rhetoric of reactionary populism onto itself and countering with a progressive populism. For others, the key is to use their multiple standpoints arising from intersectional identities, cracking the homogenous edifice of "the people." Most starkly, Lindsay Martel Montgomery encourages acting as a "bad settler," recognizing the aims of settler society and actively working to undermine them through promotion of Indigenous sovereignty. Above all, they *stay*—as long as needed to build relations, and then longer, to nurture them and see them shift and change over time. The crises of politics and the insatiable push to produce or publish from institutions must be refused in order to effectively intervene. The staying does come at a cost, so I would humbly suggest that our interventions should also target the structures and institutions that currently do not value or support this critical work, this slow archaeology and slow heritage.

I am enthusiastic about this volume because it resonates with me, and I am sure many others in the fields of archaeology and heritage management, as we have all had that experience. You know, the one where you get a question or comment at a public event revealing a view of the world you absolutely do not share. Do you dismiss it, or do you engage with it? Which action risks more harm? Which has the potential for genuine dialogue? Maybe the questioner is a family member, or a community member, or a reporter. Increasingly in the academic realm—maybe they are a donor. The answer you give or the dialogue you have may make a difference—maybe not with the person you are speaking to but to someone who is listening. Either way, the authors in this volume want you to know that what you say, and that you say it, matters rather a lot.

Katherine Hayes, Series Editor

FOREWORD

This book makes a strong appeal for a tough engagement of archaeology in politics. Certainly, some would dispute this appeal. Some believe that archaeology has nothing to do with politics, and vice versa. Others, perhaps even more wide-eyed than the former, believe that the political should be confined just within the limits of our citizenship, without transgressing into our professional or scientific actions. I imagine that the authors of this book would reject both of these positions. And I think that our authors are right. We can only answer the question "for whom is archaeology?" from a political perspective. Any question that is directed at finding out the object of something, "for whom," is political as it necessarily implies social relationships, practical concerns, meeting needs and reconciling interests.

However, let's be honest, archaeology has never been political.

It is a commonplace that humanity faces great challenges: global climate change; overcoming Classical economics once and for all; the transforming geopolitical chessboard (starting with the emergence of BRICS, it continues with the rise of reactionary populism and currently the conflicts in Ukraine, Gaza, and the Gulf of Aden); the migratory challenge, and the explosion of artificial intelligence.

We have convinced ourselves that these challenges require a global transformation that is necessarily green, energetic, political, and digital. Personally, I believe that instead we should be concerned by the root of these challenges: the equivalence of state and nation; nationalism in all of its forms (central or peripheral); the hegemony of neoliberalism, constructed over the past 40 years; the decommissioning of social democracy, reducing it to progressive neoliberalism (Butler, 2009); the temptation of anarcho-liberalism; the displacement of the forces of the Left, and particularly progressive populism; and, above all, the persistence of macho-patriarchal structures.

Still, these are not even the biggest issues because we must deal with ontologies and structures prior to them. Our greatest problem is identity—specifically, individual identity. It is rooted in the hegemony of a model of subjectivity, expressed through the exclusive preeminence of the individual agent and reconstructed in identity politics. Identity politics—created to guarantee individual security, freedom of opinion, and the rights of the individual—is used in a twisted way to attack positions that go against elite interests. Elites use the systems that guarantee these rights to confront and to co-opt progressive movements that would challenge elite privilege.

A possible hypothesis is that the liberal West is ceasing to be democratic. It has reduced democracy to a set of formal rules, including basic rights and voting. At the same time, it has forgotten responsibilities and co-responsibilities (to other people, to other living things, and to the Earth) that would be imposed by a true democratic ethos. As much as we wish freedom and well-being for ourselves, we should also wish the same for our neighbors and fellow human beings. Without this, there is no freedom and well-being for humanity.

The collective communitarianism and the ontological and logical preeminence of a relational identity (Hernando 2017) over individual identity have been forgotten. We need a new model of subjectivity. A new way of being (people) in society. The model we inherited is, along with the nation-state and patriarchy, both the product and the means that shaped the bourgeois revolution and modern capitalism.

Aside from the cases when the archaeological record has been manipulated by totalitarian ideologies, archaeology as a discipline has never been political. To create a political archaeology, we must do more than hang theories as political window dressing. We must be political people. Only then will we do political archaeology.

Why should we be political people doing a political archaeology? The main battle ahead of us confronts the paradigms of subjectivity and consciousness. Archaeology and heritage, through materiality and robust methods, are unique specialties that show history to have been different over its long course and that each society had different subjectivities. This revelation is archaeology's greatest mission. To accomplish it, we must overcome the cliché and imagine the discipline as something more than discoveries and archaeological sciences.

Issues of *Nature* and *Science* in January 2024 represented archaeology dramatically differently on their covers. *Science* fell for the magic of discovery. Its headline, "Lost City," referred to a lidar survey that identified large structures in the Amazon. *Nature,* under the headline "Steppe Change," preferred the magic of aDNA, reporting on the genetic risks of multiple sclerosis, which, according to archaeogenetics, are related to the Eurasian steppe migrations. These two covers clearly illustrate the current relevance of archaeology in sciences and society. Nevertheless, neither of these covers proclaim the great headline that archaeology deserves: "150 years of archaeological research proves that another world IS possible because other worlds have existed before." I do not believe a greater political objective exists.

We introduced the concept of reactionary populism to archaeology in a paper (González-Ruibal et al., 2018) expressing our concern after the 2016 earthquake that was Trump's victory, Brexit, and related events in other countries (Poland, Hungary, etc.). Eight years later it remains necessary to discuss heritage, archaeology, and reactionary populism. This should be done as the book's contributors have done: with empirical research, intellectual ambition, and a manifest political commitment. Good research is the best way to trump reactionary populism's narrative. Thanks to its editors for this!

Felipe Criado-Boado

References Cited

Butler, J. 2009. *Frames of War: When Is Life Grievable?* Verso. London.

González-Ruibal, A., P. A. González, and F. Criado-Boado. 2018. Against Reactionary Populism: Towards a New Public Archaeology. *Antiquity* 92(362): 507–515.

Hernando, A. 2017. *The Fantasy of Individuality: On the Sociohistorical Construction of the Modern Subject.* Springer. Berlin.

ACKNOWLEDGMENTS

The workshop upon which this book is based was funded by the Wenner-Gren Foundation. We are thankful to the foundation for its support and flexibility throughout the process. The Wenner-Gren Foundation also provided funding to help publish the paperback edition of this volume. Most especially we would thank Laurie Obbink and Danilyn Rutherford. The workshop in Santiago de Compostela benefited from the hospitality, logistics, and catering provided by the Institute of Heritage Sciences of the Spanish National Research Council, where it was celebrated. Thanks are due to its director, Felipe Criado-Boado, who also kindly agreed to write the foreword, and to Jadranka Verdonkschot for translating the foreword. During the celebration of the seminar, a trip to Cereixa (Lugo) allowed the group to have firsthand experience of a long-running community archaeology project coordinated by one of the participants, Xurxo Ayán Vila. We thank Xurxo and his uncle, Jesús Vila Regueira, for generously sharing their knowledge, food, and drink with us. Of course, neither the workshop nor the book would have existed without the colleagues who agreed to participate, share their experiences and insights, and comment on each other's work. We thank them for this and for being always attentive to our requests during the process of putting together the volume. Working with them has been an enriching experience. Special thanks to Claudia Theune, who did not participate in the workshop but agreed to write a thoughtful conclusion for the volume. Finally, we would like to thank Mary Puckett, at the University Press of Florida, for supporting this project and guiding it through completion.

1

Archaeology and the Challenge of Populism

ALFREDO GONZÁLEZ-RUIBAL AND RANDALL H. MCGUIRE

In 1978, Mexican social archaeologists Rebeca Panameño and Enrique Na-
ldo asked "¿arqueología para quien"? (archaeology for whom?) For many archaeologists this question had a simple answer: scholars created archaeological knowledge to advance science. Social archaeologists, however, sought to
build multivocal scholarship that would do political work for the "people"
by producing usable heritages that advanced the interests of communities.
Forty years later the idea that archaeologists should serve communities has
become widely accepted with a plethora of community projects in archaeology. Scholars have, however, insufficiently addressed the questions: "What is
a 'community'?" "Who are the 'people'?" (but see Waterton and Smith 2010).
Despite thoughtful reflections on public archaeology and heritage during
the last three decades, most projects in practice work with an unproblema-
tized notion of community, as if they were inherently positive and relatively
trouble-free. Under the present circumstances, this is no longer a viable option. Since the turn of the twenty-first century, a wave of reactionary populism has washed over the world. In this transformed scenario, an archaeology
collaborating with communities may not necessarily serve the liberating goals
of social archaeology. We fear that the communities that we work with have
or will embrace a populism that compromises the liberal ideals of a social
archaeology (McGuire: Chapter 6). In a new century, we therefore ask again:
"Archaeology for whom?"

We asked this question in a Wenner-Gren sponsored workshop, and this
volume develops our answers to it. Our workshop brought together 12 archaeologists from around the world, including advocates and critics of
community-based research and scholars from Spain, the United States, Canada, the United Kingdom, Colombia, Ireland, Portugal, and Germany. All
expressed the desire to produce an archaeology that makes a difference in
the world. This common goal formed the basis for an inclusive but critical

conversation that we hope will have a transformative effect on modern archaeology.

The "Archaeology for Whom?" workshop fostered a conversation about community and reactionary populism in archaeology. We discussed how archaeologists have deployed the concept of community and to what work they have harnessed it in different contexts. We identified the challenges of reactionary populism and asked if a social archaeology based in community collaboration can achieve liberating goals in the face of these challenges. How can the universal aspirations of critical political thinking be combined with the specific expectations and needs of communities? The workshop has marked out new and alternative directions for future politically engaged research in social archaeology. These directions include rethinking context, confronting new ethical dilemmas, and redefining political engagement beyond the local community.

Archaeology

The scholars writing in this book use a very broad concept of archaeology following Shanks and McGuire's (1996) definition of archaeology as a craft. The craft of archaeology is a mode of cultural production that investigates the relationship of the material world to the most diverse realms of human life. Archaeologists use their craft to understand how the material world (artifacts, features, ecofacts, landscapes, etc.) interact with human actions, emotions, consciousness, and relations to make and remake culture and society from ancient times to the modern world. This craft leads to multiple archaeologies, diverse archaeological products, and varied relationships with communities. The chapters in this book reflect this multiplicity of products, with case studies from prehistory, history, and the contemporary.

Populism

Defining populism is not easy, and political scientists themselves disagree strongly on how to characterize it (Pappas 2016). This is not surprising because, as we will see, populism means many different things—often diametrically opposed—and in the same country this phenomenon may have meant radically different things in different moments (like nineteenth-century US populism and Trumpism). We can, however, minimally define populism as the idea that political sovereignty belongs to and should be exercised by "the people," who are considered to be homogeneous, morally virtuous, and antagonistic against corrupt elites and dangerous "others" (Mudde 2004; Pappas 2016). For its very definition, populism is strongly opposed to liberal or constitutional democracy, which it claims to misrepresent the people's will. But populism is a global phenomenon, so trying to produce more detailed definitions may leave out some national movements that could be otherwise be characterized as populist.

Populism is not a new phenomenon. Indeed, historians and political scientists trace current populist politics to the late nineteenth century in the United States (Eatwell and Goodwin 2018; Finchelstein 2019), and forms of populism—as a critique of the elites and an appeal to the virtuous people—have existed in the West at least from fifth century BC classical Greek democracy. Despite these precedents, many scholars argue that contemporary populism has a more recent and a more specific origin. According to Federico Finchelstein (2019), it is the product of the defeat of fascism during the Second World War and the ideological realignment of the fascist base. Postwar populism rejected violence as a means of doing politics, dictatorship as a legitimate political regime, and biological racism as a way of hierarchizing human beings, and contemporary populism accepted the democratic game—indeed, it often claimed that it is the true democracy that seeks the authentic representation of people's aspirations (Mudde 2004: 560). In that, postwar populism can be distinguished from radical right-wing movements, such as neo-Nazis, who do not reject political violence or dictatorship.

Populists, however, did adopt many of the ideas and values that had characterized fascism, including charismatic leadership; ultranationalism; illiberalism; praise of the armed forces; a restricted notion of citizenship; xenophobia; visceral anticommunism; male chauvinism; a patriarchal, heteronormative notion of the family; and the idea that they—native (in Europe or India), white (in the West), Christian, heterosexual, etc.—incarnate the will of the people. Like in classical fascism, scapegoating plays an important role, today with immigrants or the LGTBQ "lobby" replacing the Jews, as does the critique of elites.

Offering a more moderate identity and parting ways with canonic fascist attitudes and symbols often helped populism grow substantially, as happened with the National Front in France (Paxton 2004: 175–187). Yet this moderation and embrace of democracy might be just apparent. After all, in few places have we been able to see a national populist government develop and mature. An exception is Hungary, and here the country is clearly on the path to a full-fledged authoritarian regime as the division of powers is severely undercut and basic freedoms are more and more restricted. It is only the absence of violent repression that separates the Hungarian regime from historical fascist regimes. Failed coup attempts, as seen in the United States, Germany, and Brazil in 2021 and 2022, also indicates that the insurrectional era is not totally over.

Populism cannot be immediately equated with extreme Right ideas or interpreted as an offshoot of right-wing extremism. There is also a left-wing populism, although it would be more adequate to talk of exclusionary and inclusionary populism, the former being an evolution of fascism and the latter a version of progressive or Marxist ideas but shaped by an antipolitical ethos. This inclusionary populism has a long history in Latin America. With origins in the Peronismo of the mid-twentieth century (which has its left-wing and right-wing versions), it has achieved success in different countries after the crisis of the neoliberal hegemony in the late 1990s, starting with Chavismo in Venezuela (since 1999) and followed by Ecuador, Bolivia, Argentina (Finchelstein 2019) and more recently Mexico under Andrés Manuel López-Obrador (since 2018). Inclusionary populism has been theorized by Argentinian thinker Ernesto Laclau (2005), whose work has had an influence in progressive populism elsewhere, most notably in Spain and Greece (Font et al. 2021). As with reactionary populism, progressive populisms also imply an essentialized vision of the (common) people it proclaims to incarnate, antagonist politics (the people versus elites), scapegoats (which can be Americans or media corporations), and a revision or even a manipulation of the past that is inevitably a simplification and a rereading of history in dichotomic terms: this is the case, for instance in Mexican president López-Obrador's appropriation of Indigenous heritage. The dangers of left-wing scapegoating have been pointed out by one of the main critics of Laclau and inclusionary populism, Slavoj Žižek (2008: 264–285). In global terms, however, it is reactionary, exclusionary, or national populism that poses the greatest threat to liberal democracy.

Populism is indeed global, but it is also diverse: there is not an essential populism, as there is not an essential fascism on which all others are based (Finchelstein 2019). This is important because the local avatars of reactionary populism can be very different and have to be addressed according to their differences. Donald Trump's America is not Viktor Orbán's Hungary or Marine Le Pen's France, even if many of their ideological principles coincide. We should not restrict national populism to Western countries, either. There are strong and successful populist movements in Africa and Asia—a good case in point being those led by Rodrigo Duterte in the Philippines and Narendra Modi in India.

The question of why populism is triumphing precisely now has elicited a long debate in the social sciences. Many reasons have been suggested, with economic ones figuring prominently (Rodrik 2018). The rise of neoliberalism in the 1980s and the progressive dismantling of the welfare state provided fuel. The financial crisis of 2008 also strengthened national populist feelings. It is probably not a coincidence that some populist movements achieved power in the decade after the beginning of the crisis, including Poland, Hungary, the United States, Brazil, and the United Kingdom. Yet economic causes per se did not determine the rise of populism (Berman 2021) and least of all its success. In some countries populists have won during times of economic prosperity (Mols and Jetten 2016) thanks to populist leaders crafting narratives of future disaster (in collaboration with the media). There are also social, political, and cultural reasons for the rise of populism: the fact that societies are more overtly heterogeneous and equal (in terms of race, culture, sex, and gender) is seen by many as a threat. There is also a perception of cultural crisis and national decline and humiliation that boost populist sentiment (Homolar and Löfflmann 2021). Not all populist grievances are figments of the imagination: the nation-state has indeed lost power in the face of multinational corporations and international institutions, which often pursue a neoliberal agenda (as is the case with the European Union). Some people see in national populism a way of countering globalization and returning power to the nation. In all cases, populism provides simple questions to complex problems.

Although populism is diverse and deeply rooted in local circumstances, it is also well connected. In the last decade it has become more transnational in part because social media strokes the flames. Modi and Trump shake hands, smiling, not because South Asian and United States populisms share cultural and historic substance but because across the world, Far-Right movements feed, support, and guide each other (Froio and Ganesh 2019). Thus, American political strategist and Trump supporter Steve Bannon has been supporting populist parties in France, Italy, and Spain. Bannon and allies have established a loose organization called "The Movement" that has partners in different European and Latin American countries. The idea is to create a right-wing international (de la Baume and Borrelli 2019). Interestingly, the concept of "movement" has been consistently used by totalitarian regimes in the 1920s–1940s (Arendt 1973). Interconnections of racism, xenophobia, antifeminism (Mamié et al. 2021), and (increasingly) transphobia link these movements. Globally, they embrace some combination of evangelical and conservative religion (Morieson 2021), racial nationalism (Berlet 2019), racialized feminism (Shepherd 2022), and in some cases ecofascism (Yakushko and De Francisco 2022), although climate negationism is more widespread. Obviously, we do not find these factors in all reactionary populist movements, but they occur in the United States and Europe, and some—especially the role of religion—

can also be found outside those contexts. The Right presents their movements as having a national character, but nationalist movements receive aid, tactics, money, and memes from beyond national borders.

Community

During the last three decades, the idea that archaeology must be a public endeavor that includes people beyond professional archaeologists has gained ground (Little and Shackel 2014; Marshall 2002; Moshenska 2010; Richardson and Almansa-Sánchez 2015). Many archaeological projects today have a public dimension or are conducted as community archaeology. It could even be argued that public—or, rather, community—archaeology is now something of a moral imperative; in fact, many grant applications and requests for proposals specifically ask which ways archaeology will practically contribute to local communities and society at large. This is at least the case in North America, Australia, Europe, and many Latin American countries (e.g., Funari and Garraffoni 2016; Little 2002; Moshenska and Dhanjal 2011; van den Dries 2014). Community archaeology is also growing steadily in sub-Saharan Africa (Schmidt and Pikirayi 2016). Yet, despite the proliferation of public archaeology projects, practitioners have often avoided definitions of the "people," the "public," or "community" or have worked with comfortable and unproblematic notions—and communities (Ayán and González-Ruibal 2014; Waterton and Smith 2010: 11–12). This has been possible because most initiatives have focused on collectives that fit liberal conceptions of the good citizen: either middle-class people with an interest in history, as is often the case in the United Kingdom (Simpson and Williams 2008), or subaltern communities with which researchers collaborate to redress symbolic injustices (e.g., Atalay 2012; Kiddey 2017; McGuire 2014). These are at least the projects that have been mostly widely publicized in collective volumes or journals like *Public Archaeology* and the *Journal of Community Archaeology and Heritage*. Little room has been devoted to communities that do not follow the liberal or emancipatory model or that are torn apart by conflict.

In most case studies, communities seem warm and fuzzy. Yet they lose some of their warmth, fuzziness, and persuasion in a reactionary populist world. We can no longer assume them as positive and supportive agents. Reactionary populism defines politics in the twenty-first century in terms of exclusive communities: it embraces nationalism, racism, and anti-intellectualism while nostalgically seeking to restore a golden age and to regain a perceived loss of privilege. The very communities that scholars embrace as vehicles of progressive social change may reject multivocality for the seduction of reactionary populism and disappoint liberal scholars by being greedy, patriarchal, xenophobic, or uninterested in the real past (González-Ruibal et al. 2018; Mc-Guire: Chapter 6).

In fact, resentment is often a very powerful force uniting communities, and it has been one of the primary drives behind populism since the 1980s (Betz 1993; Montgomery: Chapter 3). Here we follow Didier Fassin's notion of historical resentment and ideological resentment (Fassin 2013). Ressentiment (historical resentment) refers to the feelings of collectives that have experienced exploitation and oppression for centuries, like Afrodescendant communities and Indigenous groups. Ideological resentment refers to the feelings of frustration provoked by social position or perceptions of lost privilege. Ideological resentment fuels national populism: white people who feel their privileges are threatened by the social advancement of other groups, or male chauvinists who feel under attack with greater gender equality. The situation is more complicated when ressentiment and ideological resentment coincide in the same group (like white, working-class people voting for Trump). Archaeologists have been good at working with historical resentment, but they have rarely addressed ideological resentment. Indeed, they are hardly prepared to deal with communities of mixed resentment, where historical and ideological reasons coalesce. This is in part because they have not taken emotions (and particularly negative emotions) seriously enough (Ahmed 2004). At best, community archaeology has celebrated a limited range of positive affects (self-assertion, solidarity, pride) and forgotten such others as humiliation, shame, and hatred (González-Ruibal 2023).

If the positive concept of community used by community archaeology breaks apart under conditions of reactionary populism, so does its methodology: multivocality (Hodder 2008). Allowing multiple voices is fine when they accept certain norms and basic values—such as human rights or the respect for cultural difference. But what shall we do with those who embrace bigotry and male chauvinism or who defend political violence (Žižek 2005: 56)? Those of us who have worked in contexts of intense social division have seen the effects of polarization and the shortcomings of community archaeology well before populism became a problem in heritage studies (González-Ruibal 2010). Now the problem is not restricted to postconflict or postdictatorship scenarios. Does this mean that we must reject community archaeology or multivocality? Not at all. At the workshop, we discussed how to address the threat of populism. We did not reject collaboration but noted that it needs to be more reflective and critical. And rather than abandoning community archaeology, we argued that it should be joined with other practices.

Populism and Archaeology

To confront populism, archaeology needs to consider difference. Community and public archaeology were defined with a strong North American / United Kingdom bias, and we should try to avoid this Anglophone focus when redefining public archaeology to meet the populist challenge. A new public archaeology has to be attuned to both the global and local dimension of communities in an intensely connected but still strongly diverse world.

Why should populism be an issue for archaeology, and public archaeology in particular? Can we not keep addressing our familiar public as usual? Keep collaborating with liberal and subaltern communities? Of course, business as usual is still an option. We can (and should) still conduct community archaeology with those collectives with whom we have traditionally collaborated. Yet there is a risk in forgetting those political communities, often fractured, conflicted, or reactionary, that we feel less comfortable with and that may be embracing populism. It is a risk for archaeology and for society at large to forget that these communities exist. There are at least three good reasons why we should not leave aside reactionary collectives from our understanding of the public.

First, they are many. In Hungary the 2022 elections gave Fidesz, the extreme Right party, 53% of the vote: a landslide victory for a political option whose leader lashed out against the racial mixture of Europeans and non-Europeans while harassing the LGBTQ community. Populism put Donald Trump in the White House; made the British exit from the European Union, or Brexit, possible; and typically musters 30–40% of the vote in France. In Spain, populists have grown exponentially since 2018 to garner over 15% of the vote (from zero in the previous elections)—until they lost a large percentage of the vote to the conservatives in the July 2023 elections, but only after the conservatives adopted much of the populist agenda and style. In Italy, a reactionary populist party, Fratelli d'Italia, with direct links to classical fascism, won the presidential elections in 2022 and ever since has pursued an extreme Right agenda in terms of immigration, environmental policies, and LGBTQ rights. At the same time, not all those who vote for national populism are necessarily xenophobic or authoritarian, and this is yet another reason not to forget them.

A second reason to take populism seriously in archaeology is because it claims to represent "The People" as well as their needs and aspirations. In fact, this is why it is called populism in the first place. The problem is that archaeologists have often used the language of "the people" (Cherry and Rojas 2015; Montgomery: Chapter 3) to refer to the public they address or with whom they collaborate. However, "the people" of populism are very different from "the people" of liberal archaeologists. While both archaeologists and populists would argue that "the people" (the common people) have been sidelined by the powerful, "the people" of archaeology has universalist implications (including all people who have been subjected to marginalization, exploitation, or abuse). In contrast, populism defines "the people" first by national belonging and race, but second by their compliance with what populists believe to be the essential values of the nation. These are conservative values, behaviors, and identities. For instance, populists accord the heterosexual patriarchal family a prominent role in all their ideologies, along with the dominant religion. While archaeologists employ an inclusive concept of "the people," populism embraces "the people" more for what it leaves out than for what it incorporates.

Third, national populists use history all the time to support their ideologies (Niklasson and Hølleland 2018). They seek to own history itself and to control the narrative. National populist history works along three axes: (1) the projection of the nation to the deep past; (2) victimization (which is again part of the politics and effects of ideological resentment), and (3) the celebration of violence in various ways (military heroism, imperialism, war). National populists need history that says their nation is very old, that it is older (and therefore more legitimate) than others, that it is more glorious than others, and that it was victimized in the past and therefore fell from their position of dominance to the state of disarray and weakness in which it is found today. Archaeologists and historians cannot provide support to this sort of narrative. But amateurs are eager to replace them. Reactionary populists often substitute historical accounts produced by nonprofessionals for academic ones. Populists write these narratives not to make people think critically but rather to make them feel proud. Archaeologists, in turn, have endeavored to provide material substance to the historicity of Indigenous, subaltern, and marginalized communities by showing that they have a history on equal footing with mainstream society. In this process, they have often derided the historical pride of members of mainstream society for being nationalist and simplistic. Archaeologists and historians, in addition, have often emphasized the negative side of history (state violence, colonialism, historical injustices) in their attempts to produce a critical account of the past. It is reactionary amateurs who are providing narratives with which dominant society can identify in positive terms—although they are exclusionary, simplistic, and based on myths rather than empirical facts (Popa 2016).

We see this war to own history around the globe. It can take the form of tearing down the material manifestations of heritage or the rewriting of history. In 1992 in India, the demolition of the sixteenth-century Babri Mosque (Bernbeck and Pollock 1996) marked the rise of the national populist Bharatiya Janata Party that now controls the nation. In 2020, in the United States, Trump attacked the 1619 project (a *New York Times* project that enlisted academics and journalists to center the telling of US history around the effects of slavery and the contributions of Black individuals) and critical race theory. He organized a "1776 Commission" to advance a populist agenda that emphasizes pride in a patriotic United States.

Conventional public and community archaeology fails to address the challenges of reactionary populism. To start with, national populism exceeds the local scale where community archaeologists work. It is a national and global problem. It also global when it is about history and heritage.

Consider the case of statues: the toppling down of statues has been a movement against reactionary, nationalist, and populist narratives that have had many centers. Although *damnatio memoriae* (condemnation of memory) has been around for millennia, the way it has been practiced has not always been the same. Thus, most monument destruction has to do with a regime—or a sovereign—overthrowing another regime. The removal of statues of imperial agents, racist figures, or slave traders is being carried out by subaltern groups within societies, such as Indigenous peoples and Afrodescendants. This is original. And so is the fact that there are transnational connections between the groups; thus, statues have fallen more or less at the same time in the United Kingdom, the United States, Colombia, Chile, and Spain (Ballantyne 2021; Langland 2021; McAnany: Chapter 11; McGuire 2023; Riaño 2021). In turn, the statues have been defended by national populists, eager to maintain traditional hierarchies and forms of oppression. Toppling statues has created transnational networks of solidarity.

Archaeology against Reactionary Populism

Archaeologists should seek ways of dealing with these global phenomena by adopting forms of social engagement that go beyond local communities. This does not mean that we cannot continue to do community archaeology. We can and we should. On the one hand, however, we must reflect more on the nature of communities, on which people we exclude by working with certain groups and not others, and on the ivory towers (social this time, not epistemic) in which we seek refuge. On the other hand, we should take the larger picture into account. We cannot work with our small subaltern or liberal collective as if the world outside were a simple extension of it (or a dark world that we prefer not to deal with).

The new scenarios ask for new strategies. One is a return to grand narratives. This has already been noticed by historians (Guldi and Armitage 2014). They argue that the rise of microhistories and the local in the 1970s left the production of grand accounts to people with limited historical knowledge, including political scientists, economists, and geographers, often with conservative agendas. With the rise of national populism, non-academics with obvious reactionary ideologies now produce these narratives and their stories reach a very wide public. Edgar Straehle (2021) uses the apt term of "historiographical populism" to refer to this phenomenon, which is present in many countries and is characterized by a moralizing discourse, the use of simple dichotomies ("us" versus "them," "good" versus "evil"), intolerance, and victimization. In the case of Spain, an ultranationalist and imperialist rant (*Imperiofobia y leyenda negra*) written in 2016 by a philologist, Elvira Roca Barea, has had over 40 editions in a few years. In typical populist vein, Spain (the Spanish Empire) is presented as a victim of hatred by other powers, a hatred that persists to our day and that can only be counteracted with nationalist pride and a positive reading of Spain's civilizing mission in the world. In France, extreme Right politician Éric Zemmour wrote a book (*Destin français*) in 2018 on the history of France that sold 100,000 copies the year it was published. The narrative intends to discredit academic historians for hijacking the greatness of French history and develops a polarized scenario in which Islam and France fight an eternal battle.

In archaeology, we run the risk of our narratives being written, in the best case, by geneticists, psychologists, or geographers, often in politically dangerous ways (Wagner et al. 2020), or, at worst, by racist propagandists. In this context, David Graeber and David Wengrow's celebrated *The Dawn of Everything* (2021), despite its shortcomings, shows the way to follow. We cannot fight reactionary bestsellers with academic papers in journals that are read by a handful other academics. And mere criticism of populist narratives has very little appeal for the public. We are reminded of V. Gordon Childe, who wrote popular grand narratives in challenge to a developing German fascism (Childe 1936, 1942). There is indeed a huge potential market for grand archaeological narratives produced by archaeologists (Hofmann et al. 2021: 521).

Writing popular books with ambitious, long-term narratives that provide hope and critique in equal measure is an important step. But we should not forget that only a fraction of the population reads books, especially thick books. This is also the case with populists. Reactionary history volumes are purchased as self-help manuals that corroborate one's own prejudices without one having to read the entire book. They work more as a charm against cognitive dissonance than a piece of literature.

The internet has proven effective (and dangerous) in spreading reactionary populist narratives during the last decade. Social media such as Facebook and Twitter and message services such as WhatsApp and Telegram have done much to spread both fake news and fake history, to create national populist communities and in some cases to put presidents in power. It is imperative for archaeologists to participate in this game, using imagination, empirical rigor, and the tools of the discipline to craft and disseminate alternative accounts. Digital public archaeology and heritage provides new opportunities for the dissemination of archaeology (Richardson 2013), but it entails its own risks, both political and ethical.

In Spain, a particularly successful example is that of PutoMikel, an archaeologist with a doctorate from Leicester University, and YouTuber with 248,000 followers, mainly young people.[1] His videos, some of which have over 400,000 views, debunk nationalist myths while proposing more complex and inclusionary readings of the past. He resorts to a provocative and irreverent pop style, which does not prevent him from exploring the past through high theory—from Deleuze to posthumanism. PutoMikel is a sort of antidote against national populist YouTubers, particularly Academia Play, a reactionary platform that broadcasts Spanish history from a nationalist lens, often resorting to outdated clichés that had been rejected by academic historians for decades. This is a crucial battle of narratives that has to do with more than history or archaeology; it has to do with the model of society that we want for the present and for the future: one based on values of inclusion and tolerance, or one based on chauvinism, patriarchy, and the sublimation of violence.

In Ireland the Right has used social media to enhance and spread a myth of white slavery. They claim that seventeenth- and eighteenth-century English plantation owners in the Caribbean held Irish people in bondage as they did Africans and Indigenous peoples.[2] Liam Hogan, a librarian based at the University of Limerick in Ireland, has written factual histories to counter "white slaves" narratives (Hogan et al. 2016). As part of these efforts, he has traced how and why the Right created the "white slave" narrative' and how they circulated it on social media. His use of social media and especially using freely accessible and shareable texts means that when people start "white slave" narratives, his followers inundate the myth with challenges. Based on Hogan's work they can provide easily digestible text to indicate how and why the myth is wrong. This media challenge to the myth seems to be working. Laura McAtackney (personal communication 2022) has noticed that the circulation of "white slave" memes and texts have lessened in number and impact in more recent years (you can predict when they will appear—any controversial police killing of a Black civilian in the United States, St. Patrick's Day, and so on).

That we have to fight in the terrain of grand narratives (in the physical as well as in the virtual world) where the cultural battles of our time are being fought does not mean that we have to forget the local. It is simply that we cannot present communities alone as the privileged or only space for the political struggles of archaeology. The local and the global are two scales in which the politics of the past are played out. They are strongly intertwined, and we have to pay attention to both. A new public archaeology should include both if it wants to be socially useful in these dark times.

Key Concepts and Questions

Having identified the challenges of reactionary populism, this book asks if a social archaeology based in community collaboration can achieve liberating goals in the face of these challenges. If not, how do we do an engaged archaeology in the face of reactionary populism? Our workshop identified a series of key concepts and questions that our authors have developed in their chapters.

First, a critical reflection on community is essential to tackle reactionary populism because ideas of community—both national and local—are foundational to populist thinking (McAtackney: Chapter 8). In this volume the notion is problematized by each of the contributors, who examine a diversity of communities: small, rural groups (Ayán: Chapter 5); Indigenous communities (Montgomery: Chapter 3; Van Dyke: Chapter 10); marginalized urban groups (Kiddey: Chapter 7; González-Ruibal: Chapter 2); working-class people, including those espousing reactionary ideas (McGuire: Chapter 6); and activists (Bernbeck: Chapter 12), but also well-to-do, conservative whites (González-Ruibal: Chapter 2; Van Dyke: Chapter 10) and even (very) rich people (Ayán: Chapter 5). How do we deal with different kinds of communities, particularly those that do not fit the liberal model of community public archaeologists are used to working with? An aspect that is emphasized in this book is diversity. We cannot approach communities in Germany and Palestine, Indigenous and settler groups, and the powerful and the dispossessed in the same way. This is why some of the chapters take a comparative approach (Bernbeck: Chapter 12; Van Dyke: Chapter 10).

Populism in its different avatars is, of course, present throughout the volume and analyzed from different perspectives. We explore different manifestations of reactionary populism, which, as noted above, is the most widespread and threatening at a global level at the moment. We map its relations with phenomena that have long concerned archaeologists, such as neoliberalism, imperialism, nationalism, and racism. But we also ask: is it possible to use progressive populism or elements of populism to counteract reaction (Ayán:

Chapter 5)? What are the ethical, political risks? Is there a critical populism? A tactical use of populism by archaeologists may draw from archaeology's own popularity and the popular tropes associated with the discipline (Holtorf 2005).

Nationalism and imperialism have been consubstantial to the birth of archaeology since Bruce Trigger's seminal work (Trigger 1984), and they have been the topic of a plethora of publications ever since (Díaz-Andreu and Champion 1996). Interest, however, has somewhat dwindled during the last decade, at least regarding nationalism, as it seemed less relevant in a globalized neoliberal world. Yet they have come back with force—and in close association to each other: nation and empire are indissolubly linked in many populist movements, from the United Kingdom to Spain, and are crucial in the new culture wars (González-Ruibal: Chapter 2; McAtackney: Chapter 8). Both imply a romanticization of the past, which is depicted as socially homogeneous and full of glory—a glory based on the domination of others (internal or external). In this context, we can wonder: is a postnational archaeology possible (Hofmann et al. 2021: 523–524)? And in a world that is more and more obsessed with borders and roots, how can we reclaim the place of those who do not have a place (refugees, migrants, displaced people) (Kiddey: Chapter 7; McGuire 2020)?

History and heritage are central to reactionary populist programs. In populists' hands history becomes a device to separate those who belong in the nation from those who do not, and heritage becomes a way of naturalizing racial, class, gender, and sexual injustices. Both history and heritage reinforce national pride through simplistic narratives that oscillate between heroization and victimization while engaging in a general whitewashing of the past. Archaeology complicates things by showing the darker side of history (Bernbeck: Chapter 12; McAtackney: Chapter 8; Moshenska et al.: Chapter 9). But by complicating things, archaeology may alienate people from their past. How do we produce historical narratives that challenge national populism while remaining truthful, socially useful, and attractive? Finding other heroes (common people versus warriors and kings) and new epics (of liberation and resistance) might be a way (Ayán: Chapter 5; McGuire: Chapter 6). Within heritage, statues and public monuments have played an outstanding role recently in the cultural wars pitting national populism and progressive movements against each other (González-Ruibal: Chapter 2; McAnany: Chapter 11). Indeed, statues have become the epitome of what heritage is in the eyes of populists, who tend to conflate history and its monumental representation (as happens with Confederate statues in the United States). Archaeology, with its focus on materiality and its long experience working with past monuments and monumental landscapes, is in a good position to deconstruct this kind of heritage and the role it plays in perpetuating social injustice.

The impact of populism in Indigenous communities is of the utmost relevance, yet it has been rarely given the attention it deserves in archaeology and heritage studies. Indigenous groups are more likely to suffer from reactionary populist politics (see Gnecco: Chapter 4; Montgomery: Chapter 3; Van Dyke: Chapter 10), which considers them not part of the authentic body of the nation—defined as white and of European ancestry. With the rebirth of imperial imaginaries, native communities are also likely to be revictimized, not only in the Global North but also in the South (Moshenska et al: Chapter 9), at least symbolically, as their histories are again negated and their sufferings downplayed. At the same time, progressive populism can also misuse Indigenous heritage and identities, as has been the case in México and Ecuador (Cusicanqui 2018).

Capitalism (and neoliberalism more specifically) is another phenomenon without which it is difficult to understand populism (McGuire: Chapter 6). As noted above, the rise of reactionary populism is indissociable from the rise of neoliberalism and the crises of capitalism. While some populist movements criticize the neoliberal elites and defend protectionism, the truth is that most populism thrives with the dominant economic regime and shows no intention of overthrowing it (a fact that is also true in most cases of progressive populism). Archaeology has been complicit with neoliberalism in different ways (Aparicio Resco 2016): by supporting its cultural logic (multiculturalism) and by participating in extractivist capitalism through CRM and contract archaeology (Gnecco 2018, Gnecco: Chapter 4). From this point of view, it is legitimate to ask how much is actually changing with the advent of populism.

Class needs to be considered, including the class position of the archaeologist herself (Ayán Vila: Chapter 5; McGuire 2008, McGuire: Chapter 6). How do we relate with people from other social classes (below, but also above the social ladder)? What are the potential misunderstandings, grievances, and resentments (Montgomery: Chapter 3) that emerge from interclass encounters? What are the risks of forgetting class in community archaeology?

Organization of Book

The archaeologists in this volume have applied their craft to a variety of communities, at differing scales and with varying temporalities and commitments. Three look broadly at the relations of archaeology and community at a national level. Two focus on long-term collaborative research to advance the interest of communities. Three studies examine negative heritage and challenge oppression. Three archaeologists compare and contrast archaeology's traditional study of past societies with more avant-garde studies of contemporary material worlds. All of the studies include a consideration of the author's own positionality vis-à-vis community collaborators and co-creators and political actors and agents.

Archaeology and Communities on a National Level

In the first chapter of part 1, "Nation, Empire, and Reactionary Populism: An Archaeological Critique," Alfredo González-Ruibal argues that the return of nationalism through reactionary populism poses new challenges to archaeologists as the past is crucial to populist projects. Along with it has come a vindication of empire, which is often indissolubly linked to national identity. The chapter first examines the relationship between archaeology and nationalism, it then presents the case of neo-imperialism in Spain, and finally suggests ways to counteract national-imperialist narratives through archaeology.

In Chapter 3, "'Constellations of Co-Resistance': Taking Power and Making Power in American Archaeology," Lindsey Martel Montgomery discusses how archaeologists have increasingly drawn on such liberal frameworks as restoration, social justice, and reconciliation to be more reflexive and responsive to historically marginalized communities. In contrast, a right-wing populist discourse villainizes minoritarian rights and makes nostalgic claims to heritage. Montgomery argues for a race-radical feminist approach that uses decolonial and abolitionist politics as emancipatory tools.

In Chapter 4, "Heritage, Archaeology, and Local Communities in Times of Reactionary Populism: Learnings from Brazil," Cristóbal Gnecco contends that reactionary populism has deepened the subjugation of the state to development and the market. He sees this in the dismantling of regulations to protect heritage. This trend dramatically increased lately in Brazil. Here public opinion is obsessively concerned with health issues related to the pandemic that began in 2020—to the exclusion of other concerns. Reactionary populism has relaxed environmental and heritage regulations.

Long-Term Archaeological Studies of Contemporary Communities

Part 2 begins with, "Reality Bites: The Insufferable Lightness of Being a Community Archaeologist." Here Xurxo M. Ayán Vila analyzes a project based on the explosive cocktail of myth, science, and community. Every night a saint flees the Cereixa church to rush back home to an Iron Age hillfort. Despite having been Christianized in the Middle Ages, mythical dwellers—the *mouros* (moors)—still live on the hillfort. In 2016 the villagers of Cereixa decided to recuperate this archaeological site. His chapter reviews the crucial role played by community archaeology in this process of heritage empowerment.

Randall H. McGuire discusses, in Chapter 6, "Solidarity, the Craft of Archaeology, and Reactionary Populism," the 1914 Ludlow Massacre in Colorado, where National Guard troops fired machine guns into a tent camp killing 21 people. From 1994 to 2002, the Ludlow Collective excavated the camp and a company town. In 2016 Donald Trump preached a reactionary populism that appealed to many working-class people and he especially courted coal miners. McGuire asks, can we practice the craft of archaeology in solidarity with the miners and challenge reactionary populism?

The Archaeology of Repression and Negative Heritage

Part 3 opens with Chapter 7, "Archaeology as Deterritorialized Community: Using Cultural Heritage Methods to Challenge Reactionary Populism in the Made in Migration Project (2018–2022)," where Rachael Kiddey discusses her multisited, multimodal, community archaeology project Migrant Materialities. The project collaborated with diverse groups of forcibly displaced people in three European locations. Migrant Materialities tackles some of the problems inherent in undertaking political engagement in a hypermobile world by creating a virtual and at times sited-together community from otherwise disempowered and displaced individuals, scattered by geopolitics. It reasserts humanity and demands equal rights.

In Chapter 8, "Conducting Community Archaeology in Ireland: Working with Marginalized and Vulnerable Communities," Laura McAtackney maintains that we must ask two questions: who is the "community" and why are we collaborating? She focuses on structural issues in Ireland and the analysis of Magdalene Laundries. In highlighting collaborations with marginalized, disenfranchised, and vulnerable groups, she argues that we can use community projects to address past wrongs, ignored injustices, and difficult (recent) pasts, but we should do so with caution.

In Chapter 9, "Contending with Colonial Heritage as a Transnational Activist Network: The Museum of British Colonialism," Gabriel Moshenska, Anthony Maina, Hannah McLean, Andrea Potts, Beth Rebisz, and Chao Tayiana Maina argue that nationalist myth is a powerful tool of reactionary populist movements, and the most widespread myth in contemporary Britain is the belief that the British Empire was an overwhelmingly benign institution. The United Kingdom–Kenya digital heritage nongovernmental organization, the Museum of British Colonialism, is an international network that works across 3-D digital modeling, archaeological survey, and filmmaking to challenge this myth in 1950s Kenya.

Comparing and Contrasting Archaeology's Study of Past Societies with the Study of Contemporary Material Worlds

The first chapter of part 4, Ruth M. Van Dyke's "Ancient Chaco, Historic Texas: A Self-Reflexive Tale," compares and contrasts two experiences with collaborative, community-engaged archaeology. At Chaco Canyon, in the Native American Southwest United States, she works closely with Indigenous descendant communities. She has also instigated an archaeological project in rural south Texas at the Alsatian settler village of Castroville. These two contrasting cases demonstrate that archaeology is always political; archaeologists can never escape the need to take an ethical position.

In Chapter 11, "Hurtful Heritage: Materializing a Past to Sediment/Unsettle Exclusionary Practices," Patricia A. McAnany investigates why certain monuments transition from symbols of power and domination to sites of conscience or of dark heritage while others can only be neutralized by their disposal or unceremonious warehousing. McAnany compares contentious manifestations of tangible heritage in the southeastern United States with the Maya region. Before starting this comparison, she considers some of the broader issues surrounding heritage, memory, and monuments.

Reinhard Bernbeck discusses two widely divergent contexts where he does archaeological research in Chapter 12, "Archaeology against Right-Wing Extremism: Lessons from a Nazi Terror Site." His discussion addresses the conceptual issues of positionality and epistemology in West Asia and Germany. In the second half of the chapter, he elaborates on these issues by referring to different voices around the excavations of a Nazi forced-labor camp. He proposes to give populism a positive turn by focusing on the value of heritage disputes.

Commentary

Claudia Theune, who did not attend the workshop, provides commentary on the volume. She provides a synthesis of the volume and forward-looking statements about archaeology and reactionary populism in the final chapter.

Conclusion

The chapters in this volume show that the question "Archaeology for whom?" does not have an easy answer in real contexts. For many years archaeologists believed that science answered the question by concluding that archaeology was for scientists. The 1990s critique of this view by post-processual, Marxist, feminist, and Indigenous archaeologists argued for an archaeology for the people. That is, an archaeology for and by communities. The spread of reactionary positivism in the twenty-first century leads us to question the simple equation of community and public with goodness and light. To answer the question "Archaeology for whom?" in the twenty-first century, we must confront reactionary populism.

Notes

1 PutoMikel's (Mikel Herrán Subiñas) YouTube page is found at https://www.youtube.com/channel/UCSvkCc8rbluGVsZV-KKHCFA.
2 See Liam Hogan, All of My Work on the "Irish Slaves" meme (2015–'23), *Medium,* March 12, 2017, https://limerick1914.medium.com/all-of-my-work-on-the-irish -slaves-meme-2015-16-4965e445802a.

References Cited

Ahmed, Sara. 2004. *The Cultural Politics of Emotion.* Edinburgh University Press, Edinburgh.

Aparicio Resco, Pablo. (editor). 2016. *Archaeology and Neoliberalism.* JAS Arqueología Editorial, Madrid.

Arendt, Hannah. 1973. *The Origins of Totalitarianism.* Houghton Mifflin Harcourt, New York.

Atalay, Sonya. 2012. *Community-Based Archaeology: Research with, by, and for Indigenous and Local Communities.* University of California Press, Berkeley.

Ayán Vila, Xurxo, and Alfredo González-Ruibal. 2014. "Public" and Archaeology. In *Encyclopedia of Global Archaeology,* edited by Claire Smith, pp. 6197–6202. Springer, New York.

Ballantyne, Tony. 2021. Toppling the Past? Statues, Public Memory and the Afterlife of Empire in Contemporary New Zealand. *Public History Review,* 28: 1–8. https://doi.org/ 10.5130/phrj.v28i0.7503.

Berlet, Chip (editor). 2019. *Trumping Democracy: From Reagan to the Alt Right.* Routledge, Abingdon.

Berman, S. 2021. The Causes of Populism in the West. *Annual Review of Political Science* 24(1): 71–88.

Bernbeck, Reinhard, and Susan Pollock. 1996. Ayodhya, Archaeology, and Identity. *Current Anthropology,* 37(S1): S138–S142.

Betz, Hans-George. 1993. The New Politics of Resentment: Radical Right-Wing Populist Parties in Western Europe. *Comparative Politics* 25(4): 413–427.

Cherry, John F., and Felipe Rojas. 2015. *Archaeology for the People: Perspectives from the Joukowsky Institute.* Oxbow, Oxford.

Childe, V. Gordon. 1936. *Man Makes Himself.* Watts & Co., London.

Childe, V. Gordon. 1942. *What Happened in History.* Penguin, Harmondsworth, England.

Cusicanqui, Silvia Rivera. 2018. *Un mundo chix'i es posible: Ensayos desde un presente en crisis.* Tinta Limón, Buenos Aires.

de la Baume, Maïa, and Silvia Sciorilli Borrelli. 2019. Steve Bannon's stuttering European adventure. *Politico,* March 5. https://www.politico.eu/article/steve-bannon-european -parliament-the-movement-stuttering-european-adventure/.

Díaz-Andreu, Margarita, and Timothy Champion (editors). 1996. *Nationalism and Archaeology in Europe.* Routledge, London.

Eatwell, Roger, and Matthew J. Goodwin. 2018. *National Populism: The Revolt Against Liberal Democracy.* Pelican, London.

Fassin, Didier. 2013. On Resentment and Ressentiment: The Politics and Ethics of Moral Emotions. *Current Anthropology* 54(3): 249–267.

Finchelstein, Federico. 2019. *From Fascism to Populism in History.* University of California Press, Berkeley.

Font, Nuria, Paolo Graziano, and Myrto Tsakatika. 2021. Varieties of Inclusionary Populism? SYRIZA, Podemos and the Five Star Movement. *Government and Opposition,* 56(1): 163–183.

Froio, Caterina, and Bharath Ganesh. 2019. The Routledge Transnationalisation of Far-Right Discourse on Twitter. *European Societies* 21(4): 513–539. https://doi.org/10.1080/14616696.2018.1494295.

Funari, Pedro Paulo A., and Renata S. Garraffoni. 2016. Arqueología participativa y empoderamiento comunitario en Brasil. *Complutum* 27(2): 281–294. https://doi.org/10.5209/CMPL.54746.

Gnecco, Cristóbal. 2018. Development and Disciplinary Complicity: Contract Archaeology in South America Under the Critical Gaze. *Annual Review of Anthropology* 47: 279–293.

González-Ruibal, Alfredo. 2010. Contra la pospolítica: Arqueología de la Guerra Civil Española. *Revista de Antropología* 22(2): 9–32.

González-Ruibal, Alfredo. 2023. Walking Through the Darkest Valley: Heritage and Hatred in the Era of Reactionary Populism. In *Polarized Pasts: Heritage and Belonging in Times of Political Polarization,* edited by Elisabeth Niklasson, pp. 134–155. Berghahn, Oxford.

González-Ruibal, Alfredo, Pablo Alfonso González, and Felipe Criado-Boado. 2018. Against Reactionary Populism: Towards a New Public Archaeology. *Antiquity* 92(362): 507–515.

Graeber, David, and David Wengrow. 2021. *The Dawn of Everything: A New History of Humanity.* Penguin, London.

Guldi, Jo, and David Armitage. 2014. *The History Manifesto.* Cambridge University Press, Cambridge.

Hodder, Ian. 2008. Multivocality and Social Archaeology. In *Evaluating Multiple Narratives: Beyond Nationalist, Colonialist, Imperialist Archaeologies,* edited by Junko Habu, Clare Fawcett and John M. Matsunaga, 196–200. Springer, New York.

Hofmann, Daniela, Emily Hanscam, Martin Furholt, Martin Bača, Samantha S. Reiter, Alessandro Vanzetti, Kostas Kotsakis, et al. 2021. Populism, Identity Politics, and the Archaeology of Europe. *European Journal of Archaeology,* 24(4): 519–555.

Hogan, Liam, Laura McAtackney, and Matthew C. Reilly. 2016. The Irish in the Anglo-Caribbean: Servants or Slaves? *History Ireland* 24(2): 18–22.

Holtorf, Cornelius. 2005. *From Stonehenge to Las Vegas: Archaeology as Popular Culture.* Altamira Press, Walnut Creek, California.

Homolar, Alexandra, and Georg Löfflmann. 2021. Populism and the Affective Politics of Humiliation Narratives. *Global Studies Quarterly* 1(1): ksab002.

Kiddey, Rachael. 2017. *Homeless Heritage: Collaborative Social Archaeology as Therapeutic Practice.* Oxford University Press, Oxford.

Laclau, Ernesto. 2005. *On Populist Reason.* Verso, London.

Langland, Tuck. 2021. Toppling Statues: Iconoclasm Yesterday, Today, and Tomorrow. *Sculpture Review* 70(1): 22–26.

Little, Barbara J. 2002. *Public Benefits of Archaeology.* University Press of Florida, Gainesville.

Little, Barbara J., and Paul A. Shackel. 2014. *Archaeology, Heritage, and Civic Engagement: Working Toward the Public Good.* Left Coast Press, Walnut Creek, California.

Mamié, Robin, Manoel Horta-Ribiero, and Robert West. 2021. Are Anti-Feminist Communities Gateways to the Far Right? In *Proceedings of the 13th ACM Web Science Conference 2021,* pp. 139–147. https://doi.org/10.1145/3447535.3462504.

Marshall, Yvonne. 2002. What Is Community Archaeology? *World Archaeology* 34(2): 211–219.

McGuire, Randall H. 2008. *Archaeology as Political Action.* University of California Press, Berkeley.

McGuire, Randall H. 2014. Working Class Archaeology. In *Transforming Archaeology: Activist Prospects and Practices,* edited by Sonya Atalay, Lee Rains Clauss, Randall H. McGuire, and John R. Welch, pp. 115–132, Left Coast Press, Walnut Creek, California.

McGuire, Randall H. 2020 The Materiality and Heritage of Modern Forced Migration. *Annual Review of Anthropology* 49: 175–191. https://doi.org/10.1146/annurev-anthro-010220-074624.

McGuire, Randall H. 2023 How Do We Tell the Good Guys from the Bad Guys . . . or Not. In *Critical Heritage Studies and the Future of Europe,* edited by Nélia Dias, Rodney Harrison, and Kristian Kristiansen, pp. 289–306, UCL Press, London.

Mols, Frank, and Jolanda Jetten. 2016. Explaining the Appeal of Populist Right-Wing Parties in Times of Economic Prosperity. *Political Psychology* 37(2): 275–292.

Morieson, Nicholas. 2021. *Religion and Populist Radical Right: Secular Christianism and Populism in Western Europe.* Vernon Press, Wilmington, Delaware.

Moshenska, Gabriel. 2010. What Is Public Archaeology? *Present Pasts,* 1(1): 46–48.

Moshenska, Gabriel, and Sarah Dhanjal (editors). 2011. *Community Archaeology: Themes, Methods and Practices.* Oxbow, Oxford.

Mudde, Cas. 2004. The Populist Zeitgeist. *Government and Opposition* 39(4): 541–563.

Niklasson, Elisabeth, and Herdis Hølleland. 2018. The Scandinavian Far-Right and the New Politicisation of Heritage. *Journal of Social Archaeology* 18(2): 121–148.

Pappas, Takis S. 2016. Modern Populism: Research Advances, Conceptual and Methodological Pitfalls, and the Minimal Definition. In *Oxford Research Encyclopedia of Politics.* Published online March 3, 2016. https://doi.org/10.1093/acrefore/9780190228637.013.17.

Paxton, Robert O. 2004. *The Anatomy of Fascism.* Vintage, New York.

Popa, Cătălin Nicolae. 2016. The Significant Past and Insignificant Archaeologists: Who Informs the Public about Their "National" Past? The Case of Romania. *Archaeological Dialogues* 23(1): 28–39.

Riaño, Peio H. 2021. *Decapitados: Una historia contra los monumentos racistas, esclavistas e invasores.* Ediciones B, Barcelona.

Richardson, Lorna. 2013. A Digital Public Archaeology? *Papers from the Institute of Archaeology* 23(1): 1–12.

Richardson, Lorna-Jane, and Jaime Almansa-Sánchez. 2015. Do You Even Know What Public Archaeology Is? Trends, Theory, Practice, Ethics. *World Archaeology* 47(2): 194–211.

Rodrik, Dani. 2018. Populism and the Economics of Globalization. *Journal of International Business Policy* 1: 12–33.

Schmidt, Peter R., and Innocent Pikirayi. 2016. *Community Archaeology and Heritage in Africa: Decolonizing Practice.* Routledge, Abingdon, United Kingdom.

Shanks, Michael, and Randall H. McGuire. 1996. The Craft of Archaeology. *American Antiquity* 61(1): 75–88.

Simpson, Faye, and Howard Williams. 2008. Evaluating Community Archaeology in the UK. *Public Archaeology,* 7(2):69–90.

Shepherd, Laura J. 2022. White Feminism and the Governance of Violent Extremism. *Critical Studies on Terrorism* 15(3): 727–749. https://doi.org/10.1080/17539153.2022.2089401.

Straehle, Edgar. 2021. El populismo historiográfico como problema y síntoma del presente. *Contexto y Acción,* June 10. https://ctxt.es/es/20211001/Firmas/37438/populismo-historiografico-leyenda-negra-nacionalismo-historia.htm.

Trigger, Bruce. 1989. *A History of Archaeological Thought.* Cambridge: Cambridge University Press.

van den Dries, Monique H. 2014. Community Archaeology in the Netherlands. *Journal of Community Archaeology and Heritage,* 1(1): 69–88.

Wagner, Jennifer K., Chip Colwell, Katrina G. Claw, Anne C. Stone, Deborah A. Bolnick, John Hawks, Kyle B. Brothers, et al. (2020). Fostering Responsible Research on Ancient DNA. *American Journal of Human Genetics,* 107(2): 183–195.

Yakushko, Oksana, and Alysia De Francisco. 2022. The (Re)Emergence of Eco-Fascism: A History of White Nationalism and Xenophobic Scapegoating. In *Handbook of Racism, Xenophobia and Populism: All Forms of Discrimination in the US and Around the Globe,* edited by Adebowale Akande, pp. 457–479. Springer, New York.

Waterton, Emma, and Laurajane Smith. 2010. The Recognition and Misrecognition of Community Heritage. *International Journal of Heritage Studies* 16(1–2): 4–15.

Žižek, Slavoj. 2005. *Bienvenidos al Desierto de lo Real.* Akal, Madrid.

Žižek, Slavoj. 2008. *In Defense of Lost Causes.* Verso, London.

I

Archaeology and Communities
on a National Level

2

Nation, Empire, and Reactionary Populism

An Archaeological Critique

ALFREDO GONZÁLEZ-RUIBAL

The Return of Nationalism

In this chapter I defend that the return of nationalism to the center of politics through reactionary populism poses new challenges to archaeologists that they cannot simply ignore. The past has always been crucial to nationalist projects, and it is perhaps even more so in the case of right-wing populism considering the outstanding psychological, social, and political roles played by roots in this ideology. Along with the return of nationalism has come a vindication of empire, which is often strongly associated with national identity. I first examine the relationship between archaeology and nationalism, with particular attention to reactionary nationalism, I then provide an example of imperialist nationalism at work in Spain, and I finally suggest how to fight against it as archaeologists. I go through different forms of historical production: from statues to archaeological remains to popular books. They are all part of what Cornelius Holtorf (2005), following Jörn Rüsen, has called a certain "culture of history" or "history culture" (*Geschichtskultur*), in this case, of early twenty-first-century Spanish history culture. We tend to separate and compartmentalize the different manifestations of history cultures (academic and popular, material and immaterial, textual and iconographic), but because they are all interconnected, it is advisable to study them together.

The links between nationalism and archaeology have been widely exposed and criticized since Bruce Trigger's influential article "Alternative Archaeologies: Nationalist, Colonialist, Imperialist" (Trigger 1984). The argument, which he further elaborated in his book (Trigger 1989) and had an enormous influence in the historiography of the discipline, was that the birth of archaeology was consubstantial with the birth of the nation-state during the nineteenth century and the consolidation of its dominant social class: the bourgeoisie. Archaeology provided palpable evidence of the nation's deep history at home and legitimation to the empire abroad. Paradigmatic examples of early nationalist archaeology were the excavations promoted by French emperor Napoleon III in Gallic and Merovingian sites—both Gauls and Merovingians regarded as ancestors of the French (Dietler 1994).

Many studies have unraveled the connections between archaeology and nationalist ideologies ever since (Díaz-Andreu and Champion 1996; Hamilakis 1996; Kohl 1998). The resurgence of violent forms of nationalism during the 1990s gave special relevance to the topic and explains the plethora of studies during those years (Díaz-Andreu and Champion 1996; Meskell 2002). By the beginning of the 2000s, however, it was clear that archaeology's Faustian bargains were no longer being struck with the nation-state but rather with capitalism. While the relationship could be traced back to the origins of the discipline (Hamilakis 2015), the connection became stronger with the weakening of the nation-state and nationalist ideologies (at least in the Global North) and the triumph of globalization and neoliberalism. The discipline's uneasy relationship with global capitalism (both a threat and an opportunity) is played out in the commoditization of heritage and the past (Baram and Rowan 2004; Hall and Bombardella 2005), on one side, and cultural resource management (contract archaeology), on the other (Gnecco 2018, this volume: Chapter 4; Zorzin 2015). Both are often connected (Ayala 2015).

The idea of the culturally homogeneous nation-state inherited from the nineteenth century gave way to the celebration of global multiculturalism (Gnecco 2015) in which archaeologists often participated, overlooking its connections with the logic of advanced capitalism. The roles allotted to archaeologists and heritage managers became, rather than the construction of a glorious national past, the production of symbolic goods for international tourist consumption (e.g., Herrera 2013); the celebration of multicultural and fluid postmodern identities (which can be commodified); and the whitewashing of capitalist development (see Gnecco 2018, this volume: Chapter 4). At this stage, well-bounded and sovereign nation-states seemed more an encumbrance than an asset for global capitalism. Practitioners in turn either participated in the global economy of heritage or, more frequently, focused on the local and community archaeology, whose importance, perhaps not coincidentally, started to grow at the same time that concerns with nationalism began to diminish (Marshall 2002). In any case, they turned away from the old-fashioned nation-state: the quest for a homogeneous nation seemed an obsession of the past in many areas, including Latin America and Europe, and the need for archaeology to buttress it seemed limited to countries like Israel (Greenberg and Hamilakis 2022; Hofman 2021) or Iran (Mohammad-pour and Soleimani 2022). But is that so? Some authors have argued that we still have to take nationalism very seriously (Hanscam 2019), and the current wave of reactionary populism proves that conservative forms of nationalism are far from dead.

Reactionary or national populism, after all, has the old nation-state at the center of its discourses. Populist movements purportedly want "to reassert the primacy of the nation over distant and unaccountable international organizations" and "the cherished and rooted national identities over rootless and diffuse transnational ones" (Eatwell and Goodwin 2018: xxxii). In the case of Europe, Brexit was the proof that nationalism was never gone. Yet by the time the United Kingdom voted to leave the European Union, countries in Eastern Europe had been developing aggressive nationalist agendas for years, most notably Poland and Hungary.

Some of the nationalist discourses of populism can be traced back several decades, to the very beginning of neoliberalism. In the United Kingdom, the right was already pitting "'the people' against the 'unions,' the 'nation' against the 'class'" in the 1970s (Bruff 2014: 117). These discourses, both nationalist and exclusionary, have become largely hegemonic today. They are different from nineteenth-century nationalism. If twenty-first century nationalism is reactionary, that of the nineteenth century could be deemed progressive: it either fought against domination by larger political structures (as in Russia or the Austro-Hungarian Empire) or was an inclusionary project of sorts, as with Jacobin centralism in France. Reactionary nationalism is closer to the fascist nationalism in that it is predicated on exclusion, not inclusion, and on ethnicity and race, not citizenship. Fascist and populist nationalisms often have other elements in common, such as the idea that war, empire, and the military are the perfect embodiment of the nation. Along with other values informing reactionary populism, such as the rejection of liberal values (feminism, anti-racism, etc.), ultranationalism is part of the "cultural backlash" that for some have been decisive in the rise of populism, more so than economic inequality (Inglehart and Norris 2016). The cultural cleavage that pits populists against cosmopolitan liberals has a wildly divergent idea of the nation at its core.

As in other aspects, the main difference with the fascism of the 1920s–1940s is that populist nationalism no longer defends violence—at least publicly and officially—to achieve its ends: it does not demand the extermination or violent repression of those elements considered alien to the nation but simply their expulsion. It does not promote wars of aggression as a form of recovering the territory of the nation—although Russia's invasion of Ukraine might be evidence that differences are not clear-cut. It is worth remembering, however, that fascism in Italy and Germany started by simply disenfranchising minorities and dissidents, and violence remained within limits until the war broke out. Thus, the factor of violence that is used by political scientists to distinguish populism from fascism (Finchelstein 2019) might be less relevant than we think. After all, in the case of fascism we have the entire story; in the case of populism, we have only the beginning.

Does the return of nationalism mean that neoliberalism is no longer an issue? Not at all. While in the 1920s and 1930s fascism resorted to the rhetoric of socialism and criticized capitalism and big business (although only in theory, as large companies thrived), national populists today abhor anything that remotely resembles socialism and embrace neoliberalism—often described under the more benign term of "liberalism." The term "authoritarian neoliberalism" (Bruff 2014), which was coined to describe the policies that emerged from the 2008 financial crisis, aptly describes the combination of illiberal democracy and unrestrained capitalism at work in those countries where reactionary populism has triumphed (Lendvai-Bainton and Szelewa 2021). In fact, if we want to understand current nationalism, we must bear in mind that nation and state have been decoupled. National populism praises the nation and decries the state. More precisely, authoritarian neoliberalism at the same time weakens and strengthens the state (Bruff 2014: 124). It hollows it out of its social component (i.e., social welfare) while enhancing its repressive capabilities (army and police).

What does all this have to do with archaeology? As noted at the beginning, the past has always played an outstanding role in nationalist ideologies. This is also the case with reactionary populism. Yet, while archaeologists played a key role as purveyors of useful tales to the progressive nation-state in the nineteenth century, their role is much less important in the crafting of reactionary nationalist narratives. This is not surprising. Since the 1980s, archaeologists have either embraced emancipatory and critical paradigms, from Marxism to decoloniality (Fernández 2006), or relapsed into positivism—some never left it, others adopted it with the rise of the third scientific revolution (Kristiansen 2014). Neither are helpful to the populist program—critical archaeologies for obvious reasons, neopositivists because populism demands myths, not data. Also, the memory of the disgraceful involvement of archaeology with Nazism (Arnold 1990) has probably discouraged those ideologically inclined to populism to start any collaboration. What we see in countries were populism is hegemonic, as with Poland and Hungary, is inaction or resistance rather than active collaboration.

The situation in certain regions of the world might be different: Indian archaeologist Dilip Kumar Chakrabarti, for example, adopts an unabashedly reactionary nationalist position to defend a deep history of India going back to the Indus civilization while bemoaning "the way the Communists have been the prime dictators of ancient Indian historical research for more than 50 years" (Chakrabarti 2021: 38). This is very much in line with Narendra Modi's national populist agenda. In Russia the director of the Hermitage Museum recently showed his full support to Putin's agenda, asserting in relation to his country's invasion of Ukraine that "we are all militarists and imperials" (Ivanisko et al. 2024: 195). It is not easy to find examples that manifest such an unabashed defense of reactionary politics, but it is not unlikely that similar attitudes began to appear elsewhere. However, so far, the place of archaeologists and historians is being mostly occupied by amateurs of all kinds (González-Ruibal et al. 2018). It could be argued that this should not be a source of concern for academia, if it were not that nonacademic visions of the past are often more popular and can have more political influence and wider outreach than scholarly research. This is the case in Spain, where bestselling popular history books are written by nonprofessionals with a reactionary agenda but are widely publicized by the media and the main department stores.

In what follows, I describe a case in which public space is being appropriated by a national populist discourse on the past. I then suggest ways in which such discourse and appropriation can be challenged.

New Statues for an Old Empire

As in many other countries, Spain has been experiencing growing polarization and a rise in reactionary populism, which is marked by a strong resurgence of nationalism. In this case, the origin can be pinpointed with some precision. Since 2006, centripetal nationalism increased in Spain after Catalan nationalism turned from autonomism to independentism, a shift motivated by uncompromising central institutions in the hands of the right (Byrne 2021). In October 2017 the mounting tension between the central government and the autonomous government of Catalonia culminated in an illegal referendum of independence, which was brutally repressed by Madrid. Catalan autonomy was redressed, and several of the nationalist politicians involved in the referendum and the subsequent unilateral proclamation of independence were taken to court and eventually received long prison sentences. The atmosphere of growing nationalism and polarization materialized in an overabundance of flags that filled the balconies of Spain, particularly in Madrid and Catalonia, the two main actors in the drama. Flags were raised as well as statues.

In recent years, statues seem to be going down everywhere: from Colombia to the United Kingdom, from the United States to Martinique (McAnnany, this volume: Chapter 8; Riaño 2021). Monuments commemorating imperialism, racism, slavery, and dictatorship are no longer accepted in many parts of the world. The case of Spain is different. Here monuments celebrating Francisco Franco's dictatorship (1936–1975) have indeed been removed since 2007, when a law banned them from public space. Yet other monuments that celebrate equally controversial pasts are still standing and revered. Not only that: new statues are being erected that celebrate empire. Madrid is at the forefront of this reactionary campaign. While today the regional and city governments are national populist, the process of imperial commemoration has deeper roots. Since 2014, three statues have been erected that openly commemorate imperial heroes: Admiral Blas de Lezo (1689–1741); the last defenders of colonial Philippines (1898–1899); and a legionnaire dressed in the colonial uniform of the 1920s–1930s. Interestingly, none of them are from the heyday of the empire.

Blas de Lezo was a naval commander during the time of Philip V, the first Spanish king of the Bourbon dynasty who inflicted a serious defeat to the Royal Navy in its bid to capture Cartagena de Indias (Colombia). This thwarted further British attempts to expand in the Caribbean (Ramsey 1963). Interest in Blas de Lezo started in the early 2000s, and since then, dozens of books and articles have been published, most insisting, a bit incongruently, on the oblivion into which the commander has fallen (Giménez Chueca 2010).

The last defenders in the Philippines (Figure 2.1) were a group of soldiers besieged in Baler (Luzón) during the Spanish-American War (April 21–December 10, 1898) who refused to surrender even after the end of the conflict. They thought the besiegers were trying to deceive them and therefore sustained the siege for one more year. The fall of the Philippines and Cuba meant the end of a four-centuries-old empire and provoked a cultural crisis in Spain. In this context, the heroes of Baler represented the heroism of a country that had been betrayed. This was a trope that worked well during the Franco dictatorship (Muñiz Sarmiento 2018). As with Lezo, the myth has been revived recently in a plethora of books and articles in which the words "epic," "heroism," and "feat" reveal how much nationalist sentiment is behind them (e.g., López de la Asunción and Leiva 2019).

Finally, the Spanish Legion was created in 1921 as a shock unit to fight in the war of Morocco, a conflict that had dragged on since 1909 and consumed enormous amounts of resources and human lives. The unit was known for its brutality, first in the colonial conflict and then during the Spanish Civil War (1936–1939), where it imported all the atrocities of imperial violence (mass rape, killings of civilians, torture, human trophies, etc.) (Nerín 2005).

Figure 2.1. Monument to the "heroes of Baler," defenders of the last remnants of the Spanish Empire in 1898, erected in Madrid in 2020. Photo by author.

The unit was never dissolved and is still part of the Spanish Army, where it has played a remarkable role in peace missions abroad since the early 1990s. Many of its members, however, have remained loyal to extreme Right ideologies. Promoters of the statue to the legionnaire (Figure 2.2) argue that it is dedicated to the legion as a unit, not to any episode of the past, but the uniform and weapon of the soldier indicate otherwise. All three statues were private initiatives, but they were all supported by the local governments, which provided prime space in the center of the city. They fit well the Spanish Far Right historical imaginary, with its strong focus on the empire (Batalla 2021; Rodríguez-Temiño and Almansa-Sánchez 2021).

The statues, in fact, speak volumes of reactionary populist ideology and its vision of history. The choice of figures is not haphazard. On the one hand, Lezo and the "heroes" of Baler are presented in reactionary thinking as forgotten. They are forgotten, so says the claim, because Spain is ashamed of itself and refuses to acknowledge those figures who do not fit in the politically correct sensibility of the time: they are white, male warriors defending the country. This is perfectly in tune with the politics of victimization that are characteristic of national populism (Al-Ghazzi 2021). An additional merit of being forgotten is that they are less controversial than well-known figures— such as Hernán Cortés or Francisco Pizarro—and people are less likely to have an opinion on them. On the other hand, the enemies they fought were not Indigenous peoples (not even, in the last instance, in the Philippine case) but other empires: the British Empire for Lezo and the United States, who re-

Figure 2.2. Monument to a Spanish colonial legionnaire of the 1920s erected in 2022. Photo by Álvaro Minguito Palomares.

placed Spain as colonial power in the Philippines. These were "bad empires," unlike Spain. It is also a tale of David against Goliath: a weak, dwindling empire fighting against a powerful one (only that, in the second case, Goliath won). Besides, both the feats of Lezo and the men of Baler were defensive in nature: not acts of conquest or aggression but a defense of what was legitimately part of Spain—something more in tune with contemporary sensibilities and also representative of the shift from overtly aggressive fascism to more subtle populism. This narrative does not fit so well the case of the legionnaire. On the one hand, the legion is far from forgotten; on the other, it was fighting a war of occupation in the 1920s. Yet the extreme Right would argue that the military are despised and marginalized anyway and deserve to be celebrated more often—a typical example of ideological resentment (Fassin 2013). They also argue that the legionnaires were defending Spanish territory against attacking Moroccans (Melilla in North Africa is part of Spain to this day) and that the monument simply extols the timeless virtues of the Legion.

Celebrating Nation and Empire

Even though the statues are not dedicated to bloodthirsty conquistadors, they celebrate empire nonetheless, which begs questions. There are several reasons behind the erection of new statues and the defense of the old ones. The most obvious is growing Spanish nationalism, as mentioned above. But why this strong relationship between nation and an old empire? The linkage is not absent in other countries. Nostalgia of empire exists in the United Kingdom (Mitchell 2021), where it has even been backed by historians (Ferguson 2012), and in France, where the affective mixture of nationalism and imperialism is expressed through *la francophonie* and other rhetorical constructs, while at the same time the shadow of Algeria looms large (Flood and Frey 2002). This nostalgia can be explained on several grounds: empires refer to a period of political expansion, military might, and cultural hegemony in a country's history. It is not surprising, thus, that they are remembered with fondness in moments of growing nationalism and especially when the nation is perceived to be weak or not being respected enough by other nations (or its own nationals). Empires are also seen (mistakenly) as periods of homogeneity, when there was one dominant culture, language, and religion. This again tallies well with national populist agendas. Empires thus offer a promise of unity, power, and glory to a citizenry that sees its country as disunited, powerless, and lackluster. These feelings have as much to do with collective identities as with personal experiences. People are not just simply unhappy with their countries but also with their lives shaped by economic difficulties, personal alienation characteristic of late modernity, and an inability to understand rapid cultural changes (including greater gender equality, alternative sexual identities, and multiculturalism). Using German sociologist Hartmut Rosa's concepts, in a world that feels mute and cold, empire offers resonance (Rosa 2019).

In the United Kingdom or France, however, it is the recent empire that is longed for, an empire that lies within living memory and that many citizens have, in fact, experienced—although forgetting or downplaying its darkest side (see Moshenska et al., this volume: Chapter 9). In the case of France, parts of the empire were provincialized during the last part of the imperial period, and the country keeps *territoires d'outremer* that makes the distinction between colony and postcolony a subtle one. The longing for empire in the United Kingdom and France is the longing for a period of supposed ethnic homogeneity, when the colonized were in the colonies and the colonizers in the metropole. A fear of drastic ethnic change and immigration lies behind the success of national populism in most of northern Europe.

The situation in Spain is very different. On the one hand, the empire some Spaniards' long for is not the one that vanished in 1975, with the loss of the last African colony (Western Sahara). Whereas European empires grew during the second wave of imperialism in the 1870s–1880s, Spanish colonies dwindled to irrelevance. With the loss of Cuba, Puerto Rico, and the Philippines, the Spanish ultramarine possessions were reduced to a small part of

Morocco, the minuscule Equatorial Guinea, and a thinly populated expanse of desert in Western Sahara. The number of Spanish settlers was minimal, and there is no collective imagination of the colonies similar to the one existing in France or the United Kingdom. Furthermore, Spain receives relatively few immigrants from its former colonies or Africa more generally compared to other European countries, and most migrants come from the Latin American colonies (Domingo and Blanes 2015: 102), which are not seen as a threat, as are migrants and refugees from the Islamic world and sub-Saharan Africa.

The empire of Spanish nationalism, then, is an empire that vanished two centuries ago and that is not related to anxieties of ethnic or racial replacement as elsewhere in Europe. So why this revival? There are at least three reasons.

The first one is the most obvious: the need for glory. Nationalism, particularly holistic nationalism, emphasizes the great feats of the past (or what are perceived as feats). Most discourses surrounding the Spanish Empire stress its vast extension—often positing, erroneously, that it was the largest in history—and tremendous military power. Related to the imperial past is a surge of interest in the Army of Flanders, the so-called Tercios de Flandes (Batalla 2021: 224–228), an elite military unit that was victorious in the battlefields of Europe until the Battle of Rocroi in 1643—an event that is taken to signal the beginning of the decline of Spanish hegemony in the world. Military prowess and territorial expansion compensate for the lack of both things in the present. They also compensate for what is perceived as the loss of relevance of Spain abroad and its weakening and fragmentation at home—due to the independentist Catalan challenge, the vindications of peripheral nationalisms, and the supposed shame felt by Spaniards in relation to their own history and identity. Furthermore, imperial fantasies are related to the typical aggressive male-chauvinistic ideology of ultranationalism and its desire of domination. I would argue that commemorating military heroes, epic battles, and war is a way of celebrating violence that directly connects with fascism and its ideology of violence (Finchelstein 2019: 74–77), but only in the realm of the imaginary and therefore in a safe way. Unable to defend the actual exercise of violence against internal or external enemies, statues, imperial flags, and the consumption of historical or pseudohistorical material fulfill a fantasy of aggression that cannot be performed in practice.

Yet the Spanish Empire does not offer a positive self-image only because it shows the military power of Spain. Paradoxically, it is also positive because of its benevolence and leniency. The term "colonialism" is, in fact, rejected—something that can be traced back to the Franco dictatorship (Nerín 2020: 48)—under allegations that "our" empire never sought to colonize other territories, exterminate, or enslave but dealt with the locals as bona fide Spanish subjects and thus benevolently. From the nationalist perspective, then, the Spanish Empire was superior to any other not only militarily and territorially but also morally. This simplistic narrative has been revived in recent books by authors with academic credentials—most recently, Muñoz Machado (2019). In this narrative, another evidence of the moral superiority of Spaniards is that they mixed with the locals, creating a large mestizo population, something that did not happen elsewhere. The same eulogizing of racial mixture, which is taken as proof for the lack of racism, exists in Italy (Del Boca 2011). The Spanish Empire thus reflects a positive self-image that the nationalists always need—even more so in a period of uncertainty and political and ethnic divisions within the country.

The second reason for the nationalist celebration of empire is the historical engineering undertaken during the dictatorship of Franco. One of the ideological pillars of the regime was the empire of the Habsburgs. In history books and in official propaganda, the empire of the sixteenth and seventeenth centuries and the dictatorship were directly connected. In the middle was a period of decadence characterized by the loss of colonies, the rise of liberalism and Marxism, the influence of Francs-Maçons and international Jewry (*conjuración judeo-masónica*), receding Catholicism, and growing anticlericalism. This situation reached its climax by the first democratic government of Spain, the Second Republic (1931–1936). The Franco regime intended to return to the period of triumphant counter-reformist Catholicism, centralization, and military hegemony before the decadence that started with the Enlightenment. The legitimacy of the new Spanish state, then, lay in the Spanish Empire. Spanish national identity and imperialism were indissolubly linked.

Not surprisingly, perhaps, the National Day of Spain is today celebrated every October 12, coinciding with the arrival of Christopher Columbus to the Americas. Unlike in other countries, where the national day is related to resistance and survival—the defense of national borders—the day of Spain is related to colonial aggression. Interestingly enough, the national day during the Franco regime was not celebrated on October 12. It was a national holiday, the Día de la Hispanidad or "Day of Spanishness," *hispanidad* referring to a sense of shared Hispanic culture and feeling (Marcilhacy 2014). It had actually been celebrated before the dictatorship—it was first proclaimed a regular holiday in 1935, during the Republic. The Franco regime established as the National Day the eighteenth of July, which was the date that the coup against the republic was staged, leading to the civil war and the beginning of the dictatorship. The conflation of the National Day with the Day of Spanishness occurred under democracy, in 1981. It changed its name from Día de la Hispanidad to Fiesta Nacional de España in 1987 (Humlebæk 2004). The idea was to delink the nation with the dictatorship, but this resulted in national identity becoming even more strongly associated with the empire of Habsburg Spain. Thus, whereas a postcolonial mentality started to develop in other countries, mainly former British colonies, Spain was reconnecting with the empire and giving it a democratic varnish. The moral aspect of the empire (shared cultural roots, brotherhood), which was already present in the last years of the dictatorship, was emphasized and the brutal aspects of the conquest were elided. The positive, liberal image of the colonial undertaking was further reinforced during the commemoration in 1992 of the five-hundredth anniversary of the "discovery" of the Americas, which was purely celebratory and left little room for reflection or criticism. The smooth transition of imperialism from dictatorship to democracy explains that it is now difficult to evict empire from national identity.

A third reason that explains the resonance of the empire with Spanish national identity has to do with the concept of Spain itself. From the late eighteenth century a process of nation-state building started in Europe that led to well-defined, largely homogeneous political entities with which people were supposed to identify. Local languages and cultures were largely erased and survived, at best, as anecdotal phenomena in the geographic, cultural, and political margins of the modern nation-state. That was the case in the United Kingdom and France, where cultural diversity had been strong hitherto but came under attack during the nineteenth century. Spain did not make such transition. Local cultures remained strong and distinctive, and some regions retained an important measure of autonomy—most notably the Basque Country. The process of homogenization was late and incomplete, and when it started it had to compete with rising centrifugal nationalism, which was particularly robust in Catalonia and the Basque Country. After the First World War and the fall of the Austro-Hungarian Empire, it could be argued that Spain remained the last multicultural "empire" within Europe and reproduced most of the problems that had affected Austria-Hungary. It did not become either a federal nation-state (such as Switzerland) or a centralized nation-state (such as France). It remained a country with a strong cultural diversity dominated by one of the cultures—Castilian. From the mid-nineteenth century, increased centralism made the entire country orbit around Madrid. Those areas of Spain where Castilian was not spoken, or not as the primary language, and that did not share the supposedly true Spanish customs (flamenco, bullfighting) were regarded in practice as not very different from colonies, although the colonial gaze of the center also affected those that did share the customs (such as Andalusia). Thus, the expression *en provincias*, "in the provinces"—used by people from Madrid, often disparagingly, to refer to the rest of Spain—reflects this imperial mentality. Some of the most radical proposals put forward by the extreme Right in the current crisis with Catalonia were not dissimilar to colonial policies and include a thorough disarticulation of Catalonian culture and military occupation. Spanish nationalism imagines the old empire as it imagines contemporary Spain: a territory governed by a king and unified by language, faith, and customs. Regional peculiarities existed, but they were minor compared to a shared sense of Spanishness.

These, then, are three elements that make notions of empire so resilient in Spain: the glorification of the empire as a military and moral enterprise; the association of imperial and national identity enacted during the dictatorship and transitioned smoothly into democracy, and the perception of Spain itself as an empire in miniature that resonates with the large empire of the sixteenth century. These three elements are pivotal in reactionary nationalist thinking, but they are by no means restricted to the Far Right, which makes it urgent for historians and archaeologists to address them.

Shifting Competition, Subverting Discourse: Toward Another Epic

Imperial statues condense the main themes of national populism and establish them in the public space: war, empire, unity, military heroism, patriarchy. This is a past that is not only reactionary but also old-fashioned and simple. How should we, archaeologists, react to this hijacking of history?

Sheri Berman (2021: 81) describes three strategies deployed by political parties to the populist challenge. One of them is the dismissive strategy: populist parties are simply ignored along with the issues on which they focus. This is a good option if the issues are considered irrelevant by the wider public. Notions of the past, roots, and national identity are unlikely to be seen as irrelevant by people, so a dismissive attitude is probably not the best option (Ayán, this volume: Chapter 5). Another strategy is adversarial, which means a strong and open opposition against populism. This strategy works fine as long as disagreement with the central concerns of populism is greater than the opposite. Otherwise, it may give more relevance to them. Again, this is probably not the best option when dealing with nationalist/imperialist history, if only because a large majority of the population would have incorporated much of it through the ideological apparatuses of the state—television, school, family memories (Althusser 2006). A third strategy is accommodative: the established parties adapt to the policies defended by populist parties to avoid defections. In politics this has proven to move the debate closer to populism, usually without positive effects to established parties. So far archaeologists (myself included) have adopted either a dismissive or an adversarial strategy, continuing their research in the framework of cosmopolitan liberalism or community archaeology as if nothing (or little) had happened or criticizing the growing influence of the Far Right without this materializing in new ways of conducting public archaeology. Resorting to an accommodative strategy is, of course, out of the question. So what can we do?

While we should obviously not try to approach populism, we may learn from its successful strategies, particularly two: shifting competition and subverting discourses. Regarding the first, the idea is to shift competition to a new issue domain (Ward et al. 2015: 1233). This is crucial because the shift is easier in the field of culture than in economy, and culture is playing an outstanding role in the rise of populism. In the case of archaeology, it is relatively easy to find new themes that compete with reactionary narratives. After all, they tend to be repetitive and unoriginal. In the case of Spain, the same stories of empire have been circulating for 150 years with few changes. In fact, recent changes to the narrative are more formal (the use of new media) than in content.

An example of shifting competition is placing emphasis on connections instead of autochthony without leaving the focus on the nation (Emily Hanscam in Hofmann et al. 2021: 526), which is obviously important for a large part of the public. It would be a mistake to deride the need for roots and stability that is felt by many and not only reactionary populists. In fact, roots can be reclaimed from a progressive perspective, even as an antidote against fascism (Ayán, this volume: Chapter 5; González-Ruibal 2020; Weil 2002). Indeed, roots and connections have more in common than it may seem. Another example of shifting the competition would be placing emphasis on communal care, collective action, and solidarity (see McGuire, this volume: Chapter 6) as opposed to the staunch neoliberal individualism that populism leaves untouched despite all its rhetoric of national community. Archaeologists, as other social scientists, have been concerned with practices of care for a while and trace them to the earliest periods of humanity. In fact, much of what we find can be related in one way or another to caring (Montón-Subías and Sánchez-Romero 2008). This means going beyond the rhetoric of care so prevalent in academia today and actually exploring in the past and showing the public how people cared for each other and how this has been crucial to societies since prehistoric times. Along with the notion of care are that of solidarity (McGuire 2008: 45, 203–204) and hospitality, which have often been seen as indistinguishable from care (Grosso 2015). Talking about care, solidarity, and hospitality is a way of taking attention away from violence and imperial conquest so cherished by populism but of little impact to people's daily life.

As for subverting discourse, this is something in which reactionary populism excels. It was already a hallmark of fascism: the subversion—or, rather, inversion—of language to make words mean something completely different (often the reverse) from their original meaning (Klemperer 2006). An excellent example of this inversion is the populist use of the term "freedom." Populist freedoms often mean precisely the opposite: a form of servitude inasmuch as the longing for traditional values invariably entails curtailing rights. Yet this inversion has been extremely successful in the Americas and Europe, especially when "freedom" is pitted against "communism." I suggest that we do the same with those concepts that can be appropriated from the extreme Right. Such concepts include notions of heroism, bravery, and epic. The only thing is, we have to remove them from the realm of violence and aggression in which they usually work and transfer them to the realm of daily life. From this perspective, care and hospitality can be heroic and epic.

I would like to finish illustrating this double strategy, shifting competition and subverting discourse, with an archaeological example. The case is an excavation of an area of Madrid, Entrevías, that had been bombed during the Spanish Civil War. My team and I had been asked to do the excavation by a foundation associated with a socialist trade union (Fundación Anastasio de Gracia) to retrieve the remains of bombed buildings. However, the excavation exposed, in the first place, a shantytown that had been established amid the ruins of the bombed houses in the mid-1950s and abandoned in the mid-1970s. Despite extensive demolition (or perhaps because of it), the remains of the shacks were well preserved, and a large amount of material was recovered in situ from the inhabitants of the shacks (Figure 2.3). The people living in the shantytown were migrants from poor regions of southern Spain who had moved to Madrid seeking job opportunities and a better life. In that, they were not different from the current population of the neighborhood, with a large percentage of migrants—in this case from different parts of Eastern Europe, Latin America, and Africa. The excavation and testimonies from neighbors showed that practices of mutual care and hospitality were crucial for the survival and improvement of the people living in Entrevías. These practices materialized in the layout of the shacks and the organization of the wider settlement and in the objects we found inside, including many artifacts associated with hygiene, health, cleaning, and child-rearing.

When attention turned from the war ruins to the shacks, neighbors immediately became interested and supportive of the project. They saw the shan-

Figure 2.3. Excavation of a shantytown from the 1950s to 1970s in Entrevías, Madrid. Photo by author.

tytown as an essential part of their history, one they were proud of: a history of overcoming poverty. We presented this to the media in two ways: as an epic tale of heroism and as collective history. What we were digging was not just the history of the neighborhood (which indeed it was) but the history of Spain, made out of immigrants trying to create a better future in very difficult circumstances—which was actually the case: large cities in the country were socially and physically made by poor migrants during the nineteenth and twentieth centuries. This story connected in a meaningful way past and present, national and international migrants. The story was soon picked up by virtually all national media, including conservative ones. Not surprisingly, it was the Far Right that was not happy. But by not being happy (or even openly hostile) they exposed themselves. They showed that the populist rhetoric was just that: a rhetoric ungrounded in any real concern for common people. The excavation of Entrevías also showed that stories exposed by archaeologists related to the recent past and the ordinary can compete with old empires and military feats. They can be useful to construct another idea of the nation, one that is inclusionary and based on ideas of hospitality and mutual care rather than violence and aggression.

Conclusions

In this chapter I have explored the rise of nationalism in association with populism. I have argued that this new nationalism can be described as reactionary and has more points in common with fascist ideas of the nation than with the progressive, integrative nationalism of the nineteenth century. In the legitimation of this new nationalism, archaeologists play a very minor role, unlike in earlier forms. In fact, they are being replaced by nonacademics, who often have a strong popular and political impact. Along with nationalism has come a vindication of empire, which is consistent with growing xenophobia and cultural chauvinism but also with a dissatisfaction with personal life typical of late modernity—especially among men. The epic of empire promises what the dull experience of the everyday cannot. To illustrate the politics of the past of reactionary nationalism, I have presented the case of Spain—or, rather, Madrid—in which nationalism and imperialism go hand in hand and are materialized in the erection of statues in public spaces, a practice that goes against global trends. It is not a coincidence that a reactionary ideology expresses itself in a reactionary medium: historicist figurative statues depicting individuals regarded as heroes—more specifically, military men who are white, Catholic, and heterosexual. I have suggested that archaeology can counteract this and similar reactionary narratives by exposing other pasts in which it is the collective, and not only a few men, who are celebrated; and it is hospitality and reciprocal care, rather than violence, that is emphasized as constitutive of a nation. The tangible things of the past, even those of the very recent past, have an extraordinary affective power that can be usefully mobilized to construct narratives that are alternative to chauvinistic, male-centered discourses while at the same time do not renounce the notions of epic and roots. They simply subvert them and appropriate them in critical ways.

These narratives already exist, but they have been mostly written for other academics or circulated in the small circles of the already convinced (stakeholders, grassroots associations, local communities). We must strive to write them for a wider public, both in social and quantitative terms. As noted in the introduction, we can make them available through social media, new media, and trade books. Creating new narratives is not an easy task. Populist historical accounts are simple, effective, and have the support of skilled propagandists, Far Right lobbies, and mass media, and they are consumed as a form of self-help in a time of social and individual crisis. It is difficult to compete against that. But archaeologists have the unrivaled advantage of direct access to the material past. This allows us to produce more authentic, fresh, accurate, and original stories—versus the endless rehashing of populism. This is a privilege but also an enormous responsibility that we should use right: to write better narratives about the past, for sure, but also to contribute to more democratic societies in the present.

References Cited

Al-Ghazzi, Omar. 2021. We Will Be Great Again: Historical Victimhood in Populist Discourse. *European Journal of Cultural Studies* 24(1): 45–59.

Althusser, Louis. 2006. Ideology and Ideological State Apparatuses (Notes towards an Investigation). In *The Anthropology of the State: A Reader*, edited by Aradhana Sharma and Akhil Gupta, pp. 86–98. Blackwell, Oxford.

Arnold, Bettina. 1990. The Past as Propaganda: Totalitarian Archaeology in Nazi Germany. *Antiquity* 64(244): 464–478.

Ayala Rocabado, Patricia. 2015. Neoliberal Multiculturalism and Contract Archeology in Northern Chile. *International Journal of Historical Archaeology* 19(4): 775–790.

Baram, Uzi, and Yorke Rowan. 2004. Archaeology after Nationalism': Globalization and the Consumption of the Past. In *Marketing Heritage: Archaeology and the Consumption of the Past*, edited by Uzi Baram and Yorke Rowan, pp. 3–23. Routledge, London.

Batalla, Pablo. 2021. *Los nuevos odres del nacionalismo español*. Trea, Gijón.

Berman, Sheri. 2021. The Causes of Populism in the West. *Annual Review of Political Science* 24: 71–88.

Bruff, Ian. 2014. The Rise of Authoritarian Neoliberalism. *Rethinking Marxism* 26(1): 113–129.

Byrne, Steven (editor). 2021. *Identity and Nation in 21st Century Catalonia: El Procés*. Cambridge Publishing Scholars, New Castle-upon-Tyne.

Chakrabarti, Dilip Kumar. 2021. Nationalism in the Study of Ancient Indian History. *National Security* 4(1): 29–50.

Del Boca, Angelo. 2011. *Italiani, brava gente?* Neri Pozza, Roma.

Díaz-Andreu, Margarita, and Timothy Champion (editors). 1996. *Nationalism and Archaeology in Europe*. Routledge, London.

Dietler, Michael. 1994. "Our Ancestors the Gauls": Archaeology, Ethnic Nationalism, and the Manipulation of Celtic Identity in Modern Europe. *American Anthropologist* 96(3): 584–605.

Domingo, Andreu, and Amand Blanes. 2015. Inmigración y emigración en España: Estado de la cuestión y perspectivas de futuro. *Anuario CIDOB de la Inmigración en España 2014*: 91–122. https://raco.cat/index.php/AnuarioCIDOBInmigracion/article/view/312788.

Eatwell, Roger, and Matthew Goodwin. 2018. *National Populism: The Revolt against Liberal Democracy*. Penguin, London.

Fassin, Didier. 2013. On Resentment and Ressentiment: The Politics and Ethics of Moral Emotions. *Current Anthropology* 54(3): 249–267.

Ferguson, Niall. 2012. *Empire: How Britain Made the Modern World*. Penguin, London.

Fernández, Victor M. 2006. Una arqueología crítica: Ciencia, ética y política en la construcción del pasado. Barcelona: Crítica.

Finchelstein, Federico. 2019. *From Fascism to Populism in History*. University of California Press, Berkeley.

Flood, Christopher, and Hugo Frey. 2002. Defending the Empire in Retrospect: The Discourse of the Extreme Right. In *Promoting the Colonial Idea: Propaganda and Visions of Empire in France,* edited by Tony Chafer and Amanda Sackur, pp. 195–210. Palgrave Macmillan, London.

Giménez Chueca, Iván. 2010. Blas de Lezo: El marino olvidado. *Clío: Revista de historia* 109: 66–73.

Gnecco, Cristóbal. 2015. Heritage in Multicultural Times. In *The Palgrave Handbook of Contemporary Heritage Research,* edited by Emma Waterton and Steve Watson, pp. 263–280. Palgrave Macmillan, London.

Gnecco, Cristóbal. 2018. Development and Disciplinary Complicity: Contract Archaeology in South America under the Critical Gaze. *Annual Review of Anthropology* 47: 279–293.

González-Ruibal, Alfredo. 2020. What Remains? On Material Nostalgia. In *After Discourse: Things, Affects, Ethics,* edited by Bjørnar Olsen, Mats Burström, Caitlin DeSilvey, and Þora Pétursdóttir, pp. 187–203. Routledge, Abingdon.

González-Ruibal, Alfredo, Pablo González Alonso, and Felipe Criado-Boado. 2018. Against Reactionary Populism: Towards a New Public Archaeology. *Antiquity* 92(362): 507–515.

Greenberg, Raphael, and Yannis Hamilakis. 2022. *Archaeology, Nation, and Race: Confronting the past, Decolonizing the Future in Greece and Israel.* Cambridge: Cambridge University Press.

Grosso, José Luis. 2015. Excess of Hospitality: Critical Semiopraxis and Theoretical Risks in Postcolonial Justice. In *After Ethics,* edited by Alejandro Haber and Nick Shepherd, pp. 79–101. Springer, New York.

Hall, Martin, and Pia Bombardella. 2005. Las Vegas in Africa. *Journal of Social Archaeology* 5(1): 5–24.

Hamilakis, Yannis. 1996. Through the Looking Glass: Nationalism, Archaeology and the Politics of Identity. *Antiquity* 70(270): 975–978.

Hamilakis, Yannis. 2015. Archaeology and the Logic of Capital: Pulling the Emergency Break. *International Journal of Historical Archaeology* 19(4): 721–735.

Hanscam, Emily. 2019. Postnationalism and the Past: The Politics of Theory in Roman Archaeology. *Theoretical Roman Archaeology Journal* 2(1): 1–14.

Herrera, Alexander. 2013. Heritage Tourism, Identity and Development in Peru. *International Journal of Historical Archaeology* 17(2): 275–295.

Hofman, Bárbara. 2021. Entonces y ahora: El rol de la arqueología en los procesos de construcción y deconstrucción de las identidades nacionales (América Latina y Estado de Israel). *Claroscuro: Revista del Centro de Estudios sobre Diversidad Cultural* 20: 1–26. https://doi.org/10.35305/cl.vi20.14.

Hofmann, Daniela, Emily Hanscam, Martin Furholt, Martin Bača, Samantha S. Reiter, Alessandro Vanzetti, Kostas Kotsakis, et al. 2021. Populism, Identity Politics, and the Archaeology of Europe. *European Journal of Archaeology* 24(4): 519–555.

Holtorf, Cornelius. 2005. *From Stonehenge to Las Vegas: Archaeology as Popular Culture.* AltaMira, Lanham, Maryland.

Humlebæk, Carsten. 2004. La nación española conmemorada: La fiesta nacional en España después de Franco. *Iberoamericana* 4(13): 87–99.

Inglehart, Ronald F., and Pippa Norris. 2016. Trump, Brexit, and the Rise of Populism:

Economic Have-Nots and Cultural Backlash. HKS Faculty Research Working Paper No. RWP16–026. Harvard Kennedy School, Cambridge, Massachusetts.

Ivanysko, Svitlana, Gennadii Kazakevych, and Pavlo Shydlovskyi. 2024. Cultural Heritage in the Russo-Ukrainian War: A Victim in the Conflict. *Complutum* 35(1): 191–214.

Klemperer, Victor. 2006. *Language of the Third Reich: LTI: Lingua Tertii Imperii*. Blackwell, Oxford.

Kohl, Philip L. 1998. Nationalism and Archaeology: On the Constructions of Nations and the Reconstructions of the Remote Past. *Annual Review of Anthropology* 27(1): 223–246.

Kristiansen, Kristian. 2014. Towards a New Paradigm? The Third Science Revolution and Its Possible Consequences in Archaeology. *Current Swedish Archaeology* 22(1): 11–34.

Lendvai-Bainton, Noemi, and Dorota Szelewa. 2021. Governing New Authoritarianism: Populism, Nationalism and Radical Welfare Reforms in Hungary and Poland. *Social Policy & Administration* 55(4): 559–572.

López de la Asunción, Miguel Ángel, and Miguel Leiva. 2019. La gesta de la defensa de la posición de Baler, Filipinas (30 junio 1898–2 junio 1899). *Revista de Historia Militar* 2: 253–300.

Marcilhacy, David. 2014. La Hispanidad bajo el franquismo: Ell americanismo al servicio de un proyecto nacionalista. In *La Hispanidad bajo el franquismo: Ell americanismo al servicio de un proyecto nacionalista,* edited by Xosé Manuel Núñez Seixas and Stéphane Michonneau, pp. 73–102. Casa de Velázquez, Madrid.

Marshall, Y. 2002. What Is Community Archaeology? *World Archaeology* 34(2): 211–219.

McGuire, Randall. 2008. *Archaeology as Political Action*. University of California Press, Berkeley, California.

Meskell, Lynn (editor). 2002. *Archaeology under Fire: Nationalism, Politics and Heritage in the Eastern Mediterranean and Middle East*. Routledge, London.

Mitchell, Peter. 2021. *Imperial Nostalgia: How the British Conquered Themselves*. Manchester University Press, Manchester.

Mohammadpour, Ahmad, and Soleimani, Kamal. 2022. Silencing the Past: Persian Archaeology, Race, Ethnicity, and Language. *Current Anthropology* 63(2): 185–210.

Montón-Subías, Sandra, and Margarita Sánchez-Romero (editors). 2008. *Engendering Social Dynamics: The Archaeology of Maintenance Activities*. BAR IS 1862. Archaeopress, Oxford.

Muñiz Sarmiento, Ramón. 2018. Los últimos de Filipinas: La re-visitación de un mito histórico. *Filmhistoria Online* 28(1–2): 49–64.

Muñoz Machado, Santiago. 2019. *Civilizar o exterminar a los bárbaros*. Crítica, Barcelona.

Nerín, Gustau. 2005. *La guerra que vino de África*. Crítica, Barcelona.

Nerín, Gustau, 2020. La cómoda memoria colonial española: El Imperio de ayer y la España de hoy. *RiMe: Rivista dell'Istituto di Storia dell'Europa Mediterranea* 7(2): 37–51.

Ramsey, Russell W. 1963. The Defeat of Admiral Vernon at Cartagena in 1741. *Southern Quarterly* 1(3): 332.

Riaño, Peio H. 2021. *Decapitados: Una historia contra los Monumentos Racistas, Esclavistas e Invasores*. Ediciones B, Barcelona.

Rodríguez-Temiño, Ignacio, and Jaime Almansa-Sánchez. 2021. The Use of past Events as

Political Symbols in Spain. The Example of Vox and the Need for a New Archaeology of Ethnicity. *International Journal of Heritage Studies* 27(10): 1064–1078.

Rosa, Hartmut. 2019. *Resonance: A Sociology of Our Relationship to the World.* John Wiley & Sons, Oxford.

Trigger, Bruce G. 1984. Alternative Archaeologies: Nationalist, Colonialist, Imperialist. *Man* 19(3): 355–370.

Trigger, Bruce G. 1989. *A History of Archaeological Thought.* Cambridge: Cambridge University Press.

Ward, Dalston, Jeong Hyun Kim, Mathew Graham, and Margit Tavits. 2015. How Economic Integration Affects Party Issue Emphases. *Comparative Political Studies* 48(10): 1227–1259.

Weil, Simone. 2002. *The Need for Roots: Prelude to a Declaration of Duties towards Mankind.* London: Routledge.

Zorzin, Nicola. 2015. Archaeology and Capitalism: Successful Relationship or Economic and Ethical Alienation? In *Ethics and Archaeological Praxis,* edited by Cristóbal Gnecco and Dorothy Lippert, 115–139. Springer, New York.

3

Constellations of Co-Resistance

Taking Power and Making Power in American Archaeology

LINDSAY MARTEL MONTGOMERY

There is a growing cohort of archaeologists in the United States who are work-ing to addresses disciplinary power imbalances rooted in colonial structures built upon assertions of racialized privilege. Historically, archaeologists have supported these systems of power (sometimes intentionally, sometimes un-intentionally) by producing what Eve Tuck (2009: 413) has referred to as "damage-centered" research that documents individual and communal pain, loss, or lack. Early American archaeologists, such as Thomas Jefferson (1787: 138), described the "arrow points, stone hatchets, stone pipes, and half shapen images" they encountered as evidence of the failure of Indigenous people to properly cultivate the land. Although more systematic in their approach, twentieth-century anthropologists continued to write about Indigenous defi-cit in similar ways. One influential scholar in this regard was Julian Stew-ard, who used the framework of cultural ecology to argue that Shoshonean groups living in the Great Basin lacked sophisticated political and economic structures and were therefore undeserving of federal recognition (Blackhawk 1997; Clemmer 2009). Jefferson's and Steward's works exemplify how archae-ological and ethnological evidence has been used by settler intellectuals to write damage-centered narratives that ultimately justify colonial policies of removal and assimilation. Lest we are tempted to imagine that these harmful racialized practices are merely an unfortunate facet of the discipline's colonial origins, we need only turn to the now highly publicized case of the Ancient One (Kennewick Man). In the late-1990s, bioarcheological reconstructions of the Ancient One's remains were seized upon by the Asatru Folk Assem-bly, a right-wing white power religious group that argued that the remains belonged to the ancestor of contemporary Europeans (Egan 1998). The use of archaeological data (despite the protest of scholars) to support European claims to the land in North America demonstrates the fields' embeddedness within settler logics of racial privilege and associated property rights.

Today damage-centered research is often framed as part of a broader liberal project aimed at achieving social justice through the documentation of trauma or deficit. While often operating benevolently using the rhetoric of social justice, such research maintains dominant power structures rooted in whiteness—

> the conscious or unconscious, violent or subtle, individual or collective ways in which dominance is imposed upon BIPOC (Black, Indigenous, and people of color) individuals' communities, or spaces by those in privileged positions through a racial calculus, logic or structural mechanism. (Reilly 2022: 52)

As Eve Tuck and C. Ree (2013: 642) note, settler colonialism has a haunting quality that refuses the finality of liberal reforms that would hope for reconciliation or resolution. The naturalization of whiteness within North American archaeology informs current critiques of efforts to create a more equitable, inclusive, and diverse discipline. Such resistance is exemplified by a recently published op-ed that frames the incorporation of some "traditional" Indigenous practices into archaeology as explicitly sexist (Weiss 2022). This "politics of resentment" echoes the logic of right-wing populism, which valorizes individual freedoms while minimizing the continuing impacts of settler colonialism on cultural heritage management, academic institutions, and the lived experiences of BIPOC people within these spheres (Cramer 2016: 9). The growing tensions within North American archaeology mirror the widening political polarizations between liberal legislative and grassroots campaigns to redress racial, gendered, and economic injustice and right-wing populist rejections of minoritarian rights (Lowndes 2017: 244).

Inspired by Randall McGuire's (2008:14) argument that the practice of archaeology is always "politics by other means," this chapter explores how liberal and right-wing populist discourses have shaped the practice of archaeology in the United States over the last 10 years. While liberal reforms have produced new ethical frameworks and equity-based policies, they have not addressed archaeology's embeddedness in whiteness and the settler state. Alternatively, populist appeals to individual "freedoms" and rights fails to question the cultural and historical situatedness of these values and their entanglement with white supremacy. Although these approaches make distinct rhetorical arguments, liberal and right-wing populist politics converge in their use of damage-centered narratives and support of settler colonial power structures.

This convergence suggests that disciplinary transformation hinges on addressing spectral forms of settler colonialism. To deconstruct these colonial hauntings, I advocate for an anticolonial abolitionist framework grounded in Leanne Simpson's (2016) concept of "constellations of co-resistance," which is a relational approach to coalition building that creates long-term networks of solidarity across BIPOC scholars, descendant communities, and allied archaeologists. While members of these constellations of co-resistance hold diverse positionalities, they share the goal of dismantling dominant power structures rooted in whiteness, patriarchy, capitalism, ableism, and deficit.

"Politics by Other Means": Populism and Liberalism in US Archaeology

Contemporary expressions of right-wing populism in the United States are characterized by a belief in the inherent rights of "the people" to self-rule and freedom; rights that must be defended from minoritarian challenges or policies that expand the power of central governments (Lowndes 2017: 244; Ostiguy 2017). As with González-Ruibal's work on Spanish nationalism and populism (this volume: Chapter 2) and Cristóbal Gnecco's (this volume: Chapter 4) discussion of reactionary populism in Brazil demonstrate, right-wing populism is built upon nostalgic historical narratives that encourage nativism and that ignore structural imbalances created by colonialism. US president Donald Trump's 2016 campaign slogan, Make America Great Again, is emblematic of this nostalgia for empire and the free-market capitalism that propelled Europe (and later the United States) to global dominance. Trump's slogan was a strategic nod to American expansionism and military domination, an era that is temporally ambiguous and conveniently free of racial conflict or identity politics (Tharoor 2016). The framing of right-wing political interests in popular terms, naturalizes white privilege, strategically erasing the position of non-Indigenous peoples as settlers and obscuring the numerous ways settlers have benefited from the ongoing dispossession of Native lands.

Liberalism's embrace of the messiness of direct democracy provides a counterpoint to the anti-minoritarian rhetoric that underpins right-wing populism (Grande 2013: 376). From a normative perspective, liberalism seeks to build a new society in the shell of the old through justice-based initiatives centered on enhancing minority rights and redistributing power and resources to historically marginalized groups (Lafrenz-Samuels 2018: 133; Rawls 1971). The evolving agenda of multiculturalism—the presence of people from diverse racial and ethnic backgrounds—has played a leading role within these liberal reform efforts. Multiculturalism has manifested itself within the discipline of archaeology through the framework of multivocality—the "contemporaneous

Figure 3.1. Indian Creek in Bears Ears National Monument, Utah. Photograph taken August 14, 2016, by US Bureau of Land Management.

articulation of numerous different narratives or parallel discourses" (Oxford University Press 2023). Multivocality is an approach to power sharing that creates space for multiple stakeholder perspectives and values to enhance disciplinary understandings of the past (Atalay et al. 2014: 11–12).

The formation of Bears Ears National Monument and subsequent controversy that erupted around its protected status provides a window into how liberalism and right-wing populism have shaped cultural heritage management in the United States (Figure 3.1). On December 28, 2016, President Barack Obama created the Bears Ears National Monument, placing 1.35 million acres in southeastern Utah under federal protection.

Of the 129 federally created national monuments, Bears Ears was the first developed using the principles of multivocality. In crafting the monument's nomination, extensive consultation was undertaken with the Bears Ears Inter-Tribal Coalition comprising members of the Navajo Nation, Hopi Tribe, Pueblo of Zuni, Ute Mountain Ute, and the Ute Indian Tribe. By empowering different Indigenous communities to act as co-stewards of archaeological sites and knowledge derived from these sites, the monument's formation marked a significant political shift toward power sharing in matters of cultural and natural heritage preservation. In this instance, Native American concerns, knowledge, and practices took priority over the interests of natural resource companies and private development.

Less than a year after the monument's formation, President Trump reduced Bears Ears by 85%. This rollback was prompted by concerted lobbying on the part of a uranium firm hoping to reopen protected areas within the monument's boundaries for mining. In justifying the reduction of Bears Ears, President Trump critiqued the American Antiquities Act, arguing that it was a gross overextension of federal power. Underpinning Trump's argument is a right-wing populist ideology that positions the exercise of federal power and the support of minoritarian rights as the two greatest threats to social stability. The Trump administration's efforts to reduce and reallocate the traditional territories of the Bears Ears Inter-Tribal Coalition prompted three lawsuits. Plaintiffs in these cases argued that the rollback was "a systematic, planned assault on Tribal sovereignty by the Trump administration that was designed to weaken government-to-government consultation with Tribal nations and dismantle environmental and heritage regulations" (d'Alpoim Guedes, Gonzalez, and Rivera-Collazo 2021: 900). Trump's policy efforts supported capitalist interests, reinforced the rights of settlers, and solidified the authority of white-dominant structures in matters of cultural heritage management.

The Bear's Ears case demonstrates how right-wing populism and liberalism uphold settler colonial power structures despite differences in political goals and rhetoric. While Trump's villainization of big government appealed to populist values of neoliberalism and individualism, his ability to reclaim lands within Bear's Ears for private development was made possible by the very executive privileges he criticized. Passed in 1906 under the presidency of Theodore Roosevelt, the Antiquities Act was originally framed as a liberal reform effort that responded to increasing levels of European immigration in the American West and a desire to preserve the Indigenous sites and pristine natural landscapes these settlers encountered. Although the protections laid out in the Antiquities Act were seen as contributing to the public good of the nation (including Native peoples), the law reinforces federal control over Indigenous lands. As Alexis de Tocqueville (2010[1835–1840]: 527) pointedly commented in *Democracy in America,* "the dispossession of the Indians often takes place today in regular and, so to speak, [an] entirely legal manner."

The tensions and convergences between populist and liberal discourses is also reflected within the academic discipline of American archaeology. The liberal spirit of multivocality informs the Society for American Archaeology's principle of stewardship, which seeks to unite diverse perspectives under a shared identity vis-à-vis the material records. As stewards, archaeologists have a duty to facilitate the "long-term conservation and protection of the archaeological record" (SAA 1996). Although framed in inclusive terms, this principle supports an individualistic understanding of ethical practice, which asserts that the primary responsibility of archaeologists is to the profession rather than to specific communities. This definition of archaeological stewardship also reinforces whiteness by imposing a Western understanding of preservation onto the material culture of a wide range of descendant communities who may not hold a shared understanding of when and how archaeological sites should be conserved or protected.

In seeking to respect the perspectives and rights of diverse stakeholders, multivocal approaches to heritage management often gloss over the unique histories of dispossession and racialization that surround the material record in the United States. For example, the legal relationship between the government and federally recognized tribal nations has led to formal legal protections for Indigenous cultural heritage that are not currently extended to other historically marginalized communities, like African Americans (Dunnavant 2016). These historical differences have meaningful implications for how cultural and material heritage should be managed and by whom. In naturalizing dominant systems of power, multivocal approaches deny communities the opportunity to craft alternative definitions of stewardship or to refuse archaeology all together.

Multivocality has also informed concerted efforts to hire BIPOC scholars in the field of archaeology (Montgomery and Supernant 2022: 6). Current diversity, equity, and inclusion recruitment initiatives build upon earlier efforts in the 1960s and 1970s to increase the number of historically underrepresented identities within academia and professional fields more broadly. The logic behind these efforts is one of critical mass: hiring archaeologists who identify as nonwhite will transform the discipline from the inside, making it more inclusive of different perspectives, approaches, and goals along the way. Despite efforts to recruit and retain diverse identities in archaeology, over the past 10 years, the actual demographics of the discipline appear to have changed little. In 2010, 71.5% of archaeologists identified as white and 48% as male; by 2019 this ratio had shifted only slightly with 70.9% of archaeologists identifying as white and 53% identifying as male (Zippia 2022). The slow pace of diversification within archaeology reflects the failure of multivocal approaches to alter structural facets of the discipline that undermine the retention of diversity and constrain the impact of equity and inclusion initiatives. Accelerating the pace and nature of disciplinary transformation requires moving beyond multivocality toward actively deconstructing oppressive forms of whiteness within systems of promotion, frameworks of financial compensation, and imbalances in service workloads as well as combating ongoing expressions of hostility (both overt and unconscious) toward BIPOC researchers (Clark et al. 2016: 4).

Bringing historically marginalized voices into the discipline without providing them with tools or support systems to create change asks BIPOC archaeologists to "ascend" to whiteness by taking up the dominant culture and practices of the discipline. As Tiffany Lethabo King writes, if racialized others "can become the settler, then the white settler has continued to occupy the structural and ontological position of the conquistador and should be named as such" (King 2019: xii). Liberal frameworks that emphasize inclusion without transformation engage in a "politics of distraction" that shifts our attention away from the restitution of homelands, resources, and power while reinvesting in rights-based processes predicated on the legitimacy of settler colonial structures and institutions (Corntassel and Holder 2008: 472). In this sense, liberal reforms based on multivocality represent what Eve Tuck and K. Wayne Yang (2012: 9) have called a "settler move to innocence"—efforts that relieve settlers of feelings of guilt or responsibility without giving up land, power, or privilege.

In naturalizing whiteness, the moves to innocence made through multivocal policies share uncomfortable similarities to the rhetorical effects of the populist discourses of "the people." Definitions of the "people" within right-wing populism are embedded within a European humanist tradition that projects a universalized vision of society built upon the identification of humanity with white, heterosexual men (Lowndes 2017: 244). By assuming the existence of an ahistorical, classless, and racially homogeneous political entity (i.e., "the people"), populism makes a move to innocence that appeals to liberal sensibilities of solidarity and "color blindness" while naturalizing whiteness and its attendant rights and privileges.

Constellations of Co-Resistance: An Anticolonial Abolitionist Tool Kit

In addressing the damaging effects of settler colonial power structures within American archaeology and cultural heritage management, I advocate for an approach grounded in abolition, anticolonialism, and co-resistance. Anticolonial abolition rejects the right-wing populist rhetoric of individualism that reflects Western notions of legal culpability and that portray systemic inequality as a personal experience rather than as a structural problem to be dismantled (e.g., racists, not racism, are the problem) (Fanon 1963). Furthermore, anticolonial abolitionist politics does not presume that settler colonial power structures should or will always continue to exist. Instead, this approach is driven by a hopeful vision of the future that creates "space to reflect on what might be more just forms of governance, not only for Native peoples, but for the rest of the world" (Smith 2005: 311).

Anticolonialism and abolition are two distinct components of a shared struggle for social justice in the United States because of the historical and ongoing relationship between Indigenous dispossession and Black oppression. This relationship was clearly articulated by Patrick Wolfe (2006), who argued that settler colonialism is a violent structure driven by a capitalist logic that clears the land of Indigenous people so it can be transformed into settler property made profitable through the labor of Black chattel slaves. The logic of white supremacy has justified the "eliminate-to-replace" vision that drives settler colonial relations with Indigenous peoples as well as the fungibility of Black bodies (Grande 2013: 376).

Anticolonialism as a form of praxis supports the "prior, definitive, Indigenous politics of (home)land-based activism" by revealing and deconstructing the property rights which are the basis of wealth, power, and inequality within the United States (Grande 2013: 376; see also Tuck and Yang 2012: 19, 26). As Jeffrey Corntassel and Cindy Holder (2008: 471) argue, "the return of homelands and permanent sovereignty over natural resources are critical to any discussion of indigenous restitution and, by extension, reconciliation." While anticolonial activism is focused on transforming settler relationships to Native lands and resources, abolition is centered on dismantling manifestations of anti-Blackness—the unique logic of Black subjugation and repression in contemporary society (Palacios 2020: 524; Jung and Vargas 2021). Abolition entails challenging the fungibility of Black lives, dismantling oppressive institutions that disproportionately imprison and brutalize Black people, and combating systems of violence that maintain white privilege. Like anticolonialism, abolition is a place-based project that actively asserts the presence and value of Black bodies on the land in the past, present, and future.

Anticolonial abolitionist work is made possible through the formation of what Simpson (2016: 27) calls "constellations of co-resistance." Constellations of co-resistance use non-elite forms of movement-building including political education, capacity building, community engagement, and direct action to dismantle systems and practices within archaeology and cultural heritage management built upon racist, misogynistic, homophobic, ableist, and classist frameworks (Collins 2015; Crenshaw 1989; Palacios 2020: 526–527). Archaeologists should commit to co-resistance out of recognition of the injustices produced by ongoing colonial oppression *and* the promise of Black and Indigenous knowledge systems to facilitate a greater understanding of the human condition more broadly (Biermann 2011). These networks of solidarity are formed by identifying areas of shared concern (e.g., the representation of hidden histories, evidence of survivance, return of belongings and ancestors, legacies of oppression, reconciliation) across archaeologists, Indigenous peoples, and descendant communities.

Constellations of co-resistance are maintained through the Indigenous principle of relational accountability—fulfilling one's role and obligations in a relationship (Wilson 2008). Unlike support, which is occasional and easily withdrawn, relational accountability involves knowing who you are in relation with, gaining knowledge to fulfill your role in the relationship, and sustaining your commitment to these relations by acting collaboratively in support of shared interests and beliefs (hooks 1984: 64; Mohanty 2003; Wilson 2008). Enacting the principle of relational accountability requires a reorientation in archaeological research away from short-term, data-driven interactions and toward connectedness beyond convenience. The concept of co-resistance resembles in many ways the notion of "accomplices"—individuals who are fully complicit in the struggles of BIPOC peoples for equality—advocated for by archaeologists like Ayana Flewellen and colleagues (2021). Accomplices, like co-resisters, engage in coalition building, which differs from liberal forms of white allyship. Relationships based on allyship can provide support for a movement's goals but typically lack the vulnerability and longevity that long-term struggles require.

In the following subsections I draw on a feminist ethic of practical activism to identify pathways for individual action and community engagement that bridge content critiques (i.e., reformulations of archaeological narratives) and equity critiques (i.e., structural reforms within the profession) (Cobb and Crellin 2022: 268). The goal of "integrative critique" is to take power away from settler colonial institutions by identifying and deconstructing expressions of white supremacy (Palacios 2020: 536; Wylie 1997: 81–84). An anticolonial abolitionist approach also works to "make power" by generating new disciplinary regimes in which whiteness, capitalism, and science are decentered (Smith 2005: 130).

Taking power away from damaging institutionalized forms of settler colonialism involves explicitly locating ourselves and our research within colonial systems of power manifested in archaeology and cultural heritage management (Duarte et al. 2019: 165). As discussed in the introduction to this chapter, a key facet of self-reflection involves an honest disciplinary accounting of how archaeological research may be perpetuating denigrating narratives of trauma, suffering, deficit, and decline (Alfred and Corntassel 2005: 611; Tuck 2009). In reiterating colonial discourses of pain and loss, archaeological research built on deficit will have limited efficacy in constructing alternative systems. While similar calls for self-reflexivity can be found in other forms of critical scholarship (e.g., postcolonial, Marxist, and feminist critique) within anthropology, over the past five years this critique has been expanded upon by a growing group of archaeologists grounded within the politics of antiracism (the active dismantling of systemic racism in its various forms) and decolonization (the long-term process of divesting colonial power structures). These paradigms inform an emerging mode of socially engaged research that historicizes collective experiences of oppression in dialogue with grassroots movements, like Black Lives Matter, No More Stolen Sisters, and Decolonize This Place, to combat systems of inequality (e.g., Belcher et al. 2021; Gonzalez-Tennant 2018; Hamalakis 2018; Laluk et al. 2022; Little and Shackel 2016; Rankin and Gaultin 2021; Shackel 2013; Smith et al. 2019; Van Dyke and McGuire 2021). These studies employ collaborative and community-based methods to connect "psychological experience, cognition, and effect on the one hand, and the political economy of brutality on the other" in contexts where violence suffuses the entire society (Farmer 2005: 133).

In response to community fact-finding initiatives, Alicia Odewale has developed a restorative justice–based research project that documents mass graves associated with the 1921 massacre of Black residents in Greenwood, Oklahoma. Odewale's research is part of a larger collaborative endeavor with Parker VanValkenburgh and the City of Tulsa that locates and inventories evidence of race relations in the city. A key community-oriented product of this research has been the creation of publicly accessible digital maps that archive significant places and oral histories about the city. In documenting the continuous evolution of Greenwood from 1921 into the present, Odewale's (2020) research uses the multidisciplinary tools of historical archaeology to tell stories of survival and resilience that resist deficit discourses around anti-Black violence. Odewale's works builds on previous calls by Black feminist scholars like Maria Franklin (2001:116) and Whitney Battle-Baptiste (2011) to publish research that confronts harmful stereotypes and debunks misrepresentations of BIPOC personhood. This engaged mode of archaeological practice creates research that is accountable to the local community while bringing attention to often hidden or ignored aspects of their histories.

Historically oriented scholarship in African diaspora archaeology is parallel to and increasingly in dialogue with community-engaged approaches to working with Indigenous communities in the United States and Canada. These two lines of research both focus on fostering collective well-being, healing breaches, and restoring broken relationships within the ongoing context of settler colonialism (Colwell 2007: 29). These goals have been achieved within Indigenous contexts through the development of culturally relevant methodological and theoretical frameworks that offer alternatives to damage-

Figure 3.2. Stone foundations of the Lower Cut Meat Creek Day School in South Dakota visited with Rosebud tribal members. Photo by author.

centered research practices. For instance, David Schaepe and his colleagues (2017) have worked with the Stó:lō Nation to implement a form of therapeutic community-based archaeology that fosters Indigenous health and well-being, while Kisha Supernant and her coauthors (2020) have developed a heart-centered approach to practicing archaeology that integrates Indigenous concepts of relationality, respect, and care.

These holistic and community-engaged forms of research have also been used to document truths about the forced assimilation of Indigenous children in boarding schools (e.g., Cowie et al. 2019; Two Bears 2021; Wadsworth et al. 2021). In dialogue with this new line of politically engaged research, Chip Colwell and I have conducted object-based oral history interviews with community members from the Hopi, Port Gamble S'Klallam, Cheyenne, Arapaho, and Rosebud reservations (Figure 3.2).

The experiences shared during these interviews draw attention to the relationship between anti-Indigenous racism, federal policies of assimilation, and ongoing structural violence in the form of economic and educational disenfranchisement (Montgomery 2018, 2023; Montgomery and Colwell 2019). Much like Odewale and VanValkenburgh's work in Tulsa, these interviews highlight the cultural persistence of Indigenous individuals and communities who have resisted (and continue to resist) epistemic colonialism.

Acts of taking power through self-reflection and critical documentation that occur without reciprocal acts of making power will uphold settler colonial power structures. As Tuck and Yang (2012: 20) note, the unsettled feelings that accompany these individual endeavors are all too easily used as proof of systemic change without requiring settlers to relinquish control. Making power asks archaeologists and heritage professionals to act as "bad settlers" by creating alternative institutional structures and practices that are grounded in the goals of descendant and Indigenous communities (Clark et al. 2016: 7; McClaurin 2001: 57). Bad settlers enact change within the spaces where they have the most power and privilege (Quick Hall 2020: 8). For archaeologists, this may include universities, museums, cultural resource management firms, or federal office. At these various sites of influence, bad settlers are tasked with implementing policies that "alleviate conditions of oppression through scholarship and activism rather than support them" (McClaurin 2001: 57; see also Clark et al. 2016: 7). Importantly, acting as bad settlers means being willing to walk away if our unique skill sets and bonds of solidarity are unwanted in BIPOC struggles for social justice.

Over the past several years, archaeologists, curators, and lawmakers have "made power" by implementing pro-active repatriation policies rather than exploiting definitional loopholes around cultural affiliation to maintain possession of Indigenous ancestral remains and belongings. Most recently, legislation was passed in Ohio to remove legal barriers to repatriation within the state, prompting the return of more than 7,000 Indigenous ancestors by the Ohio History Connection—one of the nation's largest holders of unrepatriated remains (Jaffe et al. 2023). Under the leadership of Interior Secretary Deb Haaland, similar issues around the legal category of "culturally identifiable" remains are being addressed at the federal level through amendments to the Native American Graves Protection and Repatriation Act (Hudetz 2023). These policy shifts are a response to long-standing complaints by Native nations and grassroot efforts to reform repatriation practices in the United States. The shifting legal regimes and policies around repatriation are significant acts of making power that hold settler institutions accountable to the principles of Native sovereignty and self-determination as outlined in the United Nations Declaration on the Rights of Indigenous Peoples (UNDRIP).

Another way in which archaeologists can actualize UNDRIP is by implementing archiving policies that transfer control over the curation and dissemination of related data, including information, knowledge, ancestors, and belongings to Indigenous and descendant communities (McAnany et al. 2022).

As described by Christine McCleave and Rose Miron (Laluk et al. 2022: 667), data sovereignty involves continual consultation with communities to ensure that Indigenous information is being collected, organized, and cataloged in ways that advance community interests and well-being. For example, Peter Nelson (2020) applies a sovereignty-based framework to his collaborative research with the Federated Indians of Graton Rancheria. A key component of the Tolay Archaeological Project is the development of culturally grounded research protocols centered on relevancy, confidentiality, minimal impact, and risk management. Nelson's work demonstrates that implementing data sovereignty demands a fundamental shift in institutional power structures that prioritizes BIPOC communities rather than upholding the individual rights of scholars and governmental organizations.

Making power also entails actively challenging expressions of scientific racism that present non-European epistemologies as inferior to or outside the scope of academic knowledge (Biermann 2011: 392). Archaeologists can dismantle cultures of whiteness in the discipline by critically engaging with theories of race and integrating antiracist and culturally responsive methods into our teaching practices (Amico 2016; Blackwell 2010; Flewellen et al. 2021; Haynes 2017; Inoue 2015). Antiracist pedagogy challenges the multicultural notion that all viewpoints are equal, connects individual prejudice and bias to white supremacy as a system, and resists the tendency to center white people in discussions of racism. Implementing antiracist praxis involves decentering ourselves as instructors by inviting students to co-construct course content and learning outcomes based on their lived experiences and expertise. It also entails avoiding asking a single student or group of students to speak for any given racialized, gendered, or socioeconomic identity (Case 2022). Archaeologists can enact principles of antiracist and anticolonial praxis within their teaching by embedding nondominant epistemologies within course assignments; increasing the number of courses offered that explore BIPOC worldviews, experiences, and perspectives; and reducing barriers to working with Indigenous peoples and descendant communities (Gaudry and Lorenz 2018; Tuck and Yang 2012: 31).

Concluding Thoughts

In the United States, archaeologists have participated in settler colonial systems of Indigenous dispossession and BIPOC oppression by removing belongings and ancestors from the land as well as by producing narratives that erase the stories and traditions that serve as the basis of their unique cultural identities (Alfred and Corntassel 2005: 598). We have done so through the creation of archaeological cultures that separate past and present peoples and by imposing Western epistemologies onto the interpretation of history. We have done so by ignoring the analytical power of traditional knowledge as valid data sources and as legitimate pedagogical frameworks. We have done so by continuing to assert stewardship over the material culture and ancestral remains of Black and Indigenous peoples despite demands to the contrary. And we have done so by accepting the legitimacy of a settler colonial culture of whiteness and associated legal regimes.

In response to the entanglement of archaeology and settler colonialism, there has been a noticeable uptick over the past ten years in efforts to reform the discipline through liberal initiatives oriented around multivocality. In dialogue with these redistributive efforts is a reactionary politics which engages right-wing populist notions of individual freedoms in opposition to minoritarian rights. While liberalism and populism have distinct aims, these positions converge in upholding settler colonial structures of power and privilege. In denying the validity of historically marginalized identities and concerns, right-wing populist discourses reinforce a dominant culture of whiteness that privileges capitalist interests within the practice of heritage management and the discipline of archaeology. Alternatively, the often unfocused multivocality of liberalism falls short of creating new systems of practice that support the culturally specific epistemologies, goals, and needs of historically marginalized groups.

Unlike liberal and populist frameworks, anticolonial abolition offers a political approach that explicitly identifies how whiteness has created and maintains the privileged position of Western values within archaeological praxis. This focus on addressing white supremacy contrasts with populist politics that erases racialized privilege as well as with liberalism's tendency to decenter whiteness. Anticolonial abolition also differs from populist methods of mobilization that marshal an intentionally vague notion of "the people" to galvanize political action as well as from liberal notions of multivocality grounded in inclusivity. Instead, an anticolonial abolitionist approach to political mobilization is grounded in an Indigenous ethic of relational accountability. These constellations of co-resistance are enacted through long-term coalition building between archaeologists, Indigenous Peoples, and historically marginalized descendant communities.

Finally, anticolonial abolition eschews the reformation-based tactics used by both right-wing populists and liberals, instead advocating for archaeologists to become "bad settlers" who commit to ensuring Black and Indigenous empowerment through active forms of anticipating, recalibrating, and mobilizing that intervene in the present to impact the future (Baldwin 2012).

Anticolonial abolition offers an antidote to damage-based research by recognizing past trauma and oppression without building the future on the legacies of these injustices. Instead, coalitions of co-resistance carve out a new space in which to imagine disciplinary regimes that are not anchored in white privilege, anti-Blackness, and Indigenous dispossession. In short, an anticolonial abolitionist framework moves the discipline beyond debates over resources and rights to reimagine an archaeological future disentangled from the project of settler colonialism (Biermann 2011: 394). This is an unsettling approach precisely because it requires us as archaeologists to give up power and privilege (Simpson 2016: 20).

Acknowledgments

This work is built upon the invaluable insights and editorial support provided by Rachael Kiddey, Kathryn Lafrenz-Samuels, Randall McGuire, and Alfredo González-Ruibal.

References Cited

Alfred, Taiaiake, and Jeff Corntassel. 2005. Being Indigenous: Resurgences against Contemporary Colonialism. *Government and Opposition* 40(4): 597–614.

Amico, Robert P. 2016. *Antiracist Teaching.* Routledge, New York.

Atalay, Sonya, Lee Rain Clauss, Randall H. McGuire, and John R. Welch. 2014. Transforming Archaeology. In *Transforming Archaeology: Activist Practices and Prospects,* edited by Sonya Atalay, Lee Rain Clauss, Randall H. McGuire, and John R. Welch, pp. 7–28. Left Coast Press, Walnut Creek.

Baldwin, Andrew. 2012. Whiteness and Futurity: Towards a Research Agenda. *Progress in Human Geography* 36(2): 172–187.

Battle-Baptiste, Whitney. 2011. *Black Feminist Archaeology.* Routledge, New York.

Belcher, William R., Suzanne Falgout, Joyce Chinen, Robert K. Carriera, and Johanna Fuller. 2021. Experiences in Archaeology, Social Justice, and Democratic Principles: The 2016–2019 Archaeological Field School at the University of Hawai'i West O'ahu. *Advances in Archaeological Practice: A Journal of the Society of American Archaeology* 9(4): 354–365.

Biermann, Soenke. 2011. Knowledge, Power, and Decolonization: Implication for Non-Indigenous Scholars, Researchers and Educators. *Counterpoints* 379: 386–398.

Blackhawk, Ned. 1997. Julian Steward and the Politics of Representation. *American Indian Culture and Research Journal* 21(2): 61–81.

Blackwell, Deanna M. 2010. Sidelines and Separate Spaces: Making Education Anti-Racist for Students of Color. *Race, Ethnicity and Education* 13(4): 473–494.

Case, Kim. 2022. Case Model for Anti-Racist Pedagogy. https://docs.google.com/document/d/1CnVIufBaFaPRImOLTYZIFWsF5Os1WtbsWFiCwlRrTe0/edit, accessed on October 30, 2023.

Clemmer, Richard O. 2009. Pristine Aborigines or Victims of Progress? The Western Sho-shones in the Anthropological Imagination. *Current Anthropology* 50(6): 849–881.

Clark, Tom, Ravi de Costa, and Sarah Maddison. 2016. Non-Indigenous People and the Limits of Settler Colonial Reconciliation. In *The Limits of Settler Colonial Reconciliation,* edited by Tom Clark, Ravi de Costa, and Sarah Maddison, pp. 1–14. Springer, New York.

Colwell, Chip. 2007. Ethics, History, and Social Justice. In *Archaeology as a Tool of Civic Engagement,* edited by Barbara J. Little and Paul Shackel, pp. 23–47. Rowman & Little-field, Lanham, Maryland.

Collins, Patricia H. 2015. Intersectionality's Definitional Dilemmas. *Annual Review of Sociology* 41: 1–20.

Corntassel, Jeffrey, and Cindy Holder. 2008. Who's Sorry Now? Government Apologies, Truth Commissions, and Indigenous Self-Determination in Australia, Canada, Guatemala, and Peru. *Human Rights Review* 9: 465–489.

Cobb, Hannah, and Rachel J. Crellin. 2022. Affirmation and Action: A Posthumanist Feminist Agenda for Archaeology. *Cambridge Archaeology Journal* 32(2): 265–279.

Cowie, Sarah E., Dianne L. Teeman, and Christopher C. LeBlanc. 2019. *Collaborative Archaeology at the Stewart Indian School.* University of Nevada Press, Reno.

Cramer, Katherine J. 2016. *The Politics of Resentment: Rural Consciousness in Wisconsin and the Rise of Scott Walker.* University of Chicago Press, Chicago.

Crenshaw, Kimberlé. 1989. *Demarginalizing the Intersection of Race and Sex: A Black Feminist Critique of Antidiscrimination Doctrine, Feminist Theory, and Anti-Racist Politics.* University of Chicago Legal Forum, Chicago.

d'Alpoim Guedes, Jade, Sara Gonzalez, and Isabel Rivera-Collazo. 2021. Resistance and Care in the Time of COVID-19: Archaeology in 2020. *American Anthropologist* 123(4): 898–915.

De Tocqueville, Alexis. 2010[1835–1840]. *Democracy in America.* Edited by Eduardo Nolla, Translated by James T. Schleifer. Liberty Fund, Indianapolis.

Duarte, Marisa Elena, Morgan Vigil-Hayes, Sandra Littletree, and Mirand Belarde-Lewis. 2019. "Of course, data can never fully represent reality": Assessing the Relationship between Indigenous Data and Indigenous Knowledge, Traditional Ecological Knowledge, and Traditional Knowledge. *Human Biology* 91(3): 163–178.

Dunnavant, Justin. 2016. African Americans and NAGPRA: The Call for an African American Graves Protection and Repatriation Act. Presented at the Society for Historical Archaeology Conference, January 6–9, Washington, DC.

Egan, Timothy. 1998. Old Skull Gets White Looks, Stirring Dispute. *New York Times,* April 2, 1998. https://www.nytimes.com/1998/04/02/us/old-skull-gets-white-looks-stirring-dispute.html.

Farmer, Paul. 2005. *Pathologies of Power: Health, Human Rights, and the New War on the Poor.* University of California Press, Berkeley.

Fanon, Frantz. 1963. *The Wretched of the Earth.* Grove Press, New York.

Flewellen, Ayana O., Justin P. Dunnavant, Alicia Odewale, Alexandra Jones, Tsione Wolde-Michael, Zoe Crossland, and Maria Franklin. 2021. "The Future of Archaeology Is Antiracist": Archaeology in the Time of Black Lives Matter. *American Antiquity* 86(2): 224–243.

Franklin, Maria. 2001. A Black Feminist-Inspired Archaeology? *Journal of Social Archaeology* 11: 108–125.

Gaudry, Adam, and Danielle Lorenz. 2018. Indigenization as Inclusion, Reconciliation, and Decolonization: Navigating the Different Visions for Indigenizing the Canadian Academy. *AlterNative: An International Journal of Indigenous Peoples* 14(3): 218–227.

Gonzalez-Tennant, Edward. 2018. *The Rosewood Massacre: An Archaeology and History of Intersectional Violence.* University Press of Florida, Gainesville.

Grande, Sandy. 2013. Accumulation of the Primitive: The Limits of Liberalism and the Politics of Occupy Wall Street. *Settler Colonial Studies* 3(3–4): 369–380.

Hamilakis, Yannis. 2018. Decolonial Archaeology as Social Justice. *Antiquity* 92(362): 518–520.

Haynes, Chayla. 2017. Dismantling the White Supremacy Embedded in Our Classrooms: White Faculty in Pursuit of More Equitable Educational Outcomes. *International Journal of Teaching and Learning in Higher Education* 29(1): 87–107.

hooks, bell. 1984. *Feminist Theory: From Margin to Center.* Southend Press, Boston.

Inoue, Asao B. 2015. *Antiracist Writing Assessment Ecologies: Teaching and Assessing Writing for A Socially Just Future.* Parlor Press / WAC Clearinghouse, Fort Collins.

Jaffe, Logan, Ash Ngu, and Mary Hudetz. 2023. The Remains of Thousands of Native Americans Were Returned to Tribes This Year. *ProPublica*, December 26, 2023. https://www.propublica.org/article/repatriation-progress-in-2023.

Jefferson, Thomas. 1787. *Notes on the State of Virginia.* Edited by William Peden. University of North Carolina Press, Chapel Hill.

Jung, Moon-Kie, and João H. Costa Vargas (editors). 2021. *Antiblackness.* Duke University Press, Durham, North Carolina.

Hudetz, Mary. 2023. New Federal Rules Aim to Speed Repatriation of Native Remains and Burial Items. *ProPublica,* December 8, 2023.https://www.propublica.org/article/interior-department-revamps-repatriation-rules-native-remains-nagpra.

King, Tiffany Lethabo. 2019. *The Black Shoals: Offshore Formations of Black and Native Studies.* Duke University Press, Durham, North Carolina.

Laluk, Nicholas C., Lindsay M. Montgomery, Rebecca Tsosie, Christine McCleave, Rose Miron, Stephanie Russo Carroll, Joseph Aguilar, et al. 2022. Archaeology and Social Justice in Native America. *American Antiquity* 87(4): 1–24.

Lafrenz-Samuels, Kathryn. 2018. *Mobilizing Heritage: Anthropological Practice and Transnational Prospects.* University Press of Florida, Gainesville.

Little, Barbara J., and Paul A. Shackel. 2016. Heritage, Civic Engagement, and Social Justice. In *Archaeology, Heritage, and Civic Engagement,* pp. 33–45. Routledge, New York.

Lowndes, Joseph. 2017. Populism in the United States. In *The Oxford Handbook of Populism,* edited by Cristobal Rovira Kaltwasser, Paul Taggart, Paulina Ochoa Espejo, and Pierre Ostig Ostiguy. Oxford University Press, Oxford.

McAnany, Patricia A., George Nicholas, Dorothy Lippert, Michael Wilcox, Larry J. Zimmerman, Lindsay M. Montgomery, Randall McGuire, Patricia Ayala Rocabado, Margaret Conkey, and Chip Colwell. 2022. Reading the Fine Print: What You Should Know about UNDRIP. *SAA Archaeological Record:* 14–17.

McGuire, Randall H. 2008. *Archaeology as Political Action.* University of California Press, Berkeley.

McClaurin, Irma. 2001. Theorizing a Black Feminist Self in Anthropology: Toward an Autoethnographic Approach. In *Black Feminist Anthropology: Theory, Politics, Praxis and Poetics,* edited by Irma McClaurin. Rutgers University Press, New Brunswick.

Mohanty, Chandra T. 2003. *Feminism without Borders: Decolonizing Theory, Practicing Solidarity.* Duke University Press, Durham, North Carolina.

Montgomery, Lindsay M. 2018. Memories That Haunt: Reconciling with the Ghosts of the American Indian School System. *International Journal of Heritage Studies* 25(7): 736–749. https://doi.org/10.1080/13527258.2018.1544166.

Montgomery, Lindsay M. 2023. "You Have Harmed Us": Stories of Violence, Narratives of Hope among the Port Gamble S'Klallam Tribe. *American Anthropologist* 125(2): 346–360.

Montgomery, Lindsay M., and Chip Colwell. 2019. *Objects of Survivance: A material history of the American Indian School Experience.* University Press of Colorado, Boulder.

Montgomery, Lindsay M., and Kisha Supernant. 2022. Archaeology in 2021: Repatriation, Reclamation, and Reckoning with Historical Trauma. *American Anthropologist* 124(4): 1–13.

Nelson, Peter. 2020. Refusing Settler Epistemologies and Maintaining an Indigenous Future for Tolay Lake, Sonoma County, California. *American Indian Quarterly* 44(2): 221–242.

Odewale, Alicia. 2020. New Efforts in Restorative Justice Archaeology: Tulsa, OK. *Society of Black Archaeologists Newsletter* 2(1): 12–13.

Ostiguy, Pierre. 2017. Populism: A Socio-Cultural Approach. In *The Oxford Handbook on Populism,* edited by Cristobal Rovira Kaltwasser, Paul Taggart, Paulina Ochoa Espejo, and Pierre Ostiguy. Oxford University, Oxford.

Oxford University Press. 2023. Multivocality. In *The Concise Oxford Dictionary of Archaeology.* Oxford University Press, Oxford. https://www.oxfordreference.com/display/10.1093/oi/authority.20110803100216225, accessed November 5, 2023.

Palacios, Lena. 2020. Challenging Convictions: Indigenous and Black Race-Radical Feminists Theorizing the Carceral State and Abolitionist Praxis in the United States and Canada. *Meridians* 19: 522.

Quick Hall, K. Melchor. 2020. *Naming a Transnational Black Feminist Framework.* Routledge, New York.

Rankin, Lisa, and Barry Gaulton. 2021. Archaeology, Participatory Democracy and Social Justice in Newfoundland and Labrador, Canada. *Archaeologies* 17: 79–102.

Rawls, John. 1971. *A Theory of Justice.* Belknap Press, Cambridge, Massachusetts.

Reilly, Matthew C. 2022. Archaeologies of Whiteness. *Archaeological Dialogues* 29: 51–66.

Schaepe, David M., Bill Angelbeck, David Snook, and John R. Welch. 2017. Archaeology as Therapy: Connecting Belonging, Knowledge, Time, Place, and Well-Being. *Current Anthropology* 58(4): 502–533.

Shackel, Paul A. 2013. A Historical Archaeology of Labor and Social Justice. *American Anthropologist* 115(2): 317–320.

Simpson, Leanne B. 2016. Indigenous Resurgence and Co-Resistance. *Critical Ethnic Studies* 2(2): 19–34.

Smith, Andrea. 2005. Native American Feminism, Sovereignty, and Social Change. *Feminist Studies* 31(1): 116–132.

Smith, Claire, Heather Burke, Jordan Ralph, Belinda Liebal, Alice Gorman, Christopher Wilson, Steve Hemming, et al. 2019. Pursuing Social Justice Through Collaborative Archaeologies in Aboriginal Australia. Archaeologies 15(3): 536–569.

Society for American Archaeology (SAA). 1996. Principles of Archaeological Ethics. https://www.saa.org/career-practice/ethics-in-professional-archaeology.

Supernant, Kisha, Jane E. Baxter, Natasha Lyons, and Sonya Atalay (editors). 2020. *Archaeologies of the Heart*. Springer, New York.

Tharoor, Ishaan. 2016. The Other Side of the Global Right-Wing Surge: Nostalgia for Empire. *Washington Post,* December 2, 2016. https://www.washingtonpost.com/news/worldviews/wp/2016/12/02/the-other-side-of-the-global-right-wing-surge-nostalgia-for-empire/.

Tuck, Eve. 2009. Suspending Damage: A Letter to Communities. *Harvard Educational Review* 79(3): 409–427.

Tuck, Eve, and C. Ree. 2013. A Glossary of Haunting. In *Handbook of Autoethnography,* edited by Stacy Holman Jones, Tony E. Adams, and Carolyn Ellis, pp. 639–658. Left Coast Press, Walnut Creek, California.

Tuck, Eve, and K. Wayne Yang. 2012. Decolonization Is Not a Metaphor. *Decolonization: Indigeneity, Education & Society* 1(1): 1–40.

Two Bears, Davina R. 2021. Researching My Heritage: The Old Leupp Boarding School Historic Site. *Kiva* 87(3): 336–353.

Van Dyke, Ruth M., and Randall H. McGuire. 2021. Settler Colonialism and Archaeology in North America: Challenges and Progress. In *Pearls, Politics and Pistachios: Essays in Anthropology and Memories on the Occasion of Susan Pollock's 65th Birthday,* edited by Aydin Abar, Maria Bianca D'Anna, Georg Cyrus, Vera Egbers, Barbara Huber, Christine Kainert, Johannes Köhler, et al., pp. 643–652. Propylaeum, Heidelberg.

Wadsworth, William, Kisha Supernant, Ave Dersch, and the Chipewyan Nation, Chipewyan. 2021. Integrating Remote Sensing and Indigenous Archaeology to Locate Unmarked Graves: A Case Study from Northern Alberta, Canada. *Advances in Archaeological Practice* 9(10): 10–17.

Weiss, Elizabeth. 2022. The Problem of Sex Discrimination in Indigenous Archaeology. *Quillette,* February 16, 2022. https://quillette.com/2022/02/16/the-problem-of-sex-discrimination-in-indigenous-archaeology/, accessed September 16, 2024.

Wilson, Shawn. 2008. *Research Is Ceremony: Indigenous Research Methods*. Fernwood, Halifax.

Wolfe, Patrick. 2006. Settler Colonialism and the Elimination of the Natives. *Journal of Genocide Research* 8(4): 387–409.

Wylie, Alison. 1997. The Engendering of Archaeology: Refiguring Feminist Science Studies. *Osiris* 12: 80–99.

Zippia. 2022. Archaeologist Demographics and Statistics in the U.S. https://www.zippia.com/archaeologist-jobs/demographics/, accessed October 25, 2022.

4

Heritage, Archaeology, and Local Communities in Times of Reactionary Populism

Learnings from Brazil

CRISTÓBAL GNECCO

Reactionary populism has deepened the already unabashed delivery of the state to development and the market. This has been seen in the dismantling of extant protective regulations on the many fronts in which the presence of the state was paramount. In Brazil this trend materialized with the Bolsonaro government, in office between 2019 and 2022. Changes in public policies affected several stakeholders. This chapter describes the deeds of reactionary populism in Brazil regarding the relaxation of environmental and heritage regulations; while the former was strongly faced by local (mostly Indigenous) communities and environmental activists, the latter worried professional guilds, including the archaeologists. The chapter also describes how these changes affected the differential positionings of the various actors vis-à-vis the state, and vis-à-vis each other, including issues of power, identity, and representation. These changes and the consequent positionings affected the former timid rapprochement between local communities, heritage agents (especially heritage educators), and archaeologists because different, sometimes diverging interests were at stake—interest that were previously compromised, mostly through a multicultural logic, but then revealed themselves in an apparent, perhaps strategic incommensurability. Yet, to grasp the events of the Bolsonaro term, a perusal of the previous governments is called for.

The Partido dos Trabalhadores Governments

After the neoliberal two terms of Fernando Henrique Cardoso (1995–2003) came 13 years of PT (Partido dos Trabalhadores, Worker's Party) governments: the two terms of Lula da Silva and the unfinished two terms of Dilma Rousseff. The progressive Left now in power, in fact a social democracy, increased government spending, strengthened and widened public education, took steps (some of them polemical, such as subsidies) to diminish poverty and to increase consumption, but kept many of the neoliberal policies established by Cardoso. PT governments excelled, for a while, in what Idelber Avelar (2021) has called administration of antagonisms and contradictions. As for the former, the PT negotiated its agenda with disparate parties and social sectors, such as evangelicals and communists. The latter, the administration of contradictions, was even finer. The most salient of all was the strengthening of the welfare state while at the same time embracing an almost unchecked capitalism. PT governments fell prey to "a process of 'perverse convergence' between two distinct projects of society: on the one hand, the democratic project and, on the other, the project of liberalization of the global economy" (Bronz et al. 2020: 15). The losses in such a difficult equilibrium were many, but I highlight later in this chapter Indigenous and peasant rights and a brutal attack on the environment. The course of archaeology and heritage was also affected. Academic archaeology dominated disciplinary practice up until then, rarely siding with anything other than professional concerns; yet, as capitalist expansion was accompanied by (mostly) bureaucratic environmental regulations, contract archaeology (CA) exploded, and so did heritage education.

In 2007 Lula launched the Programa de Aceleração do Crescimento (PAC, Growth Acceleration Program) to boost economic growth, a purely capitalist undertaking. But economic growth is a bad ally for the fate of other socially sensitive policies. PT governments drew a slim line around heritage and the environment, thus setting a precarious equilibrium between nature/history and the economy. When economic growth demanded swift actions, the other member of the equation bore the consequences. The National Historical and Artistic Heritage Institute (IPHAN) was responsible for ensuring mediation between economic interests and their compliance with heritage legislation mostly through the activation of the archaeological leviathan: contract archaeology. As in most countries, PAC development projects had to obtain environmental licensing, a component of which was the archaeological evaluation of the areas to be intervened. However, the "quality control" of contract archaeology (that is, the archaeology governed by the logic of capital) was, and still is, carried out in accordance with the efficiency criteria of the contracting companies, usually committed to complying with the project schedules for which it was hired. The importance of contract archaeology for development was so sensitive (because it could stop the construction of infrastructure) that its management by IPHAN was under careful government surveillance, especially in relation to the investigations carried out in the development projects that the government considered crucial. The development agenda created a technocratic machine that controlled archaeological research and consolidated authoritarian institutional practices, including the emergence of legal loopholes that allowed companies to dispense with contract archaeology, delegating to them the final decision on what should be preserved.

Not unlike other parts of the world, in Brazil this kind of archaeology is linked to capitalist expansion. PAC projects expanded the job market for Brazilian archaeologists in an unprecedented way. In 2015 more than 95% of active archaeologists in Brazil worked on contract projects. Linked to booming capitalism and its resulting infrastructure works, hired archaeologists lost independence and critical capacity. In addition, contract archaeology rapidly transformed curricula and even traced disciplinary paths. Under the ideology of growth, which implies that the economy behaves like a living organism, PAC-related projects were promoted without considering what they found in their way. In the process, the rights of peoples and nature were summarily violated. In a country eager for development and willing to accelerate its rate of economic growth, one of the most pressing concerns was to increase energy production. As a result, huge hydroelectric plants were built. The large areas flooded were mostly located in Indigenous and peasant territories and in the Amazon basin; their construction severely affected thousands of people and thousands of hectares of fragile ecosystems (Rocha 2020). Andrea Zhouri and Raquel Oliveira (2007) denounced the situation, highlighting the enormous inequality of the forces that fought for or against those projects and created a situation in which "socially unjust and environmentally unsustainable policies are perpetuated, as riverside communities struggle against a reified logic that turns them into objects in the 'natural' landscape" (Zhouri and Oliveira 2007: 120).

Violence frequently broke out because affected communities reacted against development, with the consequent police intervention to "protect" the interest of the economic sectors involved (Rocha 2020). PAC-related projects, plagued by conflict and violence, brought academic disciplines to the fore. While some disciplines (such as anthropology and political science, and even hard sciences such as biology) took the side of defending life, solidarity, and well-being, archaeology did not. Its eloquent silence arose, for the most part, from its uncritical and instrumental relationship with development. The most significant case occurred at the beginning of this century around a huge dam that was being built in the Culuene River, in the Amazon basin. In addition to the devastating environmental effects resulting from the construction of the dam, the rights (traditional and otherwise) of the Indigenous peoples living in the area were violated. In 2004 the local Indigenous inhabitants noticed that the dam was already under construction, but they had not been consulted, which violated the provisions of Indigenous and Tribal Peoples Convention (known as the ILO Convention 169), ratified by Brazil in 2002. They moved quickly and seized the works, arguing that a sacred site was going to be flooded and fishing resources (on which they depended) would be affected. After lengthy legal battles to stop or continue construction, the Culuene dam received approval from the Brazilian environmental agency and was finally built. In the approval, the concept issued by a CA company was decisive, indicating that the sacred site for which the Indigenous people were fighting was elsewhere. The anthropologist Carlos Fausto (2017) criticized the approval of the Culuene dam for environmental and cultural reasons, and criticized the concept issued by the company, about which he pointed out profound deficiencies, if not manifest errors. In addition, he asked: "What are the public mechanisms that prevent the production of a vicious circle between entrepreneurs and consulting companies? What should be the role of public bodies and scientific associations in this process?" (Fausto 2017: 297). After considering answers to his own questions, he declared: "Thus, I can only conclude, once again, that in the science of contract the most important thing is the contract and not the science. . . . Or is it that in Brazil the contract became an end in itself?" (Fausto 2017: 301). The Culuene case exposed the insurmountable tautology in which, for reasons of economic convenience, contract archaeology is usually trapped: the construction company needed to prove in court that no sacred Indigenous sites were going to be affected by the project; for this purpose, it hired a CA company to provide the necessary information to support its claim, so the CA company stated that no sacred Indigenous sites were going to be affected by the project! This is so because CA companies often accommodate themselves to the pressures and interests of the party they work for. In doing so, they not only violate the rights of different communities and nature but also the "supreme interest" they are supposedly striving to protect: the archaeological record. The latter is compromised when and where development is present, revealing that it is development that sets the fate of the archaeological record—but rarely the other way around, as CA practitioners often argue in defending their doubtful independence and professional integrity.

Capitalism traced disciplinary practice, which alienated archaeology from most local communities. Its fate was linked to that of development, not to the alternative lives championed by them. However, a related endeavor, heritage education, took the opposite direction and did find a way—a rather twisted way, though—to community engagement. Heritage education was widely promoted as a way to "open and legitimize" academic spaces for the discipline to articulate with the community and as a way to educate the public on cultural issues that, it was assumed, only archaeology was capable of fostering. The rationale behind heritage education posited that development certainly threatens the past by threatening its material evidence (thus creating an endangered past), but that it also allows an unprecedented opportunity to investigate a past that would otherwise remain unexposed. The argument is, of course, tautological: development created an endangered past that could be profitably studied but that would not have to be studied had it not been endangered by development. Besides, it did not face the very origin of the endangerment of the past (development) but accepted as a fact that it occurred and then it sought to profit from the situation. Contract archaeology then became both an opportunistic partner and an accomplice of development.

Heritage education posited that past evidence exposed by development works and studied by contract archaeology could be converted into heritage and then taught to local populations. Heritage education programs linked to contract archaeology boomed as a means of countering the critiques received from academia, especially regarding the inaccessibility of contract-related findings and its isolation from various stakeholders, mostly local. Heritage education programs allowed contract archaeology to become socially responsible. The arrogance, coloniality, and utter modernity of heritage education linked to CA projects is obvious: it pretended that local populations were ignorant about their pasts, which could only exist if exposed by the discipline; and it made heritage educators the redeemers of the past, the history, and even the cultures of local populations. Further, heritage education legitimizes and whitewashes the logic of development (Bezerra 2015). As Henri Acselrad and colleagues (2021: 179) have noted,

The very expression progressive extractivism, for example, widely adopted during the 2000s in Latin America, did not come to mean anything other than this combination between territorial expropriation by corporations, on the one hand, and the supposedly compensatory character of economic gains that would finance policies of transfer of income to the population, within the scope of the so-called commodity consensus.

In this case the income transferred is knowledge, dressed in the Enlightened pretensions of the moderns.

"Opening and legitimizing" academic spaces for archaeology articulated with the community via heritage education and, at the same time, providing professional services to development companies that violate all kinds of rights was not contradictory but cynical. It was also a manifestation of the corporate phase archaeology had entered, in which "social responsibility" stands out. This cynicism, mixed with corporate ideology, went unnoticed or was met with complacent silence, especially since some of its perpetrators managed to infiltrate institutional and academic spaces. The complicity between the academic world and contracting companies was notorious in Brazil. Some owners, partners or employees of consulting firms also worked in academia. The situation was made worse when those same individuals also held positions in the institutions charged with setting academic policy at the national level. The result of this perverse mix was simple: Brazil witnessed an explosion of new, basically technical undergraduate programs (Bezerra 2008; Schaan 2009) clearly aimed at training the many archaeologists that the contract market desperately needed.

While contract archaeology boomed, so did academic archaeology, although in a much more modest dimension. The PT governments highly invested in public education (federal universities doubled in number and teaching positions during those years; likewise, the number in grants for undergraduate and graduate studies experimented a steady growth), and funding for research in all areas was increased. The main research institution, the National Council for Scientific and Technological Development, increased its budget by 50% between 2002 and 2013.

At the same time, and not unlike other countries, a timid multicultural archaeology began to emerge under the labels of "public" and "collaborative." As in other countries, the logic was the same. To keep up with multicultural changes, profound as they were, archaeology did four things: (1) it opened its practice to local actors; (2) it widened the circulation of it discourse; (3) it included other historical horizons in its interpretations; and (4) it gave up the exclusive control of some disputed issues. Yet, the open practice it championed—the first point—only allowed local actors to be members of research teams or, at most, to be trained in the discipline. Such openness was normally framed under the heading "collaboration," but power relations were rarely at stake. Most archaeologists were content to offer cultural crumbs to the communities (a local museum, a video, a booklet) while preserving the control of key issues (research designs, destination of findings, production and dissemination of narratives). Second, a widened circulation of archaeological discourses—which, along with collaboration, form the backbone of so-called public archaeology, part and parcel of a more comprehensive entity that I have chosen to call multicultural archaeology—had two results: it reproduced the archaeological canon more widely, and it furthered the reification and objectification of the past, such as in the case of local museums. Third, an expanded archaeological hermeneutics, achieved by incorporating non-Western conceptions of the past, enriched the explanatory potential of the discipline but did not engage intercultural understandings. Such an interpretative expansion, many times resorting to alien cosmologies that produce curious argumentative hybrids—for instance: live objects, with agency, amid rigid functional frames (see Marín-Aguilera 2021)—deepened a logocentric arrogance but did not aim to forge nonhierarchical relationships. As a result, historical diversity (that is, differential interpretations of the past, including the conception of what the past is) became an instrument for the forging of a more vigorous archaeology. And, fourth, relinquishing control over certain issues meant precisely that: certain issues and under certain circumstances. This characteristic was more commonly achieved through the selective repatriation of biological and cultural remains.

Multicultural (or liberal) archaeology in Brazil was demographically unimportant because the bulk of disciplinary practitioners (up to 95%) worked in the contract market; the remaining few pursued some kind of academic research. Liberal archaeology was indeed marginal, to say the least, and managed to survive in the wake of academic-oriented projects.

In sum, the PT era left uneven results regarding the entities this book is concerned with: it did bring together communities and heritage through education, yet in a neocolonial fashion; there was a close rapport between archaeology and heritage, but only if we consider them in their historical specificities, tinted by development and the market: contract archaeology and heritage education. And there was a perverse relationship between communities and archaeology as the latter, dressed with its contract outfit, usually sided with development companies at the expense of community interests. A liberal relationship emerged, however, as some archaeologists went public and collaborative. Yet, their move did not militate against the ontological violence of the logocentric tradition. Multicultural archaeology is a traditional academic archaeology, accommodated to the multicultural mandates of openness and tolerance, without losing its privileges. The dictum of *The Leopard* was never so true: "If we want things to stay as they are, things will have to change" (Lampedusa 1960: 31). These are the cosmetic changes that many contemporary archaeologists have produced: changes that are not changes at all but rather a disciplinary hardening. Archaeologists, members of a privileged cognitive minority, do not want to lose the privileges granted by being the owners of a form of representation that, at most, they are willing to share but never to change.

The Bolsonaro Times

And then it came Jair Bolsonaro, a mediocre right-wing extremist *deputado* who thrived in the shadows until the circumstances were ripe to bid for the presidency in 2018.[1] His electoral stronghold was mostly white and well off: he got 75% of his votes in middle- and high-income areas and won in 95% of the richest municipalities. He won in 10 of the richest cities in Brazil, where he crushed his contender, Fernando Haddad, 8 to 1. If Brazil were divided in two halves, one with the poorer municipalities and the other with the richer ones, Haddad would have won in 79% of the former and Bolsonaro in 89% of the latter. Bolsonaro's triumph not only had an economic imprint but a racial one as well: he prevailed in 9 out of 10 municipalities with a white majority; Haddad prevailed in 7 out of 10 with a nonwhite majority. Bolsonaro won in cities where almost the entire population is white, the majority in the south of the country. The PT candidate obtained meager results in those cities but won in all those where whites do not reach 20% of the population (Llaneras 2018). The gender divide was also important, especially among the young, with women supporting Haddad massively, while men voted Bolsonaro (Pinheiro-Machado and Scalco 2018). Yet, these statistics fall short of what happened in 2018, for Bolsonaro also won in some poor and Black areas (such as in four northeastern states) and gained increasing support from the poorest echelons of society during his first year in office. One explanation for this situation is the massive vote of evangelicals, usually poor and usually marginalized in terms of employment, education, and health services. The evangelical bloc grew under the PT, with which it negotiated for years, but eventually gave its support to Bolsonaro, the figure it identified as capable of curtailing violence and restoring order and Christian (patriarchal) values. The other reason springs from the explosive mix of authoritarianism and capitalism:

> It is in this tune that the supposed enemies of development are forged in the context of neoextractivism in Latin America: Indigenous peoples, quilombolas, environmentalists, inspection agents, intellectuals and social movements, indicating that capitalist development collides with democratic achievements. . . . In this socio-historical configuration, the disinherited of capitalism can become the social base of au-

thoritarianism, forging a tortuous articulation between the oppressed
and the oppressors. (Acselrad et al. 2021: 174)

Bolsonaro's presidential campaign was partly populist for it opposed a pure,
traditional, and defenseless people to a corrupted establishment that he would
put at bay.[2] The corruption against which Bolsonaro's campaign was populist
was not only political but moral (see Kalil 2018):[3] materialism, civil rights,
"gender ideology," and abortion corrupted the religious and traditional values
that he was meant to save. Up to 25% of Bolsonaro's voters were affiliated with
evangelical churches; while Haddad and Bolsonaro were even in the Catholic
vote, the final difference favoring the latter, some 11 million votes came from
the evangelicals (Spyer 2020: 53). His campaign was populist by its opposition to the political establishment of the day—the old politics, by virtue of
which he appealed to the hegemony of a large part of society articulated as an
ideological option vis-à-vis the PT—and by its praise of the Brazilian military
regimes of the 1960s and 1970s because of their strong leadership, their suppression of parties and democracy, and their pro-capitalist and nationalist
stand. In this regard, Chantal Mouffe did not see Bolsonaro as a populist but
as a fascist because

> right-wing populism is a populism that gives answers or a xenopho-
> bic articulation to democratic demands. But if they are not democratic
> demands, I would not speak of right-wing populism. In the case of
> Bolsonaro, it is complicated but I do not see that there are democratic
> demands either, for the most part it is a total rejection, rather than an
> articulation of democratic demands. (quoted in Mazzolini 2019)

Bolsonaro's regime was an expression of antidemocratic, authoritarian capitalism. The "progressive neoliberalism" that characterized the PT governments
was replaced by a "hyper-reactionary neoliberalism"—the terms are Nancy
Fraser's (2017). He never attacked neoliberalism; instead, he praised it and
supported it. Unlike radical nationalists, such as Donald Trump, Bolsonaro
did not blame unemployment and economic stagnation on neoliberalism but
on the PT "socialist" policies (Maitino 2020: 9).[4] The sum of authoritarianism
and neoliberalism is not a random relationship. Neoliberalism is always prone
"to authoritarian solutions to implement policies for the commodification of
life and economic liberalization" (Acselrad et al. 2021: 175). No wonder Bolsonaro's reactionary populism soon became reactionary capitalism—if there
really can be something like this, if we would really need to add an adjective to
what already is frankly reactionary. As an accomplished representative of the

New Right, Bolsonaro neatly merged neoliberalism and authoritarianism—a not so unlikely couple that may have been in disguise before but that now came to full light, without hesitation. Given that Latin American countries are mostly commodity producers, neoliberalism in the region essentially means neoextractivism, an economic practice responsible for a large part of the unarmed contemporary attacks against life (and not only human life) and cultural survival. As Maristella Svampa (2019: 17) notes,

> At the beginning of the twenty-first century, extractivism took on new dimensions. In that context, where it is possible to record continuities and ruptures, is that the concept appears recreated as neoextractivism. Continuities because, in the heat of successive economic cycles, the extractivist DNA with which European capital marked the long memory of the region was also feeding a certain social imaginary about nature and its benefits. Consequently, extractivism was associated not only with the large-scale dispossession and looting of natural assets, but also with the comparative advantages and economic opportunities that emerged with the rhythm of the different economic cycles and the role of the state. Not by chance, in the face of prevailing progressivism, neoextractivism forcefully reinstated the developmentalist illusion, expressed in the idea that, thanks to the opportunities provided by the new commodity boom and even more so the active role of the state, it would be possible to achieve development. Ruptures because the new phase of capital accumulation, characterized by strong pressure on natural assets and territories, even more so by the vertiginous expansion of the commodity frontier, opened up new political, social and ecological disputes, social resistance unthinkable since the dominant developmentalist imaginary; new gaps in collective action that questioned the developmentalist illusion while denouncing the consolidation of a tendentially single-producer model, which destroys biodiversity, leads to land grabbing and the destruction of territories.

Bolsonaro is what Benjamin Teitelbaum (2020) calls a traditionalist: an antimodern believer in universal, conservative, racist, patriarchal, and religious values (a free mix of Indo-European religions at whose core is the perennial idea of God), and thus a follower of René Guénon, Julius Evola, and Frithjof Schuon, whose teachings he came to know (if he ever did) through his association with the Brazilian Olavo de Carvalho, who would become his main source of inspiration. Bolsonaro embodied the cultural war against the hegemony of the left—a vague and undifferentiated block in which communism, sexual and ethnic minorities, Paulo Freire, the PT, civil right movements, fighters for land, ecologists, and social disciplines were all thrown into—to which a majority of the Brazilian electorate eventually subscribed. As Martin Maitino (2020: 9) has noted,

> the bet on "hyper-reactionary neoliberalism" would not necessarily be an abandonment of the populist strategy, but could represent a shift from populism to the field of recognition by fomenting antagonisms based on the idea of culture wars.

The final key to Bolsonaro's eventual success, however, was his unwavering support of agrobusiness and mining at the expense of the demarcation of Indigenous lands and environmental regulations. Those two collateral victims set the tone for the relationship of his government with the indigenes, with anthropology, and with archaeology/heritage. They also show that the main player in those equations was not populism but capitalism.

The old Brazilian mythology of racial democracy was recast anew in Bolsonaro's Christian nationalism—whose campaign slogan was "Brazil above all, God above us all"—which despised the politics of identity, save that of the good Brazilian, or the good citizen (Kalil 2018). All things considered, "bolsonarism grew, and was nourished and reproduced by a polarization with the PT. . . . Having given an answer to an anti-PT demand made Bolsonaro eligible" (Avelar 2021: 277). Such a demand was in the air—the worldwide publicized revolts of June 2013 during Dilma Rousseff government against corruption, poor public services, police brutality, and environmental predation, especially against the Amazon, were the apex of immense popular mobilizations before and after that date—but existed in a political vacuum until Bolsonaro seized the opportunity. The "people" Bolsonaro appealed to were not those who were defeated by globalization (as with Trump's backers) but those who were unhappy with the PT governments and their political opening—a racist, classist middle class, yes, but also the poor identified with conservative religious values and (paradoxically) with the abstract menace that predatory capitalism would worsen their already bad living standard.

Bolsonaro's disastrous government provoked many victims, the environment among them, but not in isolation; predation on the environment also meant predation on the entities with which it is linked. The regulations concerning the environment were mostly lifted (Scantimburgo 2018). Environmental deregulations are a symptom of a wider phenomenon, environmental inequalities, which, when inflicted upon indigenes and Afro-Brazilian peasants (*quilombolos*), is also an expression of environmental racism. As Acselrad et al. (2021: 170–171) have noted,

The more than proportional penalization of blacks, indigenous peoples and low-income groups reaffirmed the way in which capitalism, with greater force in its neoliberal and authoritarian stage, unequally distributed environmental and health ills. . . . The increase in environmental inequality came to be thus showing a constitutive part of the neo-extractivist project in its liberal-authoritarian phase. This is because deregulating environmental standards and releasing predatory activities implies favoring the expropriation of social groups whose material and immaterial reproduction depends on access to land, water and other environmental resources.

Environmental deregulations translated into "the dismantling of State policies aimed at protecting environmental and socio-environmental rights of traditional peoples and communities" and into an "anti-indigenous, anti-environmental and anti-science [policy], supported by conservative sectors of agribusiness, the evangelical church, large-scale mining and obscurantist groups" (Bronz et al. 2020: 9, 13). Those deregulations were set in motion in the wake of the advancement of neocolonial development—"hierarchical classification of peoples and territories based on inequalities of race/ethnicity/gender, the exploitation of work and nature . . . and the delimitation of a non-human zone" (Acselrad et al. 2021: 178) in which the Others of the post-nation are included—and its patriarchal language (civilizing mission, taming and pacification of the Others; progress and domination of the forces of nature).[5]

Life for Indigenous communities under Bolsonaro worsened. Indigenous lands were one of the collateral victims of environmental deregulations for freeing access to lands previously protected as Indigenous or federal territories. The last move against Indigenous communities and the rights of nature was the establishment of a so-called temporal frame that invalidated the demarcation of Indigenous lands after 1988, seeking to open millions of hectares in Indigenous hands, especially in the Amazon and the Pantanal, to agrobusiness and mining. Yet, on September 22, 2023, the Supreme Court of Brazil voted against such a frame and upheld all the demarcations carried so far and set the legal conditions to respect demarcations to come. This is a remarkable triumph for Indigenous activism and its academic allies, which in any case responded to Bolsonaro with force, from denouncing (before the International Criminal Court and the United Nations' Human Rights Council) his policies against them as genocidal to mobilizations in different cities, portraying the struggle against the temporal frame as "the most important of the century" (see APIB 2021). The moment was so serious that it brought together leaders from most Brazilian Indigenous groups for the first time in the last 40 years—they coalesced in the late 1980s to ensure that Indigenous rights were included in the constitutional frame being discussed at the time.

Bolsonaro overstepped the unstable limits drawn by PT governments between environment/heritage and economic growth. Environmental deregulations dragged heritage along. The issue was not just that the appointed head of IPHAN was a tourism specialist overtly sided with Bolsonaro's policies but that the institute was deprived of most of the tools it had to curtail heritage destruction—which is an overstatement, given that heritage destruction linked to capitalist expansion was rampant even during PT times.

Archaeology was also a victim in its two main guises. The environmental deregulations put in place by the Bolsonaro government had a great impact on the archaeological contract market and, consequently, also on heritage education. If they grew up together during the PT governments, the time came for them to separate and to launch isolated struggles for their share of the economic pie. This move showed, incidentally, that their former cohabitation was circumstantial, not ideological (or disciplinary, for that matter). Social/human sciences (not my term) were a preferred target of Bolsonaro's inflammatory rhetoric, charging them with indoctrination and with spreading the imprecise but useful, when it comes to discrediting progressive policies, "gender ideology" (Alves and Silva 2020). In 2021 the National Council for Scientific and Technological Development's budget was less than half of what it was in 2013. The cuts affected the distribution of research grants, mostly social science–related. As a result, academic archaeology was hit hard. Liberal archaeology, which enjoyed a modest boom during the PT governments alongside the promotion and support of social science projects, all but disappeared—save in the Amazon, where the multicultural approach to Indigenous peoples was prominent due to their indigeneity (not a redundancy, however) and the role, no matter how modest, archaeology had played in "the current debates about the management of the Amazonian forest" (Bezerra 2020: 61; see also Cabral 2015, 2016; Lima 2019).

If environmental predation and the assault on ethnic communities resulting from the intimate relation between authoritarianism and neoliberalism/neoextractivism was so obvious in Brazil as to "occupy a growing space in democratic struggles" (Acselrad et al. 2021: 172), what did archaeologists do in that regard? Nothing. As had been the case before, they pretended that those events happened in another context, to which they were impervious. Ultimately, they still believed that they dealt with the past as past, unrelated to the evils of the present (or the future). This is not fresh news, however. In years past neither them nor heritage specialists did anything to counter the alliance between predatory capitalism and social democracy during PT governments; rather, they profited from such an alliance, especially as it infused millions of dollars into contract archaeology and heritage education. However, faced with the virtual dismantling of the contract market following the relaxation of environmental regulations during Bolsonaro's term, they just defended class and guild positions.

Closing Thoughts

How do they get together, the three entities I have been dealing with, archaeology, heritage, and local communities? Their relationship is not self-evident or (of course) historically determined. They get together, if they do, for circumstantial reasons that are not always political or even philosophical; they can be as prosaic as the surrender to capitalism—not the higher motifs so cherished by the discipline but mere dabbles in the earthly midden of mercantile exchange. After reading the previous pages for sketching these closing notes, I have the feeling that their joint presence in this chapter marked by reactionary politics during Bolsonaro is due to my idiosyncratic historical reading of the recent past, but also of the future. That is, it is tinted both by my analysis and by my wishful thinking.

Those three entities were subjected to heavy artillery fire under Bolsonaro. However, they did not respond jointly, as perhaps could be expected if their relationship were organic. But it was not. Their responses were mixed and ultimately separated them (if they were ever together). Before environmental deregulation, (contract) archaeology came forward to defend its interests (which are at odds with those of local communities), protesting the shrinking of the contract market and the deterioration of working conditions. Heritage (education) remained basically mute, hoping that the conditions that made it possible (environmental licensing) could someday regain their pace. And local communities have reacted as much as they can, especially Indigenous peoples, by far the better organized and the ones with clearer goals. One could only expect that those disciplinary variances more engaged with them, such as liberal (public, collaborative) archaeology, would accompany their struggles. Did that happen?

The fate of liberal archaeology can be assessed using the Brazilian case. To begin with, Brazil seems to endorse the claim by González and colleagues (2018: 510), which states that "predatory capitalism does not need archaeologists, simply because it does not need legitimizing narratives." But Brazil was an exception in that regard in the region: predatory capitalism (here dressed as neoextractivism) indeed enlisted archaeologists and heritage agents in its ranks. What made Brazil different was the hyperneoliberalism espoused by Bolsonaro at the expense of mostly everything else. It thus can be fair to say that, unlike most other Latin American countries, Brazil sustained its predatory capitalism without resorting much to archaeology and heritage, which is not tantamount to saying that "as producers of economic value through heritage, archaeologists are largely irrelevant to global capitalism; as producers of symbolic value through multivocality and multiculturalism, archaeologists are politically harmless" (González et al. 2018: 513). They may be irrelevant economically but not "as producers of symbolic value." Not only archaeology and heritage *can* help to whitewash development, but it has already done it worldwide—and Brazil was no exception. This is what a few engaged activists/scholars, such as Rich Hutchings and Marina La Salle (e.g., 2019, 2021), have been loudly saying for a number of years now, without being much heard—after all, for discipline practitioners, they are little more than harmless noise, to be easily dispensed with.

González and colleagues (2018:510) state, "We believe that archaeology has the opportunity to redefine its relationship with society. But this will only be possible if we dispose of epistemic populism." Archaeology may have opportunity to redefine its relationship with society, but that may not necessarily pass by dispensing of epistemic populism, the minor of all evils that affect the discipline—and, well, the world at large. In Brazil, as elsewhere, the archaeological task has been largely defined (and narrowed down) by its relation to neoliberalism. Independently of how neoliberalism is nuanced as progressive or reactionary, archaeology has provided valuable services to the market. What should concern an archaeology that wants to follow other paths is the discipline's relation with neoliberalism. In the end, for archaeology as its overwhelmingly practiced worldwide, it matters little if the neoliberalism it engages dresses as a social democracy (as in the three terms of the PT) or as fascism (Bolsonaro), provided it does not alter the social contract they signed some three decades ago. This is a terribly sad and worrisome situation.

The main player in this larger picture is not populism but neoliberal capitalism, the real force that archaeology (whether mainstream, alternative, or the like), critical heritage, and communities must reckon with. Facing neoliberalism, facing development, is a tremendous task for, as Mouffe has noted,

> it could be said that, although left-wing populism in Latin America has been able to generate electoral majorities and imprint an important shift in public policies, on a deeper level, linked to a much more subtle

cultural hegemony, the populisms have not been as effective. In other words, neoliberalism wins even without being the dominant ideology anymore. (Mazzolini 2019: 138)

Difficult as it may be, "We need to go back to the roots of politics—radical dissent, conflict, inequality—and reconstruct archaeology as a public-engaged practice to make it a truly critical voice in the global stage" (González et al. 2018: 513–514). We must do it because contemporary archaeology is overtly post-political, in Mouffe's (2018) sense; that is, it partakes of the negation of any political frontier.[6] The post-political is the logic of mainstream archaeology as we now know it, from the technocracy of its contract guise to the multiculturalism of most "alternative" stances in which the energy of difference is contained by a tamed and innocuous diversity. Yet, politics are entering the disciplinary scene with force to upset it, mostly from militant quarters formerly labeled as the others of modernity-coloniality: women, African descendants, and Indigenous. As Mouffe (2018: 41) noted, "The possibility of implementing counter-hegemonic practices to bring an end to the post-political consensus requires the construction of a political frontier" (Mouffe 2018: 41).

Facing neoliberalism while retaining the modern disciplinary attire would not mean much, however. A deep transformation of archaeology—an ontological redesign—does indeed require undisciplining it, that is, moving it away from its utter modernity-coloniality. Facing reactionary populism is not enough, for it may end up reconstituting the discipline. Siding with progressive regimes (populist or not) is not the way out either, save that such regimes be clearly anti-post-political. Part of the undisciplining move is a struggle against reification, notably the reification of development and the market. Undisciplining as political means abandoning the comfortable post-political position that archaeology has enjoyed for so many years, and it means abandoning cultural reductionism. Indeed, "alternative" archaeologies—social, public, collaborative, community, or liberal—can be overtly reductive. Cultural reductionism is a trademark of anthropology (and archaeology, alas!) as an instrument for the administration of otherness. Cultural reductionism thrives in bypassing other cosmologies, in not taking them seriously, in neglecting inter-ontological understandings. Those archaeologies are a bit more of the disciplinary same. Good intentions notwithstanding, those archaeological interventions (public or otherwise) are a recapitulation of the modern colonial order. They are not alternatives to it.

Postscript

Lula da Silva is back in office. He won the 2022 Brazilian presidential election. Dreadful Bolsonaro was ousted from government. Right-wing populism is not dead (Bolsonaro's party and its allies currently control the Brazilian congress), however, but right-wing populism may well be replaced by the kind of Left populism theorized by Mouffe (2018) as a counter to the harmful effects of regressive neoliberal policies. Whether that happens or not, the odds for undisciplining archaeology are served: the contract market has shrunk to a minimum (and so has, consequently, heritage education) and the multicultural logic that feed non–contract archaeological practices is forcefully opposed by local stakeholders who find that undisciplined archaeologists are siding with them against the predations of capitalism and of modernity-coloniality at large.

Acknowledgments

Marcia Bezerra and José Alberione dos Reis provided much-needed and timely assistance with comments and key references. Alfredo González-Ruibal made extensive and welcomed comments on the manuscript. Thanks to them all!

Notes

1 A *deputado* is a member of the lower chamber of the Brazilian Congress.

2 O caminho da prosperidade: Proposta de plano de governo. https://divulgacandcontas .tse.jus.br/candidaturas/oficial/2018/BR/BR/2022802018/280000614517/proposta _1534284632231.pdf, accessed October 18, 2023.

3 This is not a perversity exclusive to Brazil. It has been enacted, time and again, wherever the Right dominates the political spectrum (see Margolis 2020 for the United States).

4 Again, this is more than just a local phenomenon. It can also be seen in Spain (Ferreira 2019) and elsewhere (Weyland 1999).

5 The deregulations are documented, step by step, in a startling dossier assembled by the Associação Nacional dos Servidores de Meio Ambiente (ASCEMA 2021). See Scantimburgo (2018).

6 Mouffe (2018: 10) writes: "Having accepted the hegemonic terrain established by Margaret Thatcher around the dogma that there was no alternative to neoliberal globalization, her famous 'TINA,' the new centre-left government ended up implementing what Stuart Hall has called a 'social-democratic version of neoliberalism.' By claiming that the adversarial model of politics and the left/right opposition had become obsolete, and by celebrating the 'consensus at the centre' between centre-right and centre-left,

the so-called 'radical centre' promoted a technocratic form of politics according to which politics was not a partisan confrontation but the neutral management of public affairs. Neoliberal globalization was seen as a fate that we had to accept, and political questions were reduced to mere technical issues to be dealt with by experts. No space was left for the citizens to have a real choice between different political projects and their role was limited to approving the 'rational' policies elaborated by those experts."

References Cited

Acselrad, Henri, Fabrina Furtado, Juliana Barros, Santo Amaro, Raquel Pinto, and Wendell Assis. 2021. Neoextrativismo e autoritarismo: Afinidades eletivas. *Antropolítica* 53: 167–194.

Alves, Alison de Sousa, and Francisco Vieira da Silva. 2020. Discursos sobre as ciências humanas no Bolsonarismo: Da repetição à prática. *Revista Eletrônica de Educação* 14: 1–20.

APIB. 2021. *Dossiê Internacional de Denúncias dos Povos Indígenas do Brasil.* Articulação dos Povos Indígenas do Brasil, Brasilia.

ASCEMA. 2021. *Cronologia de um desastre anunciado: Ações do Governo Bolsonaro para desmontar as políticas de meio ambiente no Brasil.* Associação Nacional dos Servidores de Meio Ambiente, Brasilia.

Avelar, Idelber. 2021. *Eles em nós: Retórica e antagonismo político no Brasil do Século XXI.* Record, Rio De Janeiro.

Bezerra, Marcia. 2008. Bicho de nove cabeças: Os cursos ae graduação e a formação de arqueólogos no Brasil. *Revista de Arqueologia* 21(2): 139–154.

Bezerra, Marcia. 2015. At That Edge: Archaeology, Heritage Education, and Human Rights in the Brazilian Amazon. *International Journal of Historical Archaeology* 19(4): 822–831.

Bezerra, Marcia. 2020. For a Solidary and Activist [Public] Archaeology in the Amazon. *Online Journal in Public Archaeology* 10.

Bronz, Deborah, Andrea Zhouri, and Edna Castro. 2020. Passando a boiada: Violação de direitos, desregulação e desmanche ambiental no Brasil. *Antropolítica* 49: 8–41.

Cabral, Mariana. 2015. Traces of Past Subjects: Experiencing Indigenous Thought as an Archaeological Mode of Knowledge. *Journal of Contemporary Archaeology* 2(2): S4–S7.

Cabral, Mariana. 2016. Entre passado e presente: Arqueologia e coletivos humanos na Amazônia. *Teoria & Sociedade* 24(2): 76–91.

Fausto, Carlos. 2017. De la responsabilidad social de antropólogos y arqueólogos: Sobre contratos, represas y algunas otras cosas. In *Crítica de la Razón Arqueológica: Arqueología de Contrato y Capitalismo,* edited by Cristóbal Gnecco and Adriana Dias, pp. 291–306. Instituto Colombiano de Antropología e Historia, Bogotá.

Ferreira, Carles. 2019. Vox como representante de la derecha radical en España: Un estudio sobre su ideología. *Revista Española de Ciencia Política* 51: 73–98.

Fraser, Nancy. 2017. From Progressive Neoliberalism to Trump—and Beyond. *American Affairs* 1(4): 46–64.

González-Ruibal, Alfredo, Pablo Alonso, and Felipe Criado. 2018. Against Reactionary Populism: Towards a New Public Archaeology. *Antiquity* 92(362): 507–515.

Hutchings, Richard, and Marina La Salle. 2019. Sustainable Archaeology: Soothing Rhetoric for an Anxious Institution. *Antiquity* 93(372): 1653–1660.

Hutchings, Richard, and Marina La Salle. 2021. Endgame: Contemplating Archaeology's Demise. *Revista de Arqueologia* 34(2): 2–22.

Kalil, Isabela Oliveira. 2018. Qual o poder do WhatsApp? Quem são e no que acreditam os eleitores de Jair Bolsonaro. *Boitempo* (blog), October 23. https://blogdaboitempo .com.br/2018/10/23/qual-o-poder-do-whatsapp-quem-sao-e-no-que-acreditam-os -eleitores-de-bolsonaro/.

Lampedusa, Giuseppe Tomasi de. 1960. *The Leopard.* Collins and Harvill Press, London.

Lima, Helena. 2019. Patrimônio para quem? Por uma arqueologia sensível. *Habitus* 17(1): 25–38.

Llaneras, Kiko. 2018. Bolsonaro arrasa en ciudades blancas y ricas: un mapa del voto en 5.500 municipios. *El País,* October 25. https://elpais.com/internacional/2018/10/23/ actualidad/1540291997_116759.html.

Maitino, Martin Egon. 2020. Populismo e Bolsonarismo. *Cadernos Cemarx* 13: 1–20.

Margolis, Michele. 2020. Who Wants to Make America Great Again? Understanding Evangelical Support for Donald Trump. *Politics and Religion* 13(1): 89–118.

Marín-Aguilera, Beatriz. 2021. Ceci n'est pas un subalterne: A Comment on Indigenous Erasure in Ontology-Related Archaeologies. *Archaeological Dialogues* 28(2): 133–139.

Mazzolini, Samuele. 2019. La apuesta por un populismo de izquierda: Entrevista a Chantal Mouffe. *Nueva Sociedad* 281: 129–139.

Mouffe, Chantal. 2018. *For a Left Populism.* Verso, London.

Pinheiro-Machado, Rosana, and Lucia Mury Scalco. 2018. Da esperança ao ódio: Juventude, política e pobreza do Lulismo ao Bolsonarismo. *Cadernos IHUideias* 16(278): 3–13.

Rocha, Bruna. 2020. "Rescuing" the Ground from under Their Feet? Contract Archaeology and Human Rights Violations in the Brazilian Amazon. In *Critical Perspectives on Cultural Memory and Heritage: Construction, Transformation and Destruction,* edited by Veysel Apaydin, pp. 169–188. UCL Press, London.

Scantimburgo, André. 2018. O desmonte da agenda ambiental no Governo Bolsonaro. *Perspectivas* 52: 103–117.

Schaan, Denise. 2009. A arqueologia Brasileira nos trinta anos da Sab. In *Construindo a arqueologia no Brasil: A trajetória da Sociedade de Arqueologia Brasileira,* edited by Denise Schaan and Marcia Bezerra, pp. 277–295. SAB/GK-Noronha Editora, Belém.

Spyer, Juliano. 2020. *Povo de Deus: Quem são os evangélicos e porque eles importam.* Geração Editorial, São Paulo.

Svampa, Maristella. 2019. *Las fronteras del neoextractivismo en América Latina.* Universidad de Guadalajara, Guadalajara.

Teitelbaum, Benjamin. 2020. *War for Eternity: The Return of Traditionalism and the Rise of the Populist Right.* HarperCollins, New York.

Weyland, Kurt. 1999. Neoliberal Populism in Latin America and Eastern Europe. *Comparative Politics* 31(4): 379–401.

Zhouri, Andrea, and Raquel Oliveira. 2007. Development and Environmental Conflicts in Brazil: Challenges for Anthropology and Anthropologists. *Vibrant* 9(1): 183–208.

II

Long-Term Archaeological Studies of Contemporary Communities

5

Reality Bites

The Insufferable Lightness of
Being a Community Archaeologist

Xurxo Ayán Vila

I am a white, Latin, heterosexual, and middle-aged archaeologist. I am an atheist, Left-leaning city dweller, and my entire research practice has taken place within academic institutions. I was born and raised in an underdeveloped Atlantic region that, over the last decades, has relied largely on the European Cohesion Fund to survive. My country, Galicia, is a stateless nation within the Kingdom of Spain. I have spent over 20 years working with local communities in the context of rural settings. I specialize in placing value on Iron Age fortified settlements. My own research trajectory mirrors the evolution of community archaeology in my country, always eager to adopt the chauvinistic theoretical and methodological frameworks of Anglo-Saxon academia. Over the years I have turned from a vindication of public archaeology (Ayán 2005) to practicing a true archaeological ethnography (Ayán 2012), later to espouse multivocality (Ayán et al. 2012) and the proposals of an integrating community archaeology (Ayán 2021).

Along my journey I have experienced the loss of innocence once described by David Clarke (1973). Over the past years, the economic crisis, a tsunami of neoliberal economic policies, and the ascent of populism and neofascism have been three key factors in my reassessment of my own archaeological practice in the Galician rural world. The strategy I have developed combines an activist guerrilla archaeology (Atalay et al. 2014; McGuire 2008) with the critical pragmatism championed by my colleagues at the Institute of Heritage Sciences of the Spanish National Research Council (Barreiro 2003; Criado 2012). My strategy synthesizes a riddle of contradictions, paradoxes, and renunciations. It is with this strategy that I confront the insufferable lightness of being a community archaeologist in these difficult times.

As I took part in the seminar from which this book originated, my aim was to share this experience with my colleagues. It was my intention then, as it is in the present text, to engage critically in the proposed discussion and to elaborate on the following apparent contradiction: how it is possible to combat reactionary populism precisely through an archaeological practice that itself seems populist, demagogical, and even cynical. To do so, I focus on a case study that I am particularly emotionally attached to: the project to recover the hillfort of San Lourenzo at my home village (Cereixa, A Pobra do Brollón, Terra de Lemos, Lugo, Galicia)—an endeavor in which I risk becoming a reincarnation of the Holy Trinity, as I am simultaneously part of the (Indigenous) local community, a promoter (as member of the board of the residents' association), and the specialist archaeologist (a technical representative of the state) directing the works.

Cereixa is a small rural locality in inner Galicia. At present, Cereixa's population totals 125 inhabitants. Its old population keeps growing their plots and fields. Cattle have virtually disappeared from the local economy. The young live in nearby urban centers. In this context, the promotion of cultural tourism is seen as a possible tool to build a future for the community. Cereixa is located on the pilgrimage route to Santiago and boasts notable archaeological heritage. In 2016 the residents' association decided to recover the San Lourenzo hillfort and entrusted me with the project's direction. My mother was born in Cereixa in 1948 and still lives in the village. I am one of those residents who migrated (I am currently a researcher in Portugal) but has not lost links with the community. Thanks to my team, eight archaeological campaigns have been carried out at the hillfort since 2016 as well as five volunteer camps since 2018.

In the following pages I critically analyze the work strategy followed over 2016–2022 and lay out the project's social, political, and economic conditions. I begin by describing Cereixa's microhistory in some detail (Cereixa: An Ideology Factory), then I move onto the heritage policies prevalent in Galicia (Neoliberalism) and the private sources of funding for the project (Capitalism). After this brief account of the project's origins, I examine the use I have made of the archaeological record, trying to channel Galician nationalism (Nationalism), to make the most of popular religion (Catholicism) and to cash in on the symbolic capital of ancestors (Necropolitics). The chapter ends with a final reflection where I defend the idea of progressive populism as a means of countering the hegemonic neoliberal narrative and as a useful tool for a community archaeology that can transform reality.

Cereixa: An Ideology Factory

Between the twelfth and the thirteenth centuries AD, Galicia's rural territory was organized into *parroquias* (parishes), a set of dispersed hamlets each under one Christian chapel and sharing a common cemetery. This originally ecclesiastical social unit has remained the country's inhabitants' most important identity reference. The community's history displays patterns of resilience similar to those portrayed by James Scott (1985). In the fourteenth century, Cereixa confronted the feudal power of the bishop of Lugo by supporting the rebellion of local landlady María Castaña, a character whose name the local residents' association bears proudly. The community remained combative well into contemporary times, and during Spain's first democratic experience—the so-called Liberal Triennium (1820–1823)—Cereixa put an end to the feudal yoke and declared itself an independent constitutional town council. In the years of Spain's Second Republic (1931–1939) it was dubbed the *red* parish, and during the postwar years it became a sanctuary of anti-Francoist guerrillas. Later, in the democratic times (since 1978) the Left has always won the elections here. Like all Galician parishes, Cereixa is a factory of identity (Lisón 1973), although in our case this history also underlines and connotes this identity politically. In turn, it is also a factory of ideology, of a communal feeling that manifests itself especially in the annual festive cycle through the practice of popular theater as a tool for political critique by recovering old folklore traditions and by cultivating local history (Ayán 2021).

Emigration has played an integral part in the making of this small rural community. During their lives abroad, our migrants socialized mainly at Galician centers and within their own ethnic communities, with marriage into local communities remaining exceptional. Especially in the South American experience, the inbreeding of Indigenous Galicians went hand in hand with currently persisting xenophobic attitudes toward the local Indigenous peoples. Our peasants' traumatic experience in the colonial wars of Cuba and North Morocco (where they were deployed as true cannon fodder) has been handed down through the generations and contributed to the long-term persistence of racist tropes and clichés. The last migration cycle of the 1960s and 1970s, coupled with mechanized agriculture, caused the tremendous demographic fall that has brought on what many today call the Empty Spain or the Emptied Spain (Del Molino 2020), which Cereixa exemplifies. According to the official census, in 2002 there were 186 inhabitants, and in 2019 the figure fell to 125.

In 2016 from within this aging but empowered village and as members of the residents' association, we began the project to recover an archaeological site. The hillfort of San Lourenzo stood abandoned and hidden by scrub at the place where a chapel had once honored the rainmaking saint to whom residents turned in times of drought. Here, among my own people, researching my ancestry, I strove to carry out a model project of community archaeology. And it has been no easy task, amid an economic crisis and a pandemic. Along the way I have been forced to give up many a principle, toe the line, and try to make the most of as many small cracks as I could identify in the system. Like both Cereixa and the object of study itself, the project has also become a generator of ideology.

Neoliberalism

The direct heirs of the Francoist dictatorship, the political Right, have been in power in Galicia since the country was converted into a Spanish autonomous region in 1981, except for six years. Over these 37 years, Galicia has been the testing ground of Spanish neoliberal agendas, especially after the 2008 crisis. The Galician government does not envisage heritage as a political construction that can generate conflicts of either identity or memory. The past is conceived solely as an innocuous and comfortable good, as a materiality to be commodified by using technocratic narratives of sustainable development. In this context, archaeology itself has become a surplus-generating tool that places value on a certain asset: heritage (Alonso 2019). We archaeologists feature as technicians of corporate neoliberalism, of a system seeking immediate benefits and conceiving heritages as commodities. Such a system encourages the consumption of the past and the digestion of identities without promoting learning or instilling any critical skills in its citizens (Hofmann et al. 2021). The aim is always to maximize the use of European funds, to consolidate political control over the local population, and to open up fresh markets. In this sense the economic exploitation of cultural tourism is the priority as long as heritage does not become an obstacle for the policy of systematic territory predation (extractivism, forest repopulation, wind-power stations, mini hydroelectric plants). In our area of practice this technocratic vision has focused since the late 1990s on two clear objectives: the promotion of a Jacobean route to Santiago de Compostela (the winter route) and the creation of a territorial brand image (the Ribeira Sacra) (Goy 2019; Menéndez 2017).

I have always been and remain critical about this process of top-down heritagization. Unescoism (Berliner 2012) reinforces the fossilization of this cultural landscape and the marginalization of the rural society which sustains it while consolidating the interests of private companies seeking to concentrate wine production following exclusively market criteria. Heritage becomes an excuse and history an inconvenience.

And yet I used this technocratic narrative as a way of gaining official support for our project. In 2016 the residents' association lacked the necessary funds to begin archaeological recovery works at the hillfort. On this very year, a double coincidence occurred that I tried to use in our favor: the winter route was formally recognized by the Galician autonomous government as a Jacobean route, and the same government began to seriously consider a UNESCO candidature for the Ribeira Sacra as a World Heritage Landscape. I therefore tried to capture the attention of the regional government by having a website designed with our bid to create a heritage asset at the very foot of the winter path and a site that would allow us to delve into the origins of the Ribeira Sacra. This site-asset was the San Lourenzo hillfort. Opportunism is one of the intrinsic qualities of populism. Cynicism is also a philosophical school.

Capitalism

The neoliberal management of the 2008 crisis brought about the rescue of Galician savings banks by the right-wing government's autonomic government. Such a transfer costed contributors 10,350 million Euros. Once refloated, Novacaixagalicia savings bank was bought from the government for 1.003 million by the Venezuelan bank Banesco. Such was the origin of ABANCA, currently the country's main bank. One of the owners of Banesco and the protagonist of this financial operation was banker JL. Born into a humble family of Cereixa, in the 1960s he emigrated to Venezuela and lived his own American dream. In the past years he has lived in Miami, Panama, Porto, Madrid, and Cereixa. JL is a contemporary representative of what is known in Galicia as *indianos,* successful migrants to America (Núñez Seixas 2002). As a history faculty graduate from the University Santiago de Compostela, I have studied this peculiar phenomenon of Galician emigration. I am well aware of how the mind of the successful migrant works on proudly returning to their home village. JL is passionate about Galician culture and language, a collector of contemporary Galician art, and sponsor of young artists who want to promote Cereixa's past.

In 2016 our residents' association had no economic support from the public powers. Cuts in education and culture were rampant, and cultural heritage was yet another collateral victim of the crisis. The empty space left by the state was filled, in this case, by our friend the banker. As opposed to the

Anglo-Saxon world, in Galicia sponsorship remains quite exceptional. But once presented with the project, JL put up a generous amount for the archaeological works to begin, thus creating the possibility for us to receive funds from the ABANCA foundation, and personally took charge of the project's merchandising. This donation from Cereixa's own magnate allowed us to remain economically independent to navigate the political ups and downs of the following years.

This is how I, a staunch defender of the welfare state and social democracy, ended up asking money from our own "wolf of Wall Street," our neighbor the anti-Chavista Miami exile. JL not only financed the initial excavations at the San Lourenzo hillfort but also supported the first archaeological excavation of a combat setting of the Spanish antifascist guerrilla, a confrontation that took place in Cereixa in 1949 and whose protagonists were communist guerrillas. As JL declared in his Caribbean accent, "This is our past and we must know it, we have to place Cereixa on the world radar."

Nationalism

As in the case of *indiano* JL, this smallholder patriotism—an apt expression of the dispersed rural habitat of Atlantic facade—is the driving force that causes people to recover their heritage. Placing value on a pre-Roman hillfort inside the *parroquia* is a good idea, although it does not spark everybody's interest. Despite our conscious ideas that those ancestral inhabitants are indeed our forebearers, they nonetheless appear diffused in our collective memory. Thus, despite having always been a fierce critic of the much-demoted German cultural historicist archaeology of organic-historicist claims, I have thrown myself headfirst into the essentialist discourse of continuity to win the support of all the local community (Furholt 2021). A hillfort is a cozy, comfortable past, and our ancestral Celtic forefathers are irresistibly likable (González and Alonso 2013).

However, as I discuss below, the great turning point for the project was finding the first tombs from the medieval necropolis in 2017. Even the most skeptical of residents were then moved by the deceased and convinced that their own ancestors, the "grandparents," were indeed buried there. We archaeologists had little in the way of scientific data to corroborate such historic continuity between past and present populations (although it seemed more than plausible). It was impossible to test this hypothesis through DNA, although stable isotope analyses carried out in 2022 point toward the local origin of those individuals analyzed. In any case, regardless of these results, Cereixa residents had made up their minds that these were their direct ancestors. As in any self-respecting peasant society, the dead continued to operate as territorial markers of collective identity.

Nationalism also ended up leaving its ideological mark on the project of the San Lourenzo hillfort. The municipality of A Pobra de Brollón is one of the few town councils in Galicia where the Nationalist Galician Block (*Bloque Nacionalista Galego,* or BNG) governs in absolute majority. The organization is a Left-leaning and antimonarchist coalition that brings together independentists, federalists, communists, social democrats, and stray internationalist nationalists. The BNG logically vindicates the history of ancient Roman Gallaecia and the Medieval Kingdom of Galicia (Villares 2015). Hillforts and the country's Celtic past have been a recurrent point of reference for Galician nationalism since the nineteenth century (in fact, they are the main characters of the Galician hymn) (Díaz Santana 2002; González García 2007; McKevitt 2006). As well as vindicating this prestigious past, the BNG are the trailblazers of a momentous struggle against the multiple legacies of the Francoist dictatorship and in favor of dignifying the memory of victims of fascist repression. Personally, I fully endorse this aspect of their political program. In 2019, faced with the ascent of neofascism, I decided to take part in the BNG's candidate team as an independent runner in the municipal elections. Rumors that the fascist party Vox would run in the very land of my parents spurred me into taking a step that seemed to break with the apparent political neutrality of our project with the San Lourenzo hillfort. In fact, such neutrality never existed since many members of the local residents' association's commission have also been in local political parties. My explicit support contributed to our obtaining a 15,000-euro annual grant from the provincial government (the *diputación* of Lugo province, governed by a coalition of the BNG and the Spanish Socialist Party). To a large extent, the project has survived thanks to this financial support. The council's support has also been crucial in carrying out exhumations of the victims of Francoist repression and in continuing with the project on the archaeology of anti-Francoist guerrillas in Cereixa (the project Repil 1949).

Activating and mobilizing these feelings of belonging to a territory and a common past, as I have done in this project, are also among the basic and simple strategies of populist movements of a nationalist character (González-Ruibal et al. 2018; Hanscam 2021; Hofmann et al. 2021).

Catholicism

I quickly understood that the past as told by science cannot do much to motivate and encourage the community. To tell the community that the hillfort

Figure 5.1. The procession with the saint arriving at the San Lourenzo hillfort, August 10, 2022. Photo by Agostiño Iglesias.

is interesting because it is a second-century BC fortified settlement dedicated to iron metallurgy is like speaking to them in Chinese. Scientific accounts are unintelligible to people who still believe the hillfort to be inhabited by mythical beings, the *mouros*. To reach out to the residents, it was more practical to start from oral tradition and popular religiosity (Riley et al. 2005). Our grandmothers used to tell us about the saint who escaped from the church to visit their hillfort, the one belonging to the same San Lourenzo whose statue's feet they used to wet to make it rain at times of drought. The *parroquia* still bore memories of the old chapel that once stood in the hillfort, and whose walls could still be seen hidden amid the vegetation.

Therefore, in 2016, local priest Father Don José and I decided that our first move would be to restore the carved statue of San Lourenzo and to recover the old festivity of August 10. The main objective of the first archaeological campaign was to exhume part of the old hillfort's chapel and to restore the saint back to his original location. And we did so successfully. After Sunday Mass the entire village initiated a procession from the church to the hillfort. Archaeologists in my team—some of them anarchists; others, communists; all of them atheists—were honored by the community and allowed to carry the saint on their shoulders along part of the way. The procession took place without any priests, which was unheard of and caused some residents of rival parishes to remember Cereixa's *red* past.

It is hard in Galicia to attempt to do local politics without considering this aspect of popular religion. In fact, since the 1980s, one the main public events staged by the Galician Popular Party (the aforementioned Right) is a gargantuan popular feast (a *Romaría,* popular pilgrimage in Galician) celebrated in the sanctuary of A Nosa Senõra do Faro (Our Lady of Faro) in Galicia's geographical center. This could well be considered the apex point of the populist Right. I never thought I would personally end up like this, organizing a procession at the Castro de San Lourenzo with the parish priest's blessing (Figure 5.1). As well as being an accomplice to neoliberalism and capitalism, of converting to nationalism, I also became a believer of a paleo-Christian saint.

Necropolitics

To this day we have documented 90 tombs at the hillfort. Even so, the real turning point came on December 3, 2017, during the third archaeological campaign. Inside the ancient chapel of San Lourenzo, we found a tomb where the skeletal remains of the buried individual had been preserved almost completely. As is frequent in the Spanish archaeological trade, the ancestor was immediately baptized, with the name Atilano. The choice was in no way innocent. For years, the Galician public television broadcast a contest inspired by a Chilean program. Aspiring singers would take the stage and, if they went out of tune or delivered a poor performance, a man dressed as a skeleton would sound a trumpet. The man was known as Atilano and is remembered instantly across the Galician rural world. Within hours, Atilano went viral and made the cover of the main Galician newspapers. It was the first exhumation in Spain ever to be broadcast via Facebook Live. A star was born.

Over the past few decades, the development of Indigenous archaeologies in the Americas and Africa has brought about a set of new legal, professional, and ethical norms in favor of the return of funerary remains to their legitimate stakeholders after centuries of plunder (Ayala 2008; Endere 2014; Gnecco and Ayala 2011; Lamptey and Apoh 2020). These processes of restitution and heritage empowerment have brought a notable postcolonial turn to both the realm of museum curating and to the field of archaeology itself. In the case of the former, the exhibition of mummies and skeletons is already a thing of the past; morbid manipulation of human beings is completely at odds with the ethics codes of the archaeological profession (Mytum 2021). As for the latter, many communities explicitly prohibit archaeological interventions in cemeteries, and even European archaeological entities prohibit their teams working abroad from exhuming necropolises.

Such debates are as yet absent in Spain. According to the current legislation, human remains collected at an archaeological excavation are as much an integral part of the archaeological record as ceramic and metal fragments or lithic pieces. Wrapped in their respective boxes, they sleep the sleep of the just in the humid warehouses of museums. Such has been the fate of the "grandparents" of the San Lourenzo hillfort against the will of Cereixa residents who wish to grant a dignified reburial to the remains of their forebearers in a corner of the chapel's ruins. Throughout the process, the local community of Cereixa has been in favor of excavating the necropolis and having it presented to the public in general. In this respect we have kept with the legal archaeological regulations while ethically relying on the support of a community promoting the works. We would not carry on with the project if this were not the case.

Having clarified these points, in what follows I describe yet another controversial use I have made of the archaeological record of the San Lourenzo hillfort, a necropolitical use (Mbembe 2003), since it has allowed us to grant Atilano a second social life, as if he were the Spanish knight Cid Campeador, whose corpse, legend has it, was straddled onto a horse after death so that this great warrior's silhouette could scare off the enemy. The very process of researching the skeleton became an impressive example of heritage promotion. Every new detail about it captured the interest of social networks and the media, both local and regional: his osteological study (he was a middle-aged man), his radiocarbon dating (second half of the fifteenth century), the restoration of a luxurious iron brooch on his belt, his social status (buried inside the chapel), his diet (rich in meat and fish), the analysis of remains from the ceramic pot laid at his feet (with aromatic herbs brought from the coast). All of this data brought back to life an Early Medieval individual who quickly made it into the collective imagery: local musicians wrote songs about him, children dressed up as him for carnival, he was featured in the local cultural magazine, and, at the San Lourenzo popular pilgrimage, the exact point of his tomb, which had remained covered while the chapel ruins were rehabilitated, became the natural scenery for artistic performances. Atilano himself traveled around Galicia as a resource to present the project and promote scientific culture such as the Scientific Festival at the San Pedro festivities in Santiago de Compostela in June 2018. Finally, in accordance with the Law of Cultural Heritage, Atilano was turned in with the rest of the archaeological materials at the storehouse of the Archaeological Museum of the Viladonga hillfort on November 11, 2019. In Cereixa, like everywhere else in rural Spain, when a young man was drafted by the state for military service, local youths used to organize a farewell party, a truly symbolic act through which the community marked the kidnapping of one of its members by a foreign power. In the same way, on the eve of November 11 a dinner party was organized at the restaurant O'Fogón in Cereixa: the banquet table was presided by a chair containing the remains of Atilano.

I can understand how Atilano's second life, with its comings and goings, and his exhibition and appropriation may be considered a scandal and a miscarriage by most readers of this text. But, as stated, it is the result of a fully knowing necropolitical use that has been legitimized by a local community who see themselves as the direct heir to those it considers its ancestors. This use had the clear aim of humanizing remains, which goes way beyond mere stratigraphic units, and with a healthy pedagogical intent but also as a marketing strategy to raise funds for the project. This is nothing that has not already been done by the prestigious and well-reputed team of prehistorians at Atapuerca with the fossil remains of "Miguelón" or "Elvis" (Hochadel 2015).

Thanks to his impressive media repercussion, Atilano continued to provide for the Cereixa community after his death. As a result, the project captured the attention of the autonomous Galician government's Council of Culture. At our meeting with the councillor in the winter of 2018, he could barely take his eyes off the famous skeleton (Figure 5.2). It was actually Atilano who enabled the government of Galicia's decision to organize an annual international volunteer work camp for the young, which is already in its fifth season. The event has been crucial in granting the project continuity. The work camp is always packed with volunteers because the possibility of excavating a medieval necropolis is an irresistibly attractive formative experience. Kids dream of finding the next Atilano.

Concluding Remarks

Cristóbal Gnecco has argued, quite convincingly, that community archaeology will always be a colonial practice, which cannot possibly be dis-embedded from the capitalist system of exploitation (Gnecco, in this volume: Chapter 4). Yet another symptom of the insufferable lightness of being archaeologists is that we are forced to operate as community managers more than as humanists or social scientists. However, I do not consider myself a cultural hero or a parachute archaeologist who, having been put in charge of some ephemeral project, merely gets paid their salary and then leaves. In the case study I have discussed here, I act as—and I am—a local Indigenous archaeologist helping to construct the heritage of my own community as a tool for the future. Here history has defined the community being discussed quite clearly: a rural par-

Figure 5.2. Poster for the IV Festival of San Lourenzo (2019), inspired by Atilano. Design by Juan Pablo Venditti.

ish in a globalized world, made up of its living and its dead, of the members on its census and its migrants. A group that retains its community ethos and its peasant habitus at a time of permanent economic and pandemic crisis. Within this logic, the community persists with the ideals of autarchy, self-management and independence which characterize peasant society. On these grounds, I presented my people (they are for me the People) with a project to recover the San Lourenzo hillfort as the ethical and moral watermark on the margins of the prevalent sociopolitical system. The initial economic injection from our local patron seemed to guarantee our independence in this respect. But this was far from being the case. I was soon confronted with the fact that Cereixa could only approach the past and future from within the system itself and by taking a pragmatic stance. This could only be done by making use of the tactics and the strategies of resilience, by establishing those relationships with power that our forebearers mastered as they navigated through either feudalism, the liberal state, the Francoist dictatorship, or the present. To me, the end justifies the means to achieve the very social archaeology reclaimed in this book's introduction.

The start of this project coincided with the heyday of reactionary populism in our country. Since then, the neofascist party Vox has gained considerable support in the rural world and even poses as bearer of the demands of ranchers, peasants, and other groups struggling against demographic decline. These fascists turn to identity, territorial attachment, the sense of belonging and tradition as rural values to legitimize their nationalist, racist, and sexist narrative (Rodríguez and Almansa-Sánchez 2021). Their demagoguery in this respect outdoes even that of the hegemonic right-wing Popular Party (Partido Popular), which is also strong within rural contexts. These reality bites have taught me to use similar tactics for diametrically opposed objectives: populists devise nationalist discourses, excluding simplistic narratives to give people a sense of pride, not to make them think critically (González-Ruibal and McGuire, in this volume: Chapter 1; Kotsakis 2021). In my case, my scientific practice also mobilizes identity and pride, tradition, and even mythical thought. It is a popular archaeology against populism, a performative activity that uses microhistory to try to generate a critical, integrating, and global narrative beyond the community itself.

A Pobra do Brollón is a rural locality of 1,600 inhabitants that, thanks to the ideological commitment of the municipal government, has a welcoming policy toward immigration despite the xenophobic attitudes of some of the local population. Its school includes students from such diverse backgrounds as the Philippines, Great Britain, Paraguay, Nicaragua, Morocco, Romania, and Venezuela, and an enriching multicultural and multilingual reality, with children and families (some from violence-ridden contexts) who are becoming integrated into this new cultural landscape. At the San Lourenzo hillfort, at the popular pilgrimage, at our dissemination activities with schools and on the field, these fellow citizens and countrypeople (as well as the volunteers at the international work camp) are brought in touch through the archaeological record, with the universal history of a peasant community's thousand-year-long struggle for survival. A hamlet of Upper Medieval free peasants who fell prey to the feudal trap. Libertaria, a woman living in the twelfth century, was part of an egalitarian subsistence-based community practicing primitive Christianity. Three centuries later, Atilano, an individual of status within the parish, represents an "estate," a tiered society based on inequality and feudal exploitation, with the Catholic Church in control of people's lives. Cereixa rebelled against this oppressive system over and over again, sometimes using physical violence, other times through symbolic violence (rites, carnival, popular pilgrimages, through disobedience and ridicule of the feudal lord).

The students also hear explanations for the relevance of population movements to local history, from the eighth-century arrival of the *mozárabes* to the impact of returned emigrants to America in the first third of the twentieth century. The Archaeology of the Recent Past seminar also provides materials for our region's antifascist memory by rendering visible the violence conducted by totalitarianism (sites of guerrilla combat, the exhuming of common graves). Ours is a project of emotional archaeology that also deals with uncomfortable pasts, that pokes into the scars of collective trauma and resentment, into fear and the violence of the civil war and postwar periods (Figure 5.3). This trauma lasts well into this day and is handed down through the generations. These negative emotions are to be considered to avoid endorsing idyllic Rousseau-type portrayals of the local community. Our emotional archaeology (Tarlow 2012) pays a price because whenever we approach these questions, adversarial voices emerge within the community against our research: "the dead should be left alone"—apparently even if they were murdered by fascist thugs. To reveal the truth and dismantle this politics of amnesia, one must turn from critical pragmatism to guerrilla archaeology.

I consider this micro-historical account a master narrative that goes beyond the community, an account as socially useful as it is attractive and suggestive, judging by its media coverage, by its impact on social media, and by the success of the heritage dissemination activities we have been developing over the past years. The entire narrative is grounded in empirical, factual evidence, on serious and conscientious scientific research. The dissemination of scientific methods has also been a fundamental tool in exposing the demagogical historical narrative underpinning value creation around the Ribeira

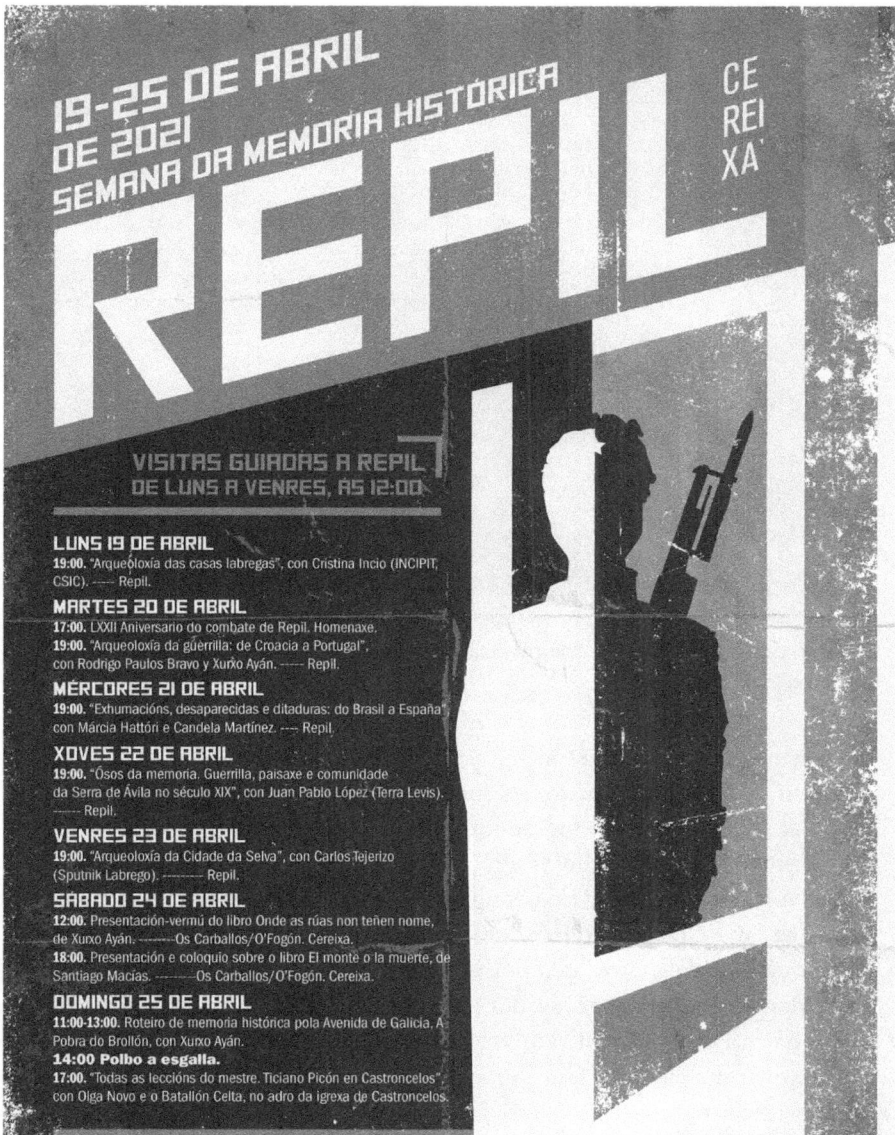

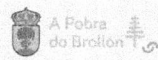

Figure 5.3. Guerrilla Archaeology: Poster for the Week of Historical Memory, organized in April 2021. Design by Juan Pablo Venditti.

Figure 5.4. Festival of San Lourenzo (August 10, 2020). This event was organized for the local community and the volunteers of the archaeological work camp. Photo by Agostiño Iglesias.

Sacra heritage. Our project at the San Lourenzo hillfort deconstructed the idea that the settlement had been built by Rome for the gold mining of the river Saa following Augustus' conquest. Our excavations have uncovered a protohistoric Iron Age hillfort with considerable mining technologies.

Using science, we have also debunked the myth of the Roman origin of this imagined landscape, a good example of a populist and oversimplifying narrative that is widely circulated outside the realm of history and archaeology professionals. In the same way, our project has exposed the arbitrariness of a biased narrative with a vested interest in the specific medieval period stretching between the eleventh and thirteenth centuries as a time of splendor for the Ribeira Sacra.

Such unpopular scientific practices cost money. To finance this, I have turned to all sorts of tactics, including some probably reproachable ones, as I exploited the paths opened up by Unescoism and the neoliberal management of heritage. I have tried to make the most of the commodification of this heritage to the point of promoting memory tourism and dark tourism so that the project, which is good for my community, could continue. The pandemic crisis has been a true litmus test. When a generalized sense of ruin took over as the result of the Covid-19 pandemic, when sociability networks broke due to confinement and perimeter closures, the project kindled a light of hope. The excavations and international work camp went on under adequate sanitary conditions, and so did the publications and the organization of the Council of Cereixa's bicentenary (2020–2023). This all attested to the resilience of a community who, against all odds, continue to believe in the future and their heritage (Figure 5.4).

As well as fulfilling these short-term goals, the project of the San Lourenzo hillfort has succeeded in promoting counterhegemonic narratives, discourses of emancipation that have contained the tide of reactionary populism. I hope to have answered one of the questions posed in this book's introduction. Yes, it *is* possible to practice a critical populism at the cost of the harsh ethical dilemmas I have had to face over these years. It is possible, if one is prepared to risk being seen as opportunistic, a cynic, a technocrat, a local development agent, a tour operator, or a tomb profaner. Such is the insufferable lightness of being a community archaeologist.

Acknowledgments

The IHC is funded by national funds through FCT—Fundação para a Ciência e a Tecnologia, I.P., under the projects UIDB/04209/2020 and UIDP/04209/2020. The Associated Laboratory IN2PAST is funded by FCT, I.P. (LA/P/0132/2020).

References Cited

Alonso González, Pablo. 2019. *The Heritage Machine: Fetishism and Domination in Maragatería, Spain.* Pluto Press, London.

Atalay, Sonja, Lee Rains Clauss, Randall H. McGuire, and John R. Welch. 2014. Transforming Archaeology. In *Transforming Archaeology. Activist practices and prospects,* edited by Sonya Atalay, Lee Rains Clauss, Randall H. McGuire, and John R. Welch, pp. 7–28. Left Coast Press, Walnut Creek, California.

Ayala, Patricia. 2008. *Políticas del pasado: Indígenas, arqueólogos y estado en Atacama.* Línea Editorial IIAM-UCN, Ocho Libros, Santiago de Chile.

Ayán Vila, Xurxo (coordinator). 2005. *Os Castros de Neixón, I: A recuperación desde a arqueoloxía dun espazo social e patrimonial.* Serie Keltia, 30. Noia, Toxosoutos.

Ayán Vila, Xurxo. 2012. Public Archaeology, Democracy and Community. Experiences from Iron Age Hillforts at Galicia (Spain). In *Integrating Archaeology: Science, Wish, Reality,* edited by Nina Schücker, pp. 41–47. Römisch-GermanischeKommission, Frankfurt A.M. des Deutschen Archäologischen Instituts, Frankfurt.

Ayán Vila Xurxo. 2021. Myth, Science and Community: The Archaeological Project of

San Lourenzo Hillfort (Galicia, Spain). *Journal of Community Archaeology and Heritage* 8(3): 145–159.

Ayán Vila, Xurxo, Martina González Veiga, and Rafael Rodríguez Martínez. 2012. Más allá de la arqueología pública: Arqueología, democracia y comunidad en el yacimiento multivocal de A Lanzada (Sanxenxo, Pontevedra). *Treballs d'Arqueología* 18: 63–98.

Barreiro Martínez, David. 2003. Arqueología y Pragmatismo Crítico. *Claves de Razón Práctica* 133: 36–41.

Berliner, David. 2012. Multiple Nostalgias: The Fabric of Heritage in Luang Prabang (Lao PDR). *Journal of the Royal Anthropological Institute* 18: 769–786.

Clarke, David. 1973. Archaeology: The Loss of Innocence. *Antiquity* 47(185): 6–18.

Criado-Boado, Felipe. 2012. *Arqueológicas: La razón perdida.* Bellaterra, Barcelona.

Del Molino, Sergio. 2020. *La España vacía: Viaje por un país que nunca fue.* Turner, Madrid.

Díaz Santana, Beatriz. 2002. *Los Celtas en Galicia: Arqueología y política en la creación de La identidad Gallega.* Toxosoutos, Noia.

Furholt, Martin. 2021. Ethnic Essentialism, Clash of Cultures, Biologization of Identities: How Flawed Concepts Affect the Archaeogenetics Discourse. *European Journal of Archaeology* 24(4): 526–529.

Endere, María de la Luz. 2014. Archaeological Heritage Legislation and Indigenous Rights in Latin America: Trends and Challenges. *International Journal of Cultural Property* 21(3): 319–330.

Gnecco, Cristóbal, and Patricia Ayala. (editors). 2011. *Indigenous People and Archaeology in Latin America.* Left Coast Press, Walnut Creek, California.

Hanscam, Emily Ruth. 2021. The Postnational Critique: A Response to Reactionary Populism? *European Journal of Archaeology* 24(4): 523–526.

González Álvarez, David, and Pablo Alonso González. 2013. The "Celtic-Barbarian Assemblage": Archaeology and Cultural Memory in the Fiestas de Astures y Romanos, Astorga, Spain. *Public Archaeology* 12(3): 155–180.

González García, Francisco Javier. 2007. Celtismo e historiografía en Galicia: En busca de los Celtas perdidos. In *Los pueblos de la Galicia Céltica,* edited by Francisco Javier González García, pp. 9–139. Akal, Madrid.

González-Ruibal, Alfredo, Pablo Alonso González, and Felipe Criado-Boado. 2018. Against Reactionary Populism: Towards a New Public Archaeology. *Antiquity* 92(362): 507–515.

Goy Diz, Ana. 2019. The Ribeira Sacra: The Definition of Its Outstanding Universal Value. In M. Crecente, J. M. (coord.): A Future for the Land: Cultural Landscapes, Rural Management and Geographical Information Systems (Expert Workshop Ribeira Sacra, November 8–9, 2018), edited by Mario Crecente, pp. 98–107. Fundación Juana de Vega, Santiago de Compostela.

Hochadel, Olivier. 2015. The Fossils of Atapuerca: Scientific Nationalism and the New Beginning of Spanish History. *Studies in Ethnicity and Nationalism* 15(3): 389–410.

Hofmann, Daniela, Emily Hanscam, Martin Furhol, Martin Bača, Samantha S. Reiter, Alessandro Vanzetti, Kostas Kostakis, et al. 2021. Forum: Populism, Identity Politics, and the Archaeology of Europe. *European Journal of Archaeology,* 24(4): 519–555.

Kotsakis, Kostas. 2021. From the Nation's Archaeology to Archaeology's People. *European Journal of Archaeology* 24(4): 537–40.

Lamptey, Pearl, and Wazi Apoh. 2020. The Restitution Debate and Return of Human Remains: Implications for Bioarchaeological Research and Cultural Ethics in Africa. *Contemporary Journal of African Studies* 7(1): 97–115.

Lisón Tolosana, Carmelo. 1973. Some Aspects of Moral Structure in Galicia Hamlets. *American Anthropological* 3: 241–273.

Mbembe, Achille. 2003. Necropolitics. *Public Culture,* 15(1): 11–40.

McGuire, Randall H. 2008. *Archaeology as Political Action.* University of California Press, Berkeley, California.

McKevitt, Kerry Ann. 2006. Mythologizing Identity and History: A Look at the Celtic Past of Galicia. *e-Keltoi: Journal of Interdisciplinary Celtic Studies* 6(art. 13). https://dc.uwm.edu/ekeltoi/vol6/iss1/13.

Menéndez Lorenzo, Aida. 2017. *A Detailed Guide: The Winter Route to Santiago.* Author's edition, Monforte de Lemos.

Mytum, Harold. 2021. Ethics and Practice in the Excavation, Examination, Analysis, and Preservation of Historical Mummified Human Remains. *Historical Archaeology,* 55: 96–109.

Núñez Seixas, Xosé Manuel. 2002. History and Collective Memories of Migration in a Land of Migrants: The Case of Iberian Galicia. *History and Memory* 14(1–2): 229–258.

Riley, Mark, David C. Harvey, Tony Brown, and Sara Mills. 2005. Narrating Landscape: The Potential of Oral History for Landscape Archaeology. *Public Archaeology* 4(1): 39–50.

Rodríguez-Temiño, Ignacio, and Jaime Almansa-Sánchez. 2021. The Use of Past Events as Political Symbols in Spain: The Example of Vox and the Need for a New Archaeology of Ethnicity. *International Journal of Heritage Studies* 27(10): 1064–1078.

Scott, James C. 1985. *Weapons of the Weak: Everyday Forms of Peasant Resistance.* Yale University Press, New Haven, Connecticut.

Tarlow, Sarah. 2012. The Archaeology of Emotion and Affect. *Annual Review of Anthropology* 41: 169–185.

Villares, Ramón. 2015. Castles vs. Castros: The Middle Ages in the Construction of Galician National Identity. In *Culture and Society in Medieval Galicia: A Cultural Crossroads at the Edge of Europe,* edited by James D'Emilio, pp. 917–946. Koninklijke Brill NV, Leiden.

6

Solidarity, the Craft of Archaeology, and Reactionary Populism

RANDALL H. McGUIRE

> Solidarity is not a matter of sentiment but a fact, cold and impassive as the granite foundations of a skyscraper. If the basic elements, identity of interest, clarity of vision, honesty of intent, and oneness of purpose, or any of these is lacking, all sentimental pleas for solidarity, and all other efforts to achieve it will be barren of results.
> —Eugene V. Debs (1914: 534)

This volume asks "archaeology for whom?" and charges us to consider the relationship between archaeology, heritage, communities, and reactionary populism. In the first decade of the twenty-first century, some archaeologists were struggling to build multivocal scholarship that would do political work for the "people" by producing usable heritages that advanced the interests of communities (McGuire 2008). By the beginning of the third decade of the twenty-first century the idea that archaeologists should serve communities has become the norm with a plethora of community projects in archaeology. Since 2016, however, a wave of reactionary populism has washed over the world. In this transformed world, an archaeology collaborating with communities may not serve liberating goals and, thus, we must critically examine our relationships. Nowhere in the world has the impact of reactionary populism been greater than among coal miners in the United States.

I was a member of the archaeological collective that investigated the 1914 Ludlow Massacre in southern Colorado (Larkin and McGuire 2009; Montoya and Larkin 2022; Saitta 2007; Saitta and Duke 1998). On this spot, Colorado National Guard troops fired machine guns into a tent camp of striking miners and their wives and children. The miners fought back, and 21 people including 11 children and two women died in the battle. For 10 days, in one of the clearest examples of class warfare in US history, a ragtag army of miners burned company buildings, killed company men, slaughtered company mules, and fought pitched battles with National Guard troops. More than 60 people died. From 1997 to 2002, the Ludlow Collective dug the remains of the tent camp and carried out excavations in a nearby company town. In our research we collaborated with the principal US coal miners' union, the United Mine Workers of America (UMWA). For a nonunion, popular audience, we employed the craft of archaeology to expose the monstrous lie that capitalism had freely given workers' rights and privileges and to reveal that workers and their families won these rights with blood (McGuire 2014). For those in the union movement, we used the craft of archaeology to build solidarity.

Solidarity unifies concerns, purposes, and sympathies among members of a group. Creating, sustaining, and expanding solidarity regularly requires compromise and putting aside conflicting identities, interests, and goals. We stood in solidarity with the UMWA in our research and accomplished much for shared goals (Montoya and Larkin 2022). In 2005, at the annual Ludlow Memorial Service, union leaders announced that they saw us as brothers and sisters in the struggle for labor justice (Saitta 2007: 105). To be brothers and sisters, however, we had to set aside or ignore significant political and class differences between us and working-class families. During and following the project, union members and archaeologists felt good about this solidarity (Larkin 2022a, 2022b). The current rise of reactionary populism, however, accentuates the class and political differences that we set aside to collaborate. This widening gap now makes me uncomfortable.

In the 2016, 2020, and 2024 presidential elections, Donald Trump preached a reactionary populism that appealed to many working-class people, and he especially courted coal miners. In 2016, Trump prevailed in part by winning over rank-and-file union members, especially from the UMWA. In this chapter, I ask whether we can practice the craft of archaeology in solidarity with the UMWA while simultaneously challenging reactionary populism. To answer this question, we must understand why coal miners embraced reactionary populism, and understand archaeology's contribution to the labor movement.

Creating Solidarity

In the mid-1990s, Phil Duke, Dean Saitta, and I developed the Archaeology of the Colorado Coalfield War Archaeological Project as an activist archaeology in support of unions and working-class families (Larkin 2022b). We recognized that activism required community collaboration.

Archaeologists frequently take the identification of a "community" for granted without critically considering how or why a group of people are a "community." Many historical archaeologists have argued that scholars are obligated to collaborate with the descendant communities of the sites that we study (Singleton and Orser 2003; Wilke and Bartoy 2000). They often, however, confuse the biological descendants of historical communities with a descendant community. In the case of Ludlow, these are two distinct groups (Larkin 2022a: 81–93). The parents of the biological descendants benefited from the great social mobility of the 1950s and 1960s, and their children left the coal-mining community and joined the middle class (Butero 2022: 63). They identify as biological descendants of the massacre and hold deep feelings about the event and its memorialization. But they do not live near each other or participate in any type of interacting group, organization, or club or in any other way form a community (Linville 2022). The unionized working people of southern Colorado make up the descendant community of the 1913–1914 coal strike. Regional director of the UMWA Region 4 Robert Butero identifies these people as the "community of interest" (Butero 2022: 61). Ernie Hernandez, past president of the Pueblo United Steelworkers called the strikers "our ancestors" (Garrett 2003). The vast majority of contemporary union workers are Chicanos who, as individuals, have no biological connection to the events of 1913–1914. In southern Colorado, we collaborated with descendants (Linville 2022) and with the community of interest—that is, union families. At that time there were two UMWA locals in southern Colorado that included retired miners and health care workers, and two United Steelworkers locals in nearby Pueblo, Colorado.

Philip Duke and I come from working-class backgrounds, and we knew that collaboration also required overcoming class differences. Duke, Saitta, and I spent almost two years traveling to Washington, DC, to Denver, and to Trinidad, Colorado, meeting people to build national-, regional-, and local-level UMWA support for our project. We learned much in this process, but two experiences stand out. They revealed that we had to overcome class antagonism and that our collaborators would only accept us if we could demonstrate how our research would support their politics.

In 1997 Saitta arrived at the UMWA local in Trinidad to introduce the project (Saitta 2007: 13). He came at a bad time. The Montana Power Company had just shuttered the last operating coal mine in southern Colorado. He carefully presented our proposal for archaeological fieldwork at the Ludlow Massacre site and stressed our support of the union. In response, one newly unemployed coal miner asserted that "all you need to know about Ludlow can be summed up in three words: they got fucked." The deep alienation and antagonism evident in this declaration revealed a class antagonism that scorned our intellectualization of the obvious.

Later that year Saitta and I met with a union professional at the UMWA regional office in Denver, Colorado (Saitta 2007: 13). There we carefully described our research plan and how our excavations would affect the memorial grounds. He listened attentively and then he said to us, "You have to understand that Ludlow is sacred ground to the UMWA, and there is one question that I have to ask you before we can approve you working there. Are you Republicans?" We hesitated a bit, taken aback by the query, then I replied, "No we are not Republicans, we are socialists." He retorted, "Fine, as long as you are not Republicans." This interaction made it clear that we were walking on sacred and politized ground where the union leadership welcomed us only if our political agenda fit that of the UMWA. Since that meeting, Trump's reactionary populist movement and promises to revive the coal industry have divided the UMWA and weakened solidarity. Following Trump, a clear majority of UMWA members have become Republicans. This leaves us to ask, what do we do when the UMWA rank and file changes its politics and a majority of UMWA members now want us to be Republicans?

Dirty Hands and Book Learning

Key attributes of reactionary populism include the criticism of elites, antipluralism, moral superiority, patriotism, and identity politics (Finchelstein 2019; Traverso 2019). These qualities do not, however, spring de novo from populism but rather originate from class relations in capitalism. They are part of the structure of capitalism, as is archaeology.

Class and class relations infuse all facets of capitalist society, and as a part of that society, archaeology embodies these relations (McGuire and Walker 1999). Archaeology has typically served middle-class interests. By middle class, I do not refer to people of middling income but rather to the structural middle class. In modern capitalism, managers, administrators, educators, and professionals who stand between the owners (or controllers) of the means of production (the bourgeois) and the workers who do the labor of production comprise the middle class. The work of the middle class is by and large intellectual labor, the application of formal knowledge or principles, commonly to tasks that working-class individuals perform. Archaeology is part of the intellectual apparatus (things such as schools, books, magazines, organizations, and arts) that generates the symbolic capital (things such as esoteric knowledge, shared experience, certification, manners, and social skills) that individuals need to be part of the middle and bourgeois classes (Bourdieu

1987). Because archaeology lives in the middle class, it principally attracts middle-class supporters and participants. It often does not appeal to working-class audiences.

The Trinidad miner's exclamation that all we needed to understand about Ludlow was that "they got fucked" reveals a key antagonism between the working and middle classes. Middle-class education usually splits learning from doing. Middle-class ideology puts a high value on the intellectual apparatus of capitalism, especially educational institutions, both because the class reproduces itself through this apparatus and because many of the class find employment in it. Working-class ideology tends to resent this apparatus as elitist, both because it hinders their own class mobility and because in the workplace their experience and skill is commonly subservient to formal knowledge. Thus, middle-class people tend to value book learning, in contrast with the working-class appreciation for knowledge won from experience. Book learning promotes thinking/talking out problems, while experience acts from the gut.

My grandfather and my uncle were union men who worked for a gas company and in a cement plant. At the dinner table, they shared many stories about their work. The anecdotes often sprang from a common trope. A practical problem had arisen with the work, and they—with their hands-on knowledge—knew how to fix it. They would have moved quickly from experience, but a college-educated engineer or supervisor stopped them and insisted that they go by the book. The book fix always took a lot of time and failed. My relatives are proud of my accomplishments in education, but they always cautioned me to be wary of too much book learning, and they encouraged me to dirty my hands with physical labor (probably the deep psychological reason I became an archaeologist).

Unionized workers in southern Colorado tend to be highly patriotic. They commonly wear T-shirts and caps with American flags, military badges, and eagles on them. The annual memorial service always begins with a color guard and flag raising. Union chapter meetings start with the Pledge of Allegiance. Such explicit patriotism made many members of the archaeological collective uncomfortable. We came to understand, however, that it is primarily working-class people who enlist in the military and die for our country. Union members' patriotism sprang from the experiences and sacrifices of fathers, mothers, brothers, sisters, sons, and daughters. Reactionary populism has co-opted this patriotism. Populists transformed it into a hyperpatriotism and used it to justify paramilitary organizations and actions. The populist stance equates patriotism with nationalism and uses the combo to justify anti-immigrant, racists, and anti-elite attitudes (Singh 2021).

The dominance of middle-class interests and ideologies in archaeology encourages archaeologists to see the middle-class perspective as universal, and to disparage other class interests and perceptions of the past. Most archaeologists perceive their audience as extensive and varied. The limited studies that have been done of the constituency for archaeology suggest that this is not the case and that, in fact, the middle class forms the primary audience for archaeology. The programs that archaeologists have developed to educate the public—exhibits, site tours, magazines, classes, and pamphlets—appeal more to middle-class individuals who look to books and authorities for knowledge, and less to working-class people, such as coal miners, who accentuate experience, practical know-how, and dirty hands.

We Dug Coal Together

Sectors of society that perceive themselves as alienated from the political system and declining in power often turn to populism (Finchelstein 2019; Traverso 2019). They embrace a nostalgia for an imagined glorious past. US coal miners are one such group.

In the United States, people tend to see coal miners as the quintessential working class. For this reason, they have become icons in, and mainstays of, US politics (Isser 2020; Martin 2018). As I write, only about 42,000 people work in the US coal industry. Despite their low numbers, coal miners have taken a pivotal role in the US political imagination and in conversations around jobs, unions, and climate change. In 2016, Donald Trump used them as a catalyst for political affect (Rose 2018). He invoked the noble coal miner as he promised to bring back coal, increase production, and secure more jobs for miners. As Arthur Rose (2018: 701) points out, "Rhetorically, his resuscitation of King Coal paralleled his appeals to white identity; both relied on a nostalgia for a past that never existed, a past untouched by either the dust of coal itself or the wider issue of racialized violence in the United States."

Despite generations of voting for Democrats ("as long as you are not Republicans"), coal miners embraced Trump's message, and he became their candidate. The American Federation of Labor and Congress of Industrial Organizations (AFL-CIO) is the largest labor federation in the United States, and it includes the UMWA. The AFL-CIO endorsed Hillary Clinton in 2016 and Joe Biden in 2020 and 2024, but the UMWA broke with the federation and endorsed no one in all three elections. In many coal towns around the country, Trump won by more than 80% of the vote. The 2024 election in coal country repeated what had happened in 2016 even though coal production and coal jobs had declined more rapidly during Trump's administration than they had during Barack Obama's presidency.

How do we account for the quintessential US working class abandoning their Democratic heritage and being swept up in Trump's reactionary populism? Were they ignorant and overcome with nostalgia for a past that never existed? Did Trump dupe them into voting against their own economic/class interests? To understand what motivated coal miners, we must understand why men want to dig coal.

When we were setting up the Colorado Coal War Project, I visited a bar in Trinidad, Colorado, wearing a T-shirt with UMWA written on it. I had barely sat down when two men stopped a game of pool and came over to me. They asked if I knew of a new mine opening. They were both unemployed miners and desperate to get back underground. After disappointing them, I had to ask myself, why would anyone want to be a coal miner? Coal mining is physically demanding and dangerous—miners deal with toxic gases and dust, plus the possibility of being crushed, drowned, or injured from fires and explosions (Pasley 2019). In the long term, many miners physically wreck their bodies and develop debilitating black lung disease.

In the American imagination, coal miners, like cowboys, symbolize masculinity. Miners find it exhilarating to work thousands of feet underground. Even with fully mechanized mining, underground miners control their machines, work largely unsupervised, and set the pace of work. Unionized coal miners are paid well; currently a union miner can earn up to $100,000 a year with overtime (compared to average working-class earnings of $35,000 to $45,000) and receive generous retirement and medical benefits. The heavy labor and dangers make the work exciting and build comradery and male bonding. In coal country, the statement "We dug coal together" signals a special relationship that outsiders cannot understand. For many, mining coal is a family tradition that goes back generations (Butero 2022). All of these factors create an experience, pride, self-esteem, and identity that most other jobs cannot match.

It probably goes without saying that coal mining is declining precipitously in the United States. Gas-powered electric plants, wind power, and solar power are all growing at coal's expense. The miners we have worked with perceive Democrats as fueling and even delighting in coal's decline because of a political divide over an environmental issue. Archaeologists tend to be avid environmentalists, and this brought us into conflict with our collaborators during the project. The miners blamed environmentalists for the declines in US coal mining. Later they easily accepted reactionary populist rhetoric that dismisses environmentalists, environmental scientists, and climate-change advocates as elites or outsiders and ties mining to job creation, economic development, and national prosperity (Ofstehage et al. 2022).

During the 2020 election, President Biden suggested that unemployed miners should learn to write computer code. His counsel was tone-deaf to what the miners have lost and wish to regain (Isser 2020). In contrast, Trump unequivocally said that he would save coal mining in the United States and bring back mining jobs. As a retired coal miner commented about Biden, "It's hard to get somebody to believe in something if your job depends on not believing in it" (Isser 2020).

Unions and the Democratic Party

Rank-and-file union discontent and support for a reactionary popularism in the United States goes far beyond coal miners. Since the Great Depression of the 1930s, the Democratic Party has been the party of unionized labor. In recent decades, however, the Democrats have taken labor's support for granted, forsaken labor's interests, and failed to block Republican efforts to erode labor rights and impede union organizing (Babineau 2019; Beauchamp 2021). People turn to populism when they do not see their concerns being addressed by their government (or union leadership) and when they are sinking toward the bottom in a burgeoning economy with increasing social inequality (Finchelstein 2019).

In the 1970s approximately 25% of American workers belonged to unions. By 1983 that number had fallen to 20.1%, and by 2023 to 10% (US Bureau of Labor Statistics). This precipitous fall resulted from two major causes—first, the decline in heavy industry and manufacturing in the United States and, second, changes in labor law that have made union organizing extremely difficult.

Heavy industry and manufacturing traditionally are the main unionized sectors of the American economy. In the first two decades of the twenty-first century, jobs in these sectors declined by one-third from 17.2 million in 2000 to 12.4 million in 2017 (Strachan and Shehadi 2021). The experience of the unionized miners who lost their jobs at the Montana Power Company Mine in southern Colorado in 1996 are the common experience of hundreds of thousands of American workers.

Many lost jobs were union jobs. Unions have been unable to replace these lost members by organizing in other employment sectors because of legal impediments put in place by Republican legislation. The Depression-era National Labor Relations Act of 1935 gave all workers the right to organize, to join a union, to engage in collective bargaining, and to engage in collective actions such as strikes. Starting with the Labor Management Relations Act of 1947, Republicans have whittled away at the rights guaranteed by the National Labor Relations Act. Federal legislation passed in the last decade has seriously hampered the ability of unions to organize workers, while state governments in many states, including Wisconsin, Iowa, Indiana, and Ohio, seek to strip public workers of the right to collective bargaining. The Democratic Party has done little to counter or roll back such legislation (Babineau 2019; Beauchamp 2021).

In this context, we should not be surprised that many rank-and-file workers feel alienated from the Democrats and from their own union leadership. The Democratic Party has treated labor badly even while union leadership remains part of the Democratic establishment. In 2016 many rank-and-file workers objected to their unions' leadership endorsing Hillary Clinton in the Democratic primary over the more radical Left populist Bernie Sanders (Babineau 2019). In 2016 2020, and 2024, Trump received only a handful of union endorsements from law enforcement unions. In the 2016, 2020, and 2024 elections the AFL-CIO endorsed the Democratic candidate. In the 2016 and 2020 elections, however, over 40% of voters from union household's broke solidarity and voted for Trump.

There is, however, room for struggle to counter the deterioration of unions and the alienation of the rank and file. Public approval for unions declined at the beginning of the twenty-first century, reaching a low of 48% in 2009 (Brenan 2020). In the last decade, however, popular support for unions has risen to 65%. There is also legislation before Congress, the Protecting the Right to Organize Act (PRO Act), that would reverse legal impediments to union organizing (Beauchamp 2021). The act prohibits employers from firing or permanently replacing striking workers, from treating employees as independent contractors, from locking out workers to stop strikes, and from unduly censoring union organizing. It would also abolish all state right-to-work laws.

What Can Archaeology Do?

What then can an activist archaeology do to participate in the struggle for labor organization and working-class rights? We can work to help increase public approval of unions and thereby muster support for legislation like the PRO Act. At Ludlow, we sought to educate archaeology's traditional middle-class constituency on how workers won their rights (Jacobson 2022; Larkin and Maher 2022; Montoya and Larkin 2022: 113–119). We need not and probably cannot change the perceived interests of coal miners. Remember, book learning. We can, however, work with our union brothers and sisters to build solidarity for labor's struggle. In the first case, we embraced already-established educational methods, while solidarity building involves a more radical praxis.

In the 1990s and 2000s the UMWA embraced our project because we helped to raise public awareness of the importance of unions. To this end, we developed interpretive signage at the site of the massacre, wrote a labor history curriculum for Colorado middle and high schools, assembled a history trunk on the massacre to tour metropolitan Denver schools, organized two teacher training institutes on the strike and massacre, and used the discoveries of our excavations to put the events of 1914 in the news again (Duke and Saitta 2009; Montoya and Larkin 2022: 113–119). We hope that, in a small way, we contributed to the greater popular knowledge of and support for unions today.

We had a simple core message: that workers won their rights with blood (McGuire 2014). Capitalists did not freely give workers the rights that many take for granted today, such as the 40-hour week, respect in the workplace, union representation, health and retirement benefits, and a safe workplace. Rather, working people won these rights with their lives and the lives of their children. The contemporary importance of this message is simple. Because capitalists did not freely give these rights and because workers secured them only through great sacrifice, we must continue to struggle to keep them. Today workers are losing this struggle, and these losses are being amplified by the gig economy. Most workers now work either substantially fewer than 40 hours a week (they are part time), work substantially more (forced overtime), or, worse, work multiple part-time jobs or gigs totaling more than 40 hours a week. Much of this work comes without benefits, especially gig work.

Archaeology can reveal the duplicity in the claim that capitalists freely gave workers rights. Archaeology makes tangible the historic struggles of working families (Duke and Saitta 2009). Archaeology offers a very productive arena for activist scholars to examine the relationships among social consciousness, lived experience, and material conditions in class struggle (Shackel 2009). Scholars often have difficulty finding detailed, systematic data on the day-to-day lived experience of home life and work of working families. Archaeologist can integrate documents and material culture to capture both the consciousness and the material conditions that formed the lived experience of working families. In the documents, people speak to us about their consciousness, interests, and struggles, but not all people do so with the same force or presence. They also rarely speak in detail about their daily lived experience. However, people create the archaeological record from the accumulation of the small actions that make up their day-to-day lives. Thus, the archaeological record consists primarily of the remains of people's everyday lives, and all people leave residues in the material record.

The miner's comment "they got fucked" tells us that we do not need to educate unionized workers in southern Colorado about the horrible price that working families paid at Ludlow. Contrary to many discussions of archaeology and education, we do not need to interest working families in this past. It is a history they already know because it is relevant to them. Our book learning will not supersede their experience. We can, however, use archaeology to toil with working families to create knowledge, to construct meaningful histories for their communities, and to help build solidarity in labor's struggle.

There are many in the United States who wish to forget or destroy the memory of the sacrifices that working families made for the rights we enjoy as workers today (Walker 2009). Labor's struggle occurs in the remembrance and forgetting of history just as it does in the court room, on the shop floor, and on the picket line. We have heard many times that the UMWA should let go of Ludlow and that we all should forget what happened there. Arguments against unions in the contemporary economy maintain that laws now protect worker's rights and that unions should be forgotten with the past.

In 1918 the United Mine Workers set the memory in stone by erecting a monument to the miners, wives, and children who died in the Ludlow Massacre (Larkin and McGuire 2009: 1–2). A granite miner, his wife, and baby stand on the monument. On the night of May 3, 2003, someone used a sledgehammer to try to erase the memory by decapitating both the miner and his wife. At the annual memorial service (June 29, 2003), Saitta represented the archaeology of the Colorado Coalfield War Archaeological Project. He spoke in solidarity with the struggles of working families and joined calls to restore the monument. Union locals and individuals contributed thousands of dollars to restore the monument, and on June 5, 2005, union leaders, rank-and-file union members, their families, visitors, and archaeologists assembled to rededicate the restored statues and the memory of the massacre.

We used memory to help build and maintain solidarity in the UMWA. We created a portable exhibit that traveled to union halls around the country (Figure 6.1). We published in the journal of the United Mine Workers (UMWAJ 1999) and in the AFL-CIO labor history journal (Walker 2000). We developed a website that both the UMWA and the AFL-CIO linked to their websites (https://www.du.edu/ludlow/cfarch.html). In 1998, when steelworkers from Locals 2102 and 3267 in Pueblo, Colorado, walked out to stop forced overtime, they made the massacre a symbol of their struggle (Figure 6.2). We addressed strike rallies to reinforce the memory of Ludlow, and we attended

Figure 6.1. Cecil Roberts, president of the UMWA, discussing our traveling exhibit with members of the Local 8965 Women's Auxiliary (2002). Photo by author.

union dinners in the steel workers' hall. They won their strike six years later in 2004.

At one memorial service, Yolanda Romero (2022), the wife of a miner and then president of Local 9856 women's auxiliary commented on our research. She remarked that the passing of the participants in the strike had severed the personal connections to the events and reduced them to the dry stuff of

Figure 6.2. Striking steelworkers arriving at the 2002 Ludlow Massacre Memorial Service. Photo by author.

books. She found that our work remade that connection as we allowed her to touch the things that the strikers had held and to follow the path of the massacre on the ground.

All of these actions remember Ludlow, and memory leads to action as working people see their contemporary struggles as a continuation of the struggle at Ludlow. They also engaged us in shared experiences with working families. Shared experience builds solidarity.

Effective activism requires a long-term commitment to the people and causes we work with. Mainly due to the work of Karin Larkin (Montoya and Larkin 2022), the Colorado Coalfield War Archaeological Project continued to collaborate with the UMWA to remember Ludlow through the one-hundredth anniversary of the massacre in 2014 (Montoya and Larkin 2022). In the summer of 2024, Larkin worked with the UMWA to obtain a Battlefield Land Acquisition Grants through the National Park Service's American Battlefield Protection Program (Yager 2024). To further collaboration in the future, we need to understand the struggles of coal-mining families and not simply dismiss their advocacy for Trump as ignorance, racism, or being dupes. In the United States, Republicans have executed the most sustained and successful assault on workers' rights and unionism since before the Great Depression. Those of us who believe in these things need to fight this attack with trowels and whisk brooms and with a persistent commitment to political action at the local and national levels.

Solidarity does not, however, mean that archaeologists should abandon our craft or our careful analytical evaluation of ourselves and the communities that we work with. We cannot abandon our ability to "speak truth to power," nor can an emancipatory archaeology ignore oppression by or within the communities that we collaborate with. Solidarity does not mean accepting rank-and-file miners' support of Trump and radical popularism. We should remember that if 40% of AFL-CIO Union families voted for Trump, that means 60% did not. We should, however, be willing to work in solidarity with Trump supporters to critique the monstrous lie that capitalists freely gave workers' rights and benefits, to demonstrate that working families won these rights with blood, to encourage popular support for unions, and to pass legislation such as the PRO Act that will assist union organizing.

Acknowledgments

The Colorado Coalfield War Archaeological Project was the work of many hands. Most importantly were the members of the Ludlow Collective. The collective included Donna Bryant, Dan Brockman, Sarah Chicone, Bonnie J.

Clark, Philip Duke, Amie Gray, Claire Horn, Michael Jacobson, Kristen Jones, Karin Larkin, Jason Lapham, Summer Moore, Paul Reckner, Beth Rudden, Dean Saitta, Mark Walker, and Margaret Wood. Dean Saitta, Karin Larkin, Ruth Van Dyke, and Patricia McAnany gave me comments on earlier versions of this chapter. The most rewarding aspects of our research came with the collaboration with the UMWA and with the working families of southern Colorado. Most especially, I want to thank Bob Butero, Mike Romero, and Yolando Romero for their help and their dedication to the memory of Ludlow. I am a member of the United University Professionals, which is affiliated with the American Federation of Teachers and the AFL-CIO.

References Cited

Babineau, Diana. 2019. Unions Have Supported Democrats for Decades. It's Time for Dems to Keep Their Promises. *In These Times,* September 5. https://inthesetimes.com/article/labor-union-endorsement-joe-biden-bernie-sanders-afl-cio-unite-democrats.

Beauchamp, Zack. 2021. Democrats Could Reverse Years of Neglecting Unions—if They're Bold Enough. *Vox,* May 17. https://www.vox.com/policy-and-politics/22307891/democrats-unions-pro-act-policy-feedback.

Brenan, Megan. 2020. At 65%, Approval of Labor Unions in US Remains High. *Gallup,* September 3. https://news.gallup.com/poll/318980/approval-labor-unions-remains-high.aspx.

Bourdieu, Pierre. 1987. *Distinctions: A Social Critique of the Judgement of Taste.* Harvard University Press, Cambridge, Massachusetts.

Butero, Robert (Bob). 2022. Interview by Fawn-Amber Montoya and Karin Larkin. In *Communities of Ludlow: Collaborative Stewardship and the Ludlow Centennial Commemoration Commission,* edited by Fawn-Amber Montoya and Karin Larkin, pp. 53–72, University Press of Colorado, Louisville.

Debs, Eugene. 1914. A Plea for Solidarity. *The International Socialist Review* 14: 534–538.

Duke, Philip, and Dean Saitta. 2009. Why We Dig: Archaeology, Ludlow and the Public. In *The Archaeology of Class War: The Colorado Coalfield Strike of 1913–1914,* edited by Karin Larkin and Randall McGuire, pp. 351–362, University Press of Colorado, Boulder.

Finchelstein, Frederico. 2019. *From Fascism to Populism in History.* University of California Press, Berkeley.

Garrett, Mike. 2003. On Hallowed Ground. *Pueblo Chiefdom.* June 30. https://www.chieftain.com/story/news/2003/06/30/on-hallowed-ground/9121273007/.

Isser, Mindy. 2020. Joe Biden Thinks Coal Miners Should Learn to Code: A Real Just Transition Demands Far More. *In These Times,* January 15, 2020. https://inthesetimes.com/article/biden-coding-coal-miners-just-transition-green-new-deal-UMWA.

Jacobson, Michael. 2022. The Story of Making a Story Map. In *Communities of Ludlow: Collaborative Stewardship and the Ludlow Centennial Commemoration Commission,* edited by Fawn-Amber Montoya and Karin Larkin, pp. 157–169. University Press of Colorado, Louisville.

Larkin, Karin. 2022a. Memory and Stewardship: Collaborative Archaeology. in Remembering Ludlow. In *Communities of Ludlow: Collaborative Stewardship and the Ludlow Centennial Commemoration Commission*, edited by Fawn-Amber Montoya and Karin Larkin, pp. 79–100. University Press of Colorado, Louisville.

Larkin, Karin. 2022b. The Power of Collaborative Public Scholarship: Evaluating the Lasting Impacts of the Colorado Coalfield War Archaeology Project. *Public Historian* 44(4): 36–62.

Larkin, Karin, and Matthew Maher. 2022. Teaching Ludlow and Reacting to the Past. In *Communities of Ludlow: Collaborative Stewardship and the Ludlow Centennial Commemoration Commission*, edited by Fawn-Amber Montoya and Karin Larkin, pp. 135–156. University Press of Colorado, Louisville.

Larkin, Karin, and Randall H. McGuire (editors). 2009. *The Archaeology of Class War: The Colorado Coalfield Strike of 1913–1914*. University of Colorado Press, Boulder.

Linville, Linda. 2022. A Descendant's Story. In *Communities of Ludlow: Collaborative Stewardship and the Ludlow Centennial Commemoration Commission*, edited by Fawn-Amber Montoya and Karin Larkin, pp. xxv–xxxviii. University Press of Colorado, Louisville.

Martin, Lou. 2018. Invoking Noble Coal Miners Is a Mainstay of American Politics. *The Conversation*, April 25, https://theconversation.com/invoking-noble-coal-miners-is-a-mainstay-of-american-politics-94281.

McGuire, Randall H. 2008. *Archaeology as Political Action*. University of California Press, Berkeley.

McGuire, Randall H. 2014. Won with Blood: Archaeology and Labor's Struggle. *International Journal of Historical Archaeology* 18: 259–271.

McGuire, Randall H., and Mark Walker. 1999. Class Confrontations in Archaeology. *Historical Archaeology* 33(1): 159–183.

Montoya, Fawn-Amber, and Karin Larkin (editors). 2022. *Communities of Ludlow: Collaborative Stewardship and the Ludlow Centennial Commemoration Commission*. University Press of Colorado, Louisville.

Ofstehage, Andrew, Wendy Wolford, and Saturnino M. Borras. 2022. Contemporary Populism and the Environment. *Annual Review of Environment and Resources* 42: 1.1–1.17.

Pasley, James. 2019. Stunning Photos Show What It's Really like to Work Deep Underground in an American Coal Mine. *Insider*, October 5. https://www.businessinsider.com/life-working-in-coal-mines-in-america-photos-2019-10.

Romero, Yolanda. 2022. Interview by Fawn-Amber Montoya and Karin Larkin. In *Communities of Ludlow: Collaborative Stewardship and the Ludlow Centennial Commemoration Commission*, edited by Fawn-Amber Montoya and Karin Larkin, pp. 32–52. University Press of Colorado, Louisville.

Rose, Arthur. 2018. Mining Memories with Donald Trump in the Anthropocene. *MFS Modern Fiction Studies* 64(4): 701–719.

Saitta, Dean. 2007. *The Archaeology of Collective Action*. University Press of Florida, Gainesville.

Saitta, Dean, and Philip Duke. 1998. An Emancipatory Archaeology for the Working Class. *Assemblage* (4), online journal, University of Sheffield. https://archaeologydataservice

.ac.uk/archives/view/assemblage/html/4/?CFID=e9f0ea79-522d-4721-ac2b -2130a04b59e8&CFTOKEN=0.

Shackel, Paul A. 2009. *An Archaeology of American Labor and Working-Class Life.* University Press of Florida, Gainesville.

Singh, Prerna. 2021. Populism, Nationalism, and Nationalist Populism. *Studies in Comparative International Development.* 56: 250–269.

Singleton, Theresa, and Charles E. Orser Jr. 2003. Descendant Communities: Linking People in the Present to the Past. In *Ethical Issues in Archaeology,* edited by Larry J. Zimmerman, Karen D. Vitelli, and Julia J. Hollowell-Zimmer, pp. 143–152, AltaMira Press, Walnut Creek, California.

Strachan, Ruth, and Sebastian Shehadi. 2021. Who Killed US Manufacturing? *Investment Monitor,* November 17. https://www.investmentmonitor.ai/manufacturing/who-killed -us-manufacturing.

Traverso, Enzo. 2019. *The New Faces of Fascism: Populism and the Far Right.* Verso, London.

United Mine Workers Journal (UMWJ). 1999. Let We Forget . . . : Ludlow Project Puts Massacre in Spotlight. *United Mine Workers Journal,* March–April: 12–13.

Walker, Mark. 2000. Labor History at the Ground Level: Colorado Coalfield War Archaeology Project. *Labor's Heritage* 11(1): 59–75.

Walker, Mark. 2009. Archaeology and Worker's Memory. In *The Archaeology of Class War: The Colorado Coalfield Strike of 1913–1914.* edited by Karin Larkin and Russell McGuire, pp. 311–331. University of Colorado Press, Boulder.

Wilkie, Laurie A., and Kevin M. Bartoy. 2000. A Critical Archaeology Revisited. *Current Anthropology* 41(5): 747–778.

Yager, Brett. 2024. NPS Awards Grant to Preserve Ludlow Massacre Site. United Mine Workers of America, July 10, 2024, https://umwa.org/news-media/news/nps-awards -grant-to-preserve-ludlow-massacre-site/.

III

The Archaeology of Repression and Negative Heritage

7

Archaeology as Deterritorialized Community

Using Cultural Heritage Methods to Challenge Reactionary Populism in the Made in Migration Project (2018–2022)

RACHAEL KIDDEY

Circling the globe in search of sustenance and attempting to settle where sustenance can be found, [the human casualties of the planet-wide victory of economic progress] offer an easy target for unloading anxieties prompted by the widespread fears of social redundancy; in the process, they are enlisted to help in the efforts of state governments to reassert their impaired and weakening authority.

—Zygmunt Bauman (2003: 63)

Increased immigration did not spur the wave of right-wing populism that continues to surge aggressively across Europe, but "People on the Move" (Hamilakis 2022: 212) are being used by European governments to manifest right-wing populism among existing populations. In the United Kingdom, successive Conservative governments have repeatedly failed to manage increased immigration and refuse to reform immigration policy to improve safe and legal routes into the country. Government failure has garnered intense media scrutiny, and in response the UK government has sought to capitalize on latent anxieties over immigration within some sections of the population (Dennison and Geddes 2018: 116), stoking fear of the "Other" through inflammatory rhetoric and oppressive language. Sustained media focus, whether sympathetic or hostile to People on the Move, often frames the "migrant crisis" in terms that favor the right-wing populist agenda, affirming immigration as a problem and making it difficult for alternative perspectives to gain widespread attention. Collaborative cultural heritage approaches to contemporary migration can make pragmatic contributions to challenging this type of reactionary populism, a claim I explore throughout this chapter.

Between 2018 and 2022 I held a British Academy–funded postdoctoral research fellowship at the School of Archaeology, University of Oxford. Combining contemporary archaeology and cultural heritage methods, my research focused on the material and visual culture of contemporary forced displacement in Europe—places and "things" that co-constitute lived experiences of displacement in Athens, Greece; Plymouth, United Kingdom; and rural northern Sweden. Working in partnership with displaced people, I co-documented the material and visual culture that they identified as significant. Together we co-curated two exhibitions: *Made in Migration* was a digital public heritage exhibition coproduced online during the Covid-19 pandemic lockdowns and that launched during Refugee Week in June 2021.[1] *Made in Migration, IRL [In Real Life]* was a live exhibit, also coproduced (online and in-person), that formed part of the British Academy Summer Showcase in London (June 2022).[2] Initially, I wanted to develop a better understanding of how people forced to flee their homes coped "through things"—that is, how small personal belongings, visual culture, familiar ritual, and utilitarian objects help people retain personal and cultural identity and how the meanings of things change through displacement (cf. Miller 2013). Experience working in close collaboration with small, internationally dispersed groups of people, subjectively ascribed the status "migrant" through historically constructed legal discourse, combined with witnessing increased hostility toward displaced people broadly led me to ask: "Can cultural heritage practices challenge reactionary populism?" Findings suggest that they can . . . a bit!

This chapter contributes to a growing body of multidisciplinary literature that argues for the deterritorialization of heritage (Chakrabarty 2000; Colomer 2017; Winter 2014) by recognizing the diachronic, often transnational character of identity in the twenty-first century (Byrne 2016; Kourelis 2016). I acknowledge problems with the concept of "community" and contend that the archaeological heritage study of contemporary forced displacement can contribute nuanced understandings of the term as globalization, conflict, and climate change scatter people across the planet, challenging what it means to "belong." Politically and ethically engaged archaeology can aid resistance to reactionary populist narrative by providing more nuanced understanding of how colonial legacies, capitalism, conflict, and climate chaos cause and exacerbate displacement, while collaborative heritage practices help to humanize the individuals affected, offering strong alternatives to derogatory narratives purported by reactionary populism.

I argue for a radical return to ethics and propose the anarchist notion of prefiguration as useful in this regard. Prefiguration insists that how we behave toward others (human/nonhuman) creates the world that we inhabit (social relations). Anarchist philosophy takes many forms and as such is often misunderstood, but some expressions pose reliable challenges to modernity, nationalism, and other ideologies of representation that form the toxic core of reactionary populism (for detailed discussion of how anarchist archaeologies offer "counter-myths for hopeful futures," see BTC et al. 2023; see also Bray 2013, for an overview of the anarchism of the Occupy Wall Street movement and its aim to "translate" anarchist principles to wider audiences). Anarchist critique of "Gods" (ideology/doctrine) and "Masters" (governments/hierarchy/state power) are useful in thinking how to decouple identity—a key component of cultural heritage—and "belonging" from territory, specifically as they are coterminous under capitalism. That is, while cultural identity in part stems from peoples' environment (geography), it is only under the property "logic" of capitalism that certain parts of the world "belong" to certain types of people, not Others. If we prize heritage and identity free from capitalist notions of territory, we can more fully complicate imposed dualities upon which reactionary populism depends, dualities such as "in/out," "us/them," "native/foreign" (sensu Labrador & Silberman 2018: 5). The editors of this volume, citing Ayán (this volume: Chapter 5) ask "is it possible to use . . . elements of populism to counteract reaction?" In using the concept of "movement," which has been consistently used by totalitarian regimes, I suggest it might be (Arendt 2017[1951]).

Populism defines "the People more by who is left out than who is incorporated" (see González-Ruibal and McGuire, this volume: Chapter 1). As archaeologists and heritage professionals, it is our ethical duty to highlight the complexity of how humans "belong" in the world. Archaeologists and heritage professionals know that the "greatest intellectual myth of the end of the twentieth century was that the twenty-first century dawned in a world of 'posts'; post-industrial, post-colonial . . . post-capitalist" (McGuire 2023: 363). As archaeologists and heritage professionals, we routinely document how recently national borders were imposed globally and how strengthened national borders have become (cf. McAtackney and McGuire 2020); we demonstrate how the museum, the map, and the census (Anderson 1983) operate as technologies of social control as well as sources of conflict (Stig Sørensen and Viejo-Rose 2015). Archaeologists and heritage professionals have much to contribute to theses that expose how ethnonationalism and racism emerged in direct support of (ongoing) colonial capitalist logic (Bradley and De Noronha 2022; El-Enany 2020; Walia 2021; see also Montgomery, this volume: Chapter 3). Now, more than ever, we have a duty to counter reactionary populism, which is often stoked by amateur, oversimplified "historical" narratives, written "not to make people think critically, but rather to make them feel proud" (González-Ruibal and McGuire, this volume: Chapter 1). In the clickbait celebrity clutches of contemporary capitalism, amateur populist "history" is often given false validity by the notoriety—or popularity—of its author(s), allowing such ludicrous claims as "one man made history" to be read far more widely than most academic tomes on, for example, Sir Winston Churchill (Johnson 2014).

As archaeologists and heritage professionals, we have the capacity to evidence the inherently mobile complexities with which we deal in the study of people, places, and things over very long expanses of time and most of the planet. If we redefine public archaeology and heritage in this way and consider difference and commonality between "the People" (all humans) more prominently, we can expose some of the inconsistencies of reactionary populism, if not defeat it.

Finally, the introduction seems a sensible place to explain why I write perhaps informally. Mine was not a typical academic trajectory. When I should have been attending undergraduate lectures, I was instead to be found with Reclaim the Streets or prepping for a weekend-long rave with banners, Day-Glo, and repetitive beats.[3] I duly received the undergraduate degree that I deserved! A decade later, my PhD found me. I had been faffing about with intention, squatting and rabble-rousing for various community initiatives in Bristol (UK) when Professor John Schofield (who later became my doctoral supervisor) suggested that I had unprecedented access to experiences of contemporary homelessness and perhaps I should undertake formal study. Now, a decade after gaining my doctorate (with no corrections), my methodological approach to academic research remains true to the ethics that I found in many squats and grassroots projects—essentially, "muck in and get your hands dirty before you expect anything in return" (cf. Grohmann 2020; Vasudevan 2017). To find "interlocutors" willing to engage in participatory academic research, I spend time on the ground, volunteering and making myself useful. I find that building the level of trust with marginalized people that is necessary for meaningful conversation only comes from giving time and building genuinely mutual relationships. This approach necessarily involves an emotional investment in people and places, and while I adhere to established methods of academic literature review and formal ethical codes of practice, my research is always fused with deep guilt that comes from my own positionality—a white, middle-class, straight, cisgender female with a British passport and a safe home. What emerges is a written style that derives in part from fieldnotes made amid someone else's lived crisis that I alone cannot address, and in part from the sense of deep unease that I then feel writing about those injustices. These are not my traumas, but they affect me. It is unconventional for academics to "show themselves" (although, see Khosravi 2010; Rizvi 2020) but our positions affect research, which is why it really matters who is involved, whose voices are amplified, and how.

Reactionary Populism and the People: A View from the United Kingdom

Populism is difficult to define and manifests differently in different parts of the world (González-Ruibal and McGuire, this volume: Chapter 1). However, at its most basic, we can agree that populism is the idea that "political sovereignty belongs to and should be exercised by 'the People,' which is considered to be homogeneous, morally virtuous, and antagonistic against corrupt elites and dangerous 'others'" (González-Ruibal and McGuire, this volume: Chapter 1). Populists argue that they are not fascist because they reject political violence or dictatorship. This, however, depends upon how one defines "political violence" and "dictatorship." For example, necropolitical policies that funnel people through the Sonoran Desert to their death (De León 2015; McGuire 2023) or that criminalize those who seek to rescue migrants from the Mediterranean Sea count, in my book, as forms of political violence (Cusumano and Bell 2021). Added to which, in the United Kingdom we have an outdated voting system that contradicts most definitions of democracy because it enshrines minority rule. Until the 2024 elections, the Conservative Party held a majority of seats in Parliament with just 43.6% of votes.[4] The "first past the post" system means that a political party that most of the voting UK public did not vote for was in power for 14 years. Over that time, the Conservatives exercised that power in antidemocratic, pseudo-fascist ways. For example, they introduced the Nationality and Borders Act 2022, which criminalizes those who attempt to enter the United Kingdom without documentation; criminalizes anyone who attempts to rescue migrants at risk of drowning at sea; enables authorities to engage in "pushbacks" (where migrant boats are "pushed back" out to sea); and allows the government to deport asylum-seekers from the United Kingdom to so-called safe countries (although this last point remains under challenge from the European Court of Human Rights). Many of the People rose in protest at such cruel legislation, and for that we were rewarded with the Public Order Act 2023, which increased police powers to arrest protestors deemed to be "disruptive" (only vaguely defined).[5] This legislation was pushed through in response to increased protest at climate devastation. Rather than listen to the People or facilitate any kind of democratic conversation, the UK government preferred to slap down new laws that strip people of their rights. This does not sound like democracy to me.

As Cas Mudde has observed,

> the populist heartland becomes active only when there are special circumstances; most notably, the combination of persisting political resentment, a (perceived) serious challenge to "our way of life," and the presence of an attractive populist leader. (Mudde 2004: 547)

Sadly, this accurately describes the political landscape in the United Kingdom in 2019, after over a decade of austerity following the 2008 financial crash. People's living standards had decreased and persisting political resentment was palpable, added to which, the increase in immigration post-2015 led to some people blaming immigrants for pressures on housing and health care. Interestingly, no one seemed very concerned about immigrants taking the low-paid jobs that UK people refused to do—for example, cleaning, fruit-picking, delivery driving, and care work. This was the climate into which Boris Johnson ascended to become the UK prime minister. While Mr. Johnson is not at all my cup of tea, he was certainly perceived by many to be an attractive populist leader. Further, Johnson had wide media experience—he knew how to use the national press to his advantage—and, not being one to let facts get in the way of a good story, he became a deadly combination of populist power and influence. The Conservative Party under Johnson was opportunistic, aiming to quickly please as many of the People as necessary to buy support—rather than looking (rationally) for the best option (Mudde 2004: 542). But who are the People to whom reactionary populism appeals? They are, according to Mudde (2004: 546), "imagined . . . much like the nation of the nationalists" (see also Anderson 1983). Populism is polarizing by its nature since "there are only friends and foes. Opponents are not just people with different priorities and values, they are *evil!*" (Mudde 2004: 544, emphasis in original). As the editors of this volume attest in their introduction, "Like classical fascism, scapegoating plays an important role [in populism] today, with immigrants and the LGBTQ+ 'lobby' replacing Jews and the critique of elites." The task then becomes to complicate the false binary that reactionary populism imposes. Contemporary archaeology and heritage approaches can help in the task of rejecting homogeneity both of populism and its imagined evils and of elitism.

How Can Contemporary Archaeology and Heritage Praxis Address the Challenges of Reactionary Populism?

Before I acknowledge problems with the concept of "community" and describe *Made in Migration* in some detail, I want first to assert the areas of reactionary populism that archaeology and heritage praxis can usefully address.

Challenging Essentialism and Exclusion

In taking up Denis Byrne's (2016) call to foster "an inclusiveness that transcends the border" (Byrne 2016: 279), *Made in Migration* (discussed in detail below) actively focused on in-between spaces, disrupting the "origin-destination dualism" that commonly occurs when "heritage practice defaults to the nation-state as the unit of analysis" (Byrne 2016: 263). *Made in Migration* did this by highlighting literal in-between spaces in which People on the Move found themselves (camps, squats, and temporary accommodation). Through ethnographic interviews and the co-curation of digital heritage artifacts, memories and testimonies were recorded to document the transnational nature of migrant identity, linking journeys that people made with places, practices, and people left behind. No longer "just" Syrian, but Syrian-Swedish-ish. No longer "just" Azeri, but "Azerbaijan-born-living-in-Britain-with-indefinite leave to remain." When we look at nationality this way, we can see how even nation-states themselves ascribe fluid legal identities and transnational belonging. This disrupts the homogeneity of reactionary populism's "People" and reasserts difference within "the People" (archaeology's people). One can be British *and* born in Sudan, even the current populist UK government says so.

Challenging the Naturalized Right to Destroy, Consume, and Not to Care (Capitalism)

One of the places where I volunteered during fieldwork in order to build trusting relationships with displaced people and gain trust from solidarity activists (many of whom function as ardent if paternalistic gatekeepers of displaced people) was the Pampiraiki warehouse (Kiddey 2023). This giant, former Olympic baseball stadium, an hour by bus out of Athens, Greece, was reused (2015–2018) as a warehouse to store clothes, food, toiletries, and other items donated by people across Europe, to be distributed among the camps and squats in which displaced people were existing. In documenting the volume of stuff that some people could afford to give away (capitalist waste) and demonstrating how it was distributed among people who, through no fault of their own, had nothing, a contemporary archaeological approach to the warehouse helps to highlight just one place where the devastating effects of capitalist destruction and rabid consumption "gather[ed] in the present" (Harrison 2011: 183); a modern "ruin" (González-Ruibal 2019: 25–48).

Heritage and Identity Independent of Ownership or a Common Territory?

Principles of collaborative approaches to the past were largely developed as an explicitly political practice by Indigenous scholars (Atalay 2006; Atalay 2012; Tuhiwei Smith 2012; Watkins 2000; Watkins 2003). Such principles have slowly influenced heritage practices and legislation in Europe. For democracy to exist in the present and future, people must be able to see themselves in the past (Lowenthal 2015) and see themselves *as they* see themselves, not how others might define them. For example, the 2000 Landscape Convention and the 2005 Faro Convention of the Council of Europe emphasize the value of public participation and establish that cultural heritage is independent of ownership. The notion of heritage communities, as set out in the Faro Convention, is particularly valuable because it enables us to think of people connected over distance despite not being from a common territory (Colomer 2017: 914). The people with whom I worked throughout the Made in Migration project are one such heritage community. But what exactly do we mean by community?

Some Problems with Community

Part of the problem is that, like "heritage" or "identity," the term "community" is inherently slippery. Community is difficult to define not least because communities (or the People) are made up of individuals who have overlapping forms of belonging. Kwame Appiah suggests that community is "connected to locale" (Appiah 2006), but we might equally define community in terms of education, hobbies, interests, sexual orientation, religious or political beliefs, or any number of other variables (Kiddey 2020: 31–33). We must also acknowledge the transformational effects of globalization on community or the term is, at best, useless (cf. Bauman 2003); at worst, it is dangerous. In his richly observed analysis of the concept of community in cultural heritage theory, Martin Mulligan calls for more reflexivity and nuance (Mulligan 2018). He demonstrates that increased global mobility has led to forms of community that are not only less stable but also likely to transform far more quickly than before, and he warns that past-facing representations of any particular community can have exclusionary effects (Mulligan 2018: 213).

Notwithstanding inherent problems with the concept of community, participatory approaches to the past must continue. Given that the past can only ever be reconstructed from traditions and fragments that persist in the present, what right does anyone have—governments very much included—to make absolute claims or decisions about how it is reconstructed?

Made in Migration: An Experiment in Community Archaeology Using Anarchist Principles

Archaeology is the study of relationships between people and things over time. Archaeology is a craft that people in the present undertake using things from the past (Shanks and McGuire 1996). If we focus on the methods employed and the data generated, the issue of how recently the things (landscapes, buildings, objects) were used by humans becomes irrelevant (Buchli and Lucas 2001: 3; Harrison and Schofield 2010). Contemporary archaeology and critical heritage approaches to the contemporary past employ the same established methods and theory as applied to archaeological sites from the deep or historic past, but they apply these to the messy materiality of the present day, viewing the material processes in the context of current sociohistorical and political relations. Throughout the Migrant Materialities project, I applied archaeological methods and theory to the sites, places, and objects identified as significant by the people with whom I was working.

For community archaeology and heritage to thrive in non-exploitative ways (cf. Watson and Waterton 2010), we need to reinvigorate an "ethic of care" (Kiddey 2017: 52–68)—care for one another, care for cultural heritage, and care for the planet that sustains it all (see also Kiddey 2020). "*Ethical* action is that in which the Subject decides and speaks *for itself*" (Badiou 2015: 404, my emphases). The best way that I have found to achieve this is through prefiguration.

Prefiguration derives from anarchist philosophy and proposes the active adoption of nonhierarchical models of social relations. Anarchism generally is receiving increased attention (see, e.g., Bray 2013; Raekstad 2020), and archaeologists are among those considering the political philosophy useful (BTC et al. 2023) not least because the (pre)history of humanity far precedes that of nation-states. Anarchists believe that societies emerge from how they are structured or prefigured—that is, the way in which we act toward one another is the result that we seek. Real change can only come from action—and prefiguration can be considered a form of action, especially when similarly minded collectives link up in physical locations (for example, the 1871 Paris Commune or the modern-day Christiania, Copenhagen; or Rojava, Syria) or digitally, thus making more space for resistance (Graeber 2002). Having worked collaboratively with marginalized communities since 2007 (Kiddey 2017, 2019, 2023), I decided to take a more explicitly activist approach to my British Academy postdoctoral research. I set out to see whether displaced people would join me in creating an international research collective developed using prefigurative practices, for example, working together using non-hierarchical decision-making processes so the direction of research and presentation of findings was decided using consensus (see Bray 2013: 99–101, for a useful discussion on the limits of consensus). The Made in Migration Collective was a loose coalition of displaced people, creative professionals, and me based in Athens, Plymouth, and rural northern Sweden. While the collective operated according to anarchist principles, not everyone in the collective identified as anarchist. Some members gained refugee status in Europe. Others remained "undocumented" throughout the project. I made no distinction between documented and undocumented members of the collective except to fully anonymize those who remained undocumented, for their safety.

While it would be wrong to suggest that no power imbalance existed between my displaced colleagues and me, everyone was enabled to participate equally in the collective. My multiskilled colleagues, displaced from Syria, Iraq, Afghanistan, Iran, Armenia, Azerbaijan, Eritrea, and Sudan, were and are people with ontological experience of displacement. I am an academic with research interests in the material and visual culture of contemporary displacement. Together we were able to speak on different aspects of the conditions that co-constitute lived experiences of contemporary forced displacement in Europe. Using a blend of ethnographic interviews, photography, drawing, memory-mapping, filmmaking, and creative writing, my colleagues and I co-documented places, buildings, and objects that they identified as significant to their experiences of displacement, and we recorded a range of digital culture (for example, text messages and digital photographs). Between late 2018 and early 2020, the collective undertook this work together, face-to-face in squats and other solidarity spaces in Greece, and in community centers and temporary accommodation in the United Kingdom and Sweden until the Covid-19 pandemic forced us to work solely online between March 2020 and June 2022.

As opposed to working collaboratively with an "imagined" (Anderson 1983) community based on national identity, The Made in Migration Collective represents the creation of a transnational community united through shared experience. The collective welcomed anyone who was willing to cooperate using broadly anarchist decision-making principles. Their contribution to the project could be direct personal or professional experience of contemporary displacement in Europe, or skills with which we might record the material and visual culture of displacement, or both. While most members of the collective had lived experience of displacement in Europe, three of us had no lived experience of forced displacement. We were of mixed gender and mixed social, ethnic, and cultural backgrounds. We were intergenerational, ranging from 18 to 72 years old. Members of the collective were of mixed sexual orientation, educational backgrounds, and political leanings. Our differences were our strength, offering necessarily complex and at times conflicting perspectives on displacement and identity. To reach consensus about how research should proceed, we engaged in protracted discussions, sometimes translating between the group, sometimes using professional translators and translation apps.

We adopted the consensus-reaching process of the anarchist archaeologist Black Trowel Collective (BTC 2021). Everyone had four options to respond to a particular suggestion: (1) vote yes, (2) vote no, (3) stand aside (choose not to be involved in the decision due to ambivalence or a conflict of interests), or (4) block. The option to "block" differs from "vote no" because to block means that the idea cannot proceed, even if everyone else votes yes. Discussions conducted using such a process are time-consuming, at best, and left unresolved, at worst. However, by prioritizing consensus, we slowly moved forward together, despite our not insignificant social, cultural, and political differences (and sometimes we moved backward or completely stalled). This approach did not comply with my original research grant time scale, but it preserved the integrity of our relationships with one another and the work coproduced, which is an important form of care.

In an effort to address epistemic injustice (Pantazatos 2019) and to avoid using displaced people as informants (Steeves 2015), the Made in Migration Collective employed prefigurative approaches to all aspects of our work together, from initial conversations about how to undertake the research, through documenting what was significant, interpreting data, and presenting and disseminating results. Prefiguration is an ethical form of care.

Three Cups of Coffee: Learning Difference, Finding Commonality

The Made in Migration Collective comprised people originally from countries across the Middle East, Africa, and Europe. Everyone drank coffee, but the ways in which we sourced, prepared, and enjoyed our coffee varied. Throughout our time working together, we shared our individual and cultural coffee rituals, which led to conversations about different ways of doing (Holloway 2010: 143). For example, for me, making coffee is a private affair that happens almost as soon as I wake up. I grind Colombian coffee beans in an

Figure 7.1. Fariha's coffee in Second School squat, Athens, 2018. Photo by author.

electric grinder and use a stovetop coffee maker. The whole process takes a little over seven minutes. I prefer a small, thin-rimmed ceramic cup because I like to have two small cups of hot coffee rather than one big warm one. I take my coffee black, no sugar. While it is not always possible, I prefer to drink my first coffee without speaking or being spoken to, ideally with birdsong and sunshine.

For Fariha, originally from Syria, coffee was much more serious and sociable. It is, in her words, "part of what makes Syrian people Syrian." I first met Fariha in a squat in Athens (Greece) in 2018. Squats are, by definition, more or less public—deterritorialized—spaces (cf. Vasudevan, 2017; see also Grohmann 2020: Chapter 4). Fariha insisted that I take coffee with her and her friends. I protested because I knew how little people at the squat had, but she replied that to decline was to deny her being Syrian, so I accepted. I sat in a circle with other women, on chairs made for primary school children, these being the only chairs available. As she made coffee in an old saucepan over a small fire, Fariha explained that, had we been at her house in Syria, she would have used a very small pot called an *ibrik*. She would have crushed cardamom seeds with coffee beans before adding boiling water, allowing the spice to meld before serving the strong black coffee in small matching cups and sharing conversation with family and friends (Figure 7.1). Back in the

Figure 7.2. Senbetu's *jebena* (coffee pot) and cups, Sweden, 2018. Photo by author.

squat in Athens, Fariha laughed melancholically as she handed me coffee in a toy cup from a children's tea set, this being what the women had to drink coffee from in the squat.

In rural northern Sweden, 2018, an Eritrean woman, Senbetu, invited me to enjoy coffee with her and her family at their home. Translated by her then 17-year-old daughter, Senbetu talked me through the coffee-making ritual as she performed it:

> First, I roast the beans and toss them on a plate . . . the aroma passes around the family and guests . . . it is the way that we [Eritreans] socialize. Come!

After some time, Senbetu mixed water with the coffee in a *jebena*, an Eritrean coffee pot. The *jebena* is not just a coffee pot (Figure 7.2). It is Senbetu's *jebena,* and it is connected to Senbetu's memories of people, places, and events (heritage), and these things are obscured if the *jebena* is not socially active (Appadurai 1986). This is basic ethnographic participant observation, but it is more than that. It is about respecting the value and meaning of objects to the people to whom they belong and respecting the time and space that using such objects traditionally take up because our lives are partly constituted through things, what we do with them, and what they do for us.

I had been invited "for coffee" and, perhaps naïvely for an anthropological archaeologist who has worked with displaced people since 2016, I thought I would be at the family home for an hour or so. But while the coffee was prepared, I was fed plates of delicious chicken and vegetables, *himbasha* (a traditional celebration bread), and rice with beans. None of the other members of the family ate, which felt extremely awkward to me, being from a background in which everyone eats together, or no one eats. My mind raced. Was I being given special treatment or, worse, was I eating their food? When would they eat? Would they have enough food to feed themselves and me? After two hours, Senbetu presented me coffee in an Eritrean style cup—a small ceramic cup with no handle. She said the coffee set was new and made her feel "at home" because she had been without a *jebena* or traditional cups for over a decade, having fled Eritrea on foot with six young children and a baby and been in a camp in Sudan until 2017. I thanked Senbetu for the food and coffee and declined her offer of sugar. The family was astonished! Senbetu pulled a face and gestured to show that she thought it would not taste good (cf. González-Ruibal 2014: 194) as her son looked up the English word "bitter" on his phone.

By focusing on a "thing" familiar to us all—in this case, the preparation and enjoyment of coffee—we found transnational commonality as the familiar was rendered very unfamiliar (Tarlow and West 1999). This enabled us to view the taken-for-granted in fresh ways. We were able to start from a place of empathy—the desire to drink coffee—and consider the "alien" cultural landscape in which it took form from a place of mutual understanding. Coffee, in this example, acted as a kind of anchor or compass, a root from which to grasp the "chaos" of another culture, a different perspective. My point in presenting these three short portraits of coffee-making is to demonstrate how community-based participatory archaeology and heritage can enable different people to come together through things. The use of anarchist principles was especially valuable because they allowed discussion that was nonhierarchical, multidirectional, and afforded the space (and time) to peaceably differ, blurring the edges of what we "know" to be true. If this can be true of coffee-making, why not many other things? How we dress, make love, relate to the past, or conceive of the future, for example?

Conclusion

Collaborative community archaeology and heritage work cannot stop reactionary populism, but it has an important role to play in challenging its supporting ideologies that seek to essentialize and exclude (ethnocentrism/nationalism) and that enshrine the right to destroy, endlessly consume, and *not* to care (capitalism).[6] If we leave cultural heritage narratives to nation-states, reactionary populists will increasingly feel validated in their opinions and social inequalities such as racism will grow. As Jonathan Seglow has stated, "State cultural policy has a symbolic authority" (Seglow 2019: 19). Reactionary populist discourse is girded by faith in amateur leaders and adherence to capitalist ideologies of ownership—"this is *my country,*" and so on—that are uncritically linked to belonging. Deterritorialized transnational archaeological heritage represents a challenge to reactionary populist myth when it functions as a form of rupture to the status quo. When it complicates colonial capitalist ideologies of belonging and identity and highlights how, prior to the recent requirement to produce documented citizenship to cross national borders (Dehm 2018), mobility has been a central feature of humanity that stretches as far back as archaeology can show.[7] As transnational deterritorialized heritage communities, we can identify and share alternative ways to conceive of the past—the different ways in which all peoples build shelter, prepare food, or relate to trees, for example (Maathai 2021)—and from commonalities we can conceive more equitable and sustainable futures.

I am not suggesting that we storm the Houses of Parliament. I am instead invoking a playfully disruptive form of radical indifference to nationalism and its prosaic cousin, reactionary populism. In the spirit of Virginia Woolf (Woolf 2019), I invoke an ethos of "choosing not to care about what we are enjoined to" (Puig de la Bellacasa 2017: 5). By choosing to be radically indifferent, we save time and energy for what matters—involving more people in the day-to-day work and debates of archaeology and heritage, which has the capacity to counter reactionary populism through exposing its inconsistencies and empowering people to recognize difference and commonalities and imagine more sociopolitically and environmentally sustainable futures. The concept of community is not unproblematic, and further research is necessary to address inherent imbalances. However, doing archaeology with all sorts of non-archaeologists remains an important space in which to continue multidirectional, multisited, intercultural, transnational learning about who "we"—humans and nonhumans of planet Earth—are, how we got here, and in which direction "we" choose to head.

Notes

1 A link to the *Made in Migration Virtual Exhibition* is found on my web page at the end of the third paragraph. https://www.plymouth.ac.uk/staff/rachael-kiddey, accessed 4/10/2024.

2 See Summer Showcase 2022 Programme and Exhibits, British Academy website, n.d., accessed 6/29/2024, https://www.thebritishacademy.ac.uk/events/british-academy -summer-showcase-2022/programme-exhibits/.

3 Reclaim the Streets is a social movement founded in Camden, London, 1995. As a collective, they believe in community ownership of public spaces and engage in non-violent, direct action, often blocking roads to have a party.

4 General Election 2019: Full Results and Analysis, January 28, 2020, House of Commons Library, UK Parliament, https://commonslibrary.parliament.uk/research -briefings/cbp-8749/.

5 The Public Order Act 2023, May 11, 2022 (updated May 16, 2022), https://www.gov .uk/government/collections/the-public-order-bill.

6 All legal systems today are derived from Roman property law, which offered three rights: *usus* (use), *fructus* (right to consume), and *abusus* (the right to destroy). Therefore, a defining feature of true legal property is the right to destroy something—the right *not* to care (Graeber and Wengrow 2021: 168).

7 The standardized international passport was not introduced by the League of Nations until 1920. On mobility, see the paper presented at the Society of American Archaeology's annual conference titled "Modelling a Collaborative Archaeological Synthesis of Human Migration for a Long-Term, Global Perspective," presented April 4, 2023, by Christopher Beekman on behalf of the Coalition for Archaeological Synthesis' Human Migration group, of which I am a member.

References Cited

Anderson, Benedict. 1983. *Imagined Communities*. London, Verso.

Appadurai, Arjun. 1986. *The Social Life of Things: Commodities in Cultural Perspective*. Cambridge, Cambridge University Press.

Appiah, Kwame Anthony. 2006. *Cosmopolitanism, Ethics in the World of Strangers*. New York, Norton.

Arendt, Hannah. 2017[1951]. *The Origins of Totalitarianism*. London, Penguin Classics.

Atalay, Sonya. 2006. Indigenous Archaeology as Decolonizing Practice. *American Indian Quarterly* 30(3): 280–310.

Atalay, Sonya. 2012. *Community-Based Archaeology: Research with, by, and for Indigenous and Local Communities*. University of California Press, Berkeley.

Badiou, Alain. 2015. Ethics and Politics. *Philosophy Today* 59(3): 401–407.

Bauman, Zygmunt. 2003. *Wasted Lives: Modernity and Its Outcasts*. Wiley, Oxford.

Black Trowel Collective (BTC). 2021. *The Black Trowel Collective Consensus Process*. Accessed February 18, 2022. https://blacktrowelcollective.wordpress.com/2021/05/06/ black-trowel-collective-consensus-process/.

Black Trowel Collective (BTC), Marian Beriheute-Azorín, Chelsea Blackmore, Lewis Borck, James L. Flexner, Catherine J. Frieman, Corey A. Hermann, and Rachael Kiddey. 2024. Archaeology in 2022: Counter-Myths for Hopeful Futures. *American Anthropologist* 126(1): 134–148.

Bradley, Gracie Mae, and Luke De Noronha. 2022. *Against Borders: The Case for Abolition*. Verso, London.

Bray, Mark. 2013. *Translating Anarchy: The Anarchism of Occupy Wall Street.* Zero Books, Winchester, England.

Buchli, Victor, and Gavin Lucas. 2001. *Archaeologies of the Contemporary Past.* Routledge, London.

Byrne, Denis. 2016. The Need for a Transnational Approach to the Material Heritage of Migration: The China–Australia Corridor. *Journal of Social Archaeology* 16(3): 261–285.

Chakrabarty, Dipesh. 2000. *Provincialising Europe: Postcolonial Thought and Historical Difference.* Princeton University Press, Princeton, New Jersey.

Colomer, Laia. 2017. Heritage on the Move: Cross-Cultural Heritage as a Response to Globalisations, Mobilities, and Multiple Migrations. *International Journal of Heritage Studies* 23(10): 913–927.

Cusumano, Eugenio, and Flora Bell. 2021. Guilt by Association? The Criminalisation of Sea Rescue NGOs in Italian Media. *Journal of Ethnic and Migration Studies* 47(19): 4285–4307.

De León, Jason. 2015. *The Land of Open Graves: Living and Dying on the Migrant Trail.* University of California Press, Oakland.

Dehm, Sarah. 2018. Passport. In *International Law's Objects,* edited by Jessie Hohmann and Daniel Joyce, 342–356. Oxford University Press, Oxford.

Dennison, James, and Andrew Geddes. 2018. A Rising Tide? The Salience of Immigration and the Rise of Anti-Immigration Political Parties in Western Europe. *Political Quarterly* 90(1): 107–116.

El-Enany, Nadine. 2020. *(B)ordering Britain: Law, Race, and Empire.* Manchester University Press, Manchester, England.

González-Ruibal, Alfredo. 2014. *An Archaeology of Resistance: Materiality and Time in an African Borderland.* Rowman & Littlefield, Lanham, Maryland.

González-Ruibal, Alfredo. 2019. *An Archaeology of the Contemporary Era.* Routledge, Abingdon, England.

Graeber, David. 2002. The New Anarchists. *New Left Review* 13 (January–February): 61–73.

Graeber, David, and David Wengrow. 2021. *The Dawn of Everything: A New History of Humanity.* Allen Lane, London.

Grohmann, Steph. 2020. *The Ethics of Space: Homelessness and Squatting in Urban England.* HAU Books, Chicago.

Hamilakis, Yannis. 2022. Border Assemblages between Surveillance and Spectacle: What Was Moria and What Comes After? *American Anthropologist* 124(1): 212–220.

Harrison, Rodney. 2011. Surface Assemblages: Towards an Archaeology in and of the Present. *Archaeological Dialogues* 18(2): 141–161.

Harrison, Rodney, and John Schofield. 2010. *After Modernity: Archaeological Approaches to the Contemporary Past.* Oxford University Press, Oxford.

Holloway, John. 2010. *Change the World without Taking Power.* 2nd edition. Pluto Press, London.

Johnson, Boris. 2014. *The Churchill Factor: How One Man Made History.* Hodder, London.

Khosravi, Shahram. 2010. *"Illegal" Traveller: An Auto-Ethnography of Borders.* Palgrave Macmillan, Basingstoke, England.

Kiddey, Rachael. 2017. *Homeless Heritage: Collaborative Social Archaeology as Therapeutic Practice.* Oxford University Press, Oxford.

Kiddey, Rachael. 2020. I'll Tell You What I Want, What I Really, Really Want! Open Archaeology That Is Collaborative, Participatory, Public, and Feminist. *Norwegian Archaeological Review* 53(1): 23–40.

Kiddey, Rachael. 2023. We Are Displaced, But We Are More Than That: Using Anarchist Principles to Materialize Capitalism's Cracks at Sites of Contemporary Forced Displacement in Europe. *International Journal of Historical Archaeology* 28, 1–26.

Kourelis, Kostis. 2016. If Place Remotely Matters: Camped in Greece's Contingent Countryside. In *The New Nomadic Age: Archaeologies of Forced and Undocumented Migration,* edited by Yannis Hamilakis, 108–120. Equinox, Bristol.

Labrador, Angela M., and Neil Asher Silberman. 2018. Introduction: Public Heritage as Social Practice. In *The Oxford Handbook of Public Heritage Theory and Practice,* edited by Angela M. Labrador and Neil Asher Silberman, 1–18. Oxford University Press, Oxford.

Lowenthal, David. 2015. *The Past Is a Foreign Country—Revisited.* Cambridge University Press, Cambridge.

Maathai, Wangari. 2021. *The World We Once Lived In.* Penguin Classics, London.

McAtackney, Laura, and Randall H. McGuire. 2020. Introduction: Walling In and Walling Out. In *Walling In and Walling Out: Why Are We Building New Barriers to Divide Us?,* edited by Laura McAtackney and Randall H. McGuire, 1–24. School for Advanced Research Press, Santa Fe, New Mexico.

McGuire, Randall. 2023. Can Archaeology Slow Down Fast Capitalism? In *What Does This Have to Do with Archaeology?,* edited by Editorial Collective, 363–368. Sidestone Press, Leiden.

Miller, Daniel. 2013. *The Comfort of Things.* Wiley, Oxford.

Mudde, Cas. 2004. The Populist Zeitgeist. *Government and Opposition* 39(4): 541–563.

Mulligan, Martin. 2018. On the Need for a Nuanced Understanding of "Community" in Heritage Policy and Practice. In *The Oxford Handbook of Public Heritage Theory and Practice,* edited by Angela M. Labrador and Neil Asher Silberman, 209–222. Oxford University Press, Oxford.

Pantazatos, Andreas. 2019. Heritage Participant Perspective, Epistemic Injustice, Immigrants and Identity Formation. In *Cultural Heritage, Ethics, and Contemporary Migrations,* edited by Cornelius Holtorf, Andreas Pantazatos, and Geoffrey Scarre, 128–143. Routledge, Abingdon, England.

Puig de la Bellacasa, María. 2017. *Matters of Care: Speculative Ethics in More Than Human Worlds.* University of Minnesota Press, Minneapolis.

Raekstad, Paul. 2020. The New Democracy: Anarchist or Populist? *Critical Review of International Social and Political Philosophy* 23(7): 931–942.

Rizvi, Uzma Z. 2020. Community-Based and Participatory Praxis as Decolonizing Archaeological Methods and the Betrayal of New Research. In *Archaeologies of the Heart,* edited by Kisha Supernant, Jane Eva Baxter, Natasha Lyons, and Sonya Atalay, 70–79. Springer, London.

Seglow, Jonathan. 2019. Cultural Heritage, Minorities and Self-Respect. In *Cultural Heri-*

tage, Ethics, and Contemporary Migrations, edited by Cornelius Holtorf, Andreas Pantazatos, and Geoffrey Scarre, 13–26. Routledge, Abingdon, England.

Shanks, Michael, and Randall H. McGuire. 1996. The Craft of Archaeology. *American Antiquity* 61: 75–88.

Steeves, Paulette. 2015. Academia, Archaeology, CRM, and Tribal Historic Preservation. *Archaeologies* 11: 121–141.

Stig Sørensen, Marie Louise, and Dacia Viejo-Rose. 2015. *War and Cultural Heritage: Biographies of Place.* Cambridge University Press, New York.

Tarlow, Sarah, and Suzie West. 1999. *The Familiar Past: Archaeologies of Later Historical Britain.* Routledge, London.

Tuhiwei Smith, Linda. 2012. *Decolonising Methodologies.* 2nd edition. Zed, London.

Vasudevan, Alexander. 2017. *The Autonomous City: A History of Urban Squatting.* Verso, London.

Walia, Harsha. 2021. *Border and Rule: Global Migration, Capitalism, and the Rise of Racist Nationalism.* Haymarket Books, La Vergne, Tennessee.

Watkins, Joe. 2000. *Indigenous Archaeology: American Indian Values and Scientific Practice.* Alta Mira Press, Walnut Creek, California.

Watkins, Joe. 2003. Beyond the Margin: American Indians, First Nations, and Anthropology in North America. *American Antiquity* 68(2): 273–285.

Watson, Steve, and Emma Waterton. 2010. Editorial: Heritage and Community Engagement. *International Journal of Heritage Studies* 16(1–2): 1–3.

Winter, Tim. 2014. Heritage Studies and the Privileging of Theory. *International Journal of Heritage Studies* 20(5): 556–572.

Woolf, Virginia. 2019. *A Room of One's Own and Three Guineas.* Penguin Classics, London.

8

Conducting Community Archaeology in Ireland

Working with Marginalized and Vulnerable Communities

LAURA MCATACKNEY

Community archaeology—however one wishes to define it—has become increasingly important not only in determining the aims and form of archaeological projects but also in shaping their proposed outcomes. Increasingly, viewing the public—in general or particular communities—as a key component in archaeological fieldwork is a means of completing research that otherwise may not be funded, but there needs to be more consideration as to what both the community and the archaeologist get from this collaboration. The widespread popularity of community projects is evident through publications such as the *Journal for Community Archaeology and Heritage* (JCAH), which has proved a highly popular outlet for community projects since 2014. The contents of the JCAH indicates not only that is there a wide interpretation of these types of projects but increasingly this type of archaeology has a "glocal" nature, which navigates between many various understandings of what "archaeology" is and local needs. But we need to critically consider how we work with communities and question how this form of archaeological practice interacts with and shapes the process of doing archaeology—for good and for ill—across different contexts.

Looking back again to the JCAH, the first editorial from this journal reveals what the editors envisioned from their new journal and how it may—or may not—map onto how we understand community archaeology now. Some of the key messages from 2014 still resonate: the idea that "community" archaeology is distinct from "public" archaeology (Thomas et al. 2014: 2), although neither are explicitly defined; a strong emphasis on "conversations" as the key to the ethos and conception of community archaeology (Thomas et al. 2014: 1); and the distrust of the journal as a vehicle solely for promoting "good work" without considering "difficult aspects" (Thomas et al. 2014: 2) of these projects. It is notable how these key attributes continue to dominate many of our preoccupations with how we think about community archaeology, especially the importance of being open and honest about how we navigate the relationship between professional and amateur archaeologists. Faye Simpson and Howard Williams argued in 2008 that good practice must ensure projects are coproduced and dialogic, but they also must include space for archaeological expertise (2008: 72). Likewise, Gabriel Moshenska and colleagues have stressed that community projects must explicitly address community needs while communicating the importance of archaeology and thereby ensuring it is sustainable (Moshenska et al. 2011: 11; this volume: Chapter 9). Such a balance is difficult in any archaeological project, but it must be especially difficult to navigate when archaeologists work with communities who are marginalized and sidelined from dominant heritage representations in their own societies, especially when the archaeologists do not come from those communities.

This chapter takes a number of points of departure to consider the role, potential, and limitations of community archaeology at this particular moment in time. As noted in the framing of the original workshop, community archaeology does not take place in a value-free bubble. We are currently living through a period in which reactionary populism is more of a threat and more mainstream than in many decades previous, and this has had an impact on archaeology as well as any other creative, arts, and humanities discipline. We are also living through a period of ongoing crisis, with the impact of a global pandemic still shaping many lives, and this has not only had a huge impact on archaeology and heritage in terms of how we function and fund but the pivot online revealed strong connections between right-wing populism, conspiracy theorists, and the misuse of the past for political opportunism. In the context of Ireland, where this chapter is situated, reactionary populists clearly extended their online reach through the pandemic and are pushing to translate it into real-world political and popular support now (Holland 2023). It is imperative that we consider how archaeology's relationship with community may need to be problematized and even reconsidered against this backdrop. Most of us are aware of the political nature of archaeology—as a historic discipline through to present day—and it has also been long acknowledged that archaeology is framed within a national consciousness that implicitly directs what we know and value from the past (Trigger 2006). Coming from a context of working on archaeologies and with various types of communities in

Ireland, I have increasingly understood that issues of training, perceptions, and outcomes from community archaeology are worth considering in wider conversations.

Community Archaeology during the Pandemic

In situating these discussions on community archaeology in the contemporary, it is important to refer to the very real and disruptive impacts of the global pandemic since the spring of 2020 (See also Kiddey, Chapter 7; Ayán Vila, Chapter 5, both this volume). Alongside the many public health issues, for those who had the privilege to work from home, we have had to find new ways to communicate due to the need to physically isolate. For many of us that meant spending more time engaging online, whether it be with our students, our colleagues, or the wider public, including on social media. It is from that vantage point that I began to consider how archaeology is perceived and potentially mis/used in the online world. A lot has been written about the pivot online during the pandemic, when many countries entered extended periods of lockdown, and for many of us our way to continue interacting with the outside world was to spend time on social media platforms such as Facebook, Twitter (now X), and Instagram. This need to focus on online audiences has been a mammoth task for many heritage and community archaeology organizations, who have faced numerous challenges in terms of maintaining their income and ongoing public engagement (Guest 2021). In the short term, some organizations were extremely creative in maintaining if not enhancing their audiences, including the UK-based DigVentures, who created online projects to address their community's social isolation by facilitating members excavating their back gardens and sharing their finds with their online community (ArchaeoBalt 2020). In some countries, community archaeology projects have been relatively undisturbed, if not enhanced, as excavations have taken place during the summer months and are situated outdoors, so they have allowed for many activities to continue to the great interest of predominantly local audiences. But despite their best efforts, many heritages and cultural organizations have often faced drastic funding and subsidy cuts across the board (Kennedy and Minguez Garcia 2020) that cannot be simply answered by moving their operations online and communicating via social media. Clearly, this has been a very challenging time for community archaeology and especially in maintaining links with communities who have their own individual and collective challenges. It has also been notable that online communities have been changed by the pandemic. The mainstreaming of conspiracy theories that were mainly restricted to the darker reaches of the internet before the pandemic have gathered momentum since 2020 and at times have become mainstream and even transgressed from Far Right to the left wing (Monbiot 2021). The move online has not simply facilitated a value-free tool for us to engage with a receptive community audience; the internet has become a different space. Most compelling with regard to considering reactionary populism is the need to be aware that white supremacists and the Far Right fundamentally underpinned and co-opted pandemic denial and antivax movements that are increasingly mainstream (Day and Carlson 2021). Archaeology is not outside of these online interactions, including the enhanced "culture wars" that have seen libertarian conservatives push back at critically engaged scholarship (Brown Centre on Education Policy 2021).

The online pivot has had a significant impact on wider societal debates and discord that archaeology has previously been involved in. As many activities moved online, so to have historical injustices been entangled with contemporary social justice movements in ways that are meaningful for archaeologists. With many societies locking down for extended periods, debates have been shaped and enhanced online by various actors from academics, journalists, activists, and members of the public so that social media has been repositioned from a distraction to a "crucial communication tool" (Shu-Feng et al. 2021: e176). It is not a coincidence that global conversations prompted by the unlawful killing of George Floyd in the United States in May 2020 extended into wider online protests, debates, and conversations as the hashtag #BlackLivesMatter (BLM) resonated from the United States to many countries with Black minority populations, often for the first time. These protests were not only enhanced by social media sharing, but the nature of protest was often appropriate to it, with online and socially distanced protests being prominent (Nakhaie and Nakhaie 2020). In England, heritage debates extended from these social injustice protests to "culture wars" on how and why the national past is remembered—and commemorated—in the present. The toppling of the statue of slaver Edward Colston into Bristol Harbour at the climax of a BLM protest in June 2020 is a well-known example of how an online social movement transformed into a real-world action. Interestingly, the statue—complete with graffiti from the toppling event—was eventually, if not uncontroversially, removed from the harbor and placed in the M Shed heritage venue as a recontextualized heritage display in June 2021 (Selvin 2021).

Right-wing government pushback at left-wing activism have resulted in overtly political attempts to ensure that controversial statues to colonizers are subject to so-called retain-and-explain policies (Harris 2021), and there have been explicit moves to shut down and prevent future funding for projects such as Colonial Countryside, which was documenting and communicating links between National Trust properties and colonial wealth (Doward 2020). In Denmark, Far Right campaigners have targeted scholars of race, colonialism, gender, and migration and have been agitating in the media for political control of university researcher activities, with significant government support. This focus on the limits of academic freedom was revealed by an artistic "happening" inspired by BLM and led by Art Academy department head Katrine Dirckinck-Holmfeld, which resulting in a bust of King Frederik V (1746–1766) being deposited into a Copenhagen canal in the autumn of 2020 (Buckley 2021). The pressure from largely online Far Right commentators resulted in demands from the Danish Parliament that universities curtail so-called academic activism (Friis and Legarth Sandorff 2021). These examples indicate that the intense social pressures experienced in many countries during the pandemic has created various pressure points around how the past is remembered and articulated that are activated on social media in new and compelling ways. Many of these stresses have implications for how archaeologists work with communities as archaeology is part of wider societal discourses on how the past is being reproduced in social injustice today.

The rest of this chapter focuses on Ireland and considers in more detail how community archaeology functions in Ireland and some of the difficulties in working with marginalized and vulnerable people.

The Politics of (Community) Archaeology in Contemporary Ireland

Due to the highly political nature of the past in Ireland, the delicate interplay between what we remember and what we forget shapes all attempts to conduct research into the recent past. In practice, working on the past in Ireland presents a conundrum: it is a highly politicized society that has a long history (and memory) of colonialism and conflict, but it is also a society that is very reticent to address the politics and enduring impacts of the past in the present as a collective endeavor. This is true of the discipline of history, which has often been criticized (including during the pandemic) for being apolitical and partial (see Hassett et al. 2021) but even more so for archaeology. While it is a common sleight of hand to simply ignore the aspects of the past that are contentious or are not agreed—and instead focus on easier elements— archaeology in Ireland largely ignores that the past is political, or at least the past that it studies.

Much of this reticence to engage with the politics of the past comes from the very structures and systems that underpin archaeology as a discipline and practice in Ireland. There is much that could be said about archaeology in Ireland that touches on the history, training, and structures of the discipline, but without expending too much space, it is important to recognize that Ireland is a small island (the Republic of Ireland with a population of nearly 5 million people; Northern Ireland, nearly 1.9 million), and archaeology is a minor discipline, which only exists as an independent department in five universities (with some outlier academics in other departments). Unlike the United States—or many settler colonial societies—archaeology is not institutionally connected to anthropology (indeed, there is only one independent anthropology department in each political jurisdiction of Ireland—at Queen's University Belfast and Maynooth University—with some outlier anthropologists elsewhere), and it is predominantly considered a scientific discipline focused on the study of the distant past. The majority of archaeologists employed in university departments specialize in prehistory through to the medieval period—essentially before the messiness of colonialism leaves extensive material traces—and there are very few explicitly historical archaeologists and no contemporary archaeologists permanently employed in universities (before mid-2022, when I was appointed as a founding member of the Radical Humanities Laboratory at University College Cork).

Alongside the lack of archaeologists interested in the recent past, there is limited training in public or community archaeology (including no master's programs), and the only real engagement with the societal context is a focus on training archaeologists to work in the private/contract archaeology sector. An entire degree program—bachelor of science in Applied Archaeology—was created in the 1990s at the Institute of Technology, Sligo, to solely produce field archaeologists for this purpose. The growth of Irish archaeology as a profession outside academia can be traced to the 1990s when the "polluter pays principle" was incorporated into the planning process and the focus of university departments split between traditional research pursuits on a pre-British island (largely excluding postmedieval archaeology) to train archaeologists to excavate the large-scale project taking place in the larger cities and European Union–funded road schemes (Doyle 2018: 47–48). To talk of "millionaire archaeologists" (Wilkins 2011) was not an outlandish concept, but this boom was over as quickly as it appeared. At its peak, 1,635 archaeologists were recorded working in the Ireland of the so-called Celtic Tiger in 2007 (mainly migrants from elsewhere), a number that crashed to 338 by 2013 (Doyle 2018: 48). The end of this "golden age" (Wilkins 2011) meant that a lot of archaeologists were forced to refocus and redeploy, which included turning to community projects (Doyle 2018: 48).

There is not a lot explicitly written about community archaeology in Ireland, primarily because it is not an overarching focus of university-based research archaeology and tends to be the domain of local authority archaeologists working with local communities with good intentions but often little explicit training and knowledge of rigorous good practice (see Baker et al. 2019; Doyle 2018). In a recent publication (Baker et al. 2019: 18), the authors stated: "In contrast to other postcolonial countries, community archaeology in Ireland has not developed in order to express a national identity, nor as a means of empowerment for minorities," which basically underlines the disavowal of the political nature of archaeology in Ireland. Of course, there is a long and well-documented history in Ireland of using ancient archaeological remains to articulate collective identity, especially one that is separate and equal to Britain. This is a well-studied area, especially focused on the use of prehistoric monuments from the nineteenth century onward, when they were frequently evoked and used as the backdrop to nationalist rallies (Cooney 1996; Hutchinson 2001; Waddell 2005). In many ways it is odd to witness how mainstream Irish history and archaeology continues to refrain from acknowledging the political nature of their disciplines, but there is long precedent to this position due to a fear of confronting the enduring legacies of colonialism and conflict in the recent past (see Gnecco, this volume: Chapter 4). University College Dublin professor of Celtic Archaeology, Gabriel Cooney, noted in 1996 that the "failure" of "Irish academic historians" across the political spectrum from communicating the more complex nature of the past was due to "removing itself from a concern with present-day society" (1996: 159). It is significant that Cooney's piece was published two years before the conflict in the North—the so-called Troubles—officially ended in 1998.

This enduring disavowal of the inherently political nature of archaeology in the Republic of Ireland, in particular, means it is very easy to reduce community-focused archaeology to small, apolitical projects that address "local concerns" (Baker et al. 2019: 18). In contrast, in Northern Ireland, community archaeology is even more delicately balanced and in some ways is even more keenly aware of its political nature and is extra cautious to acknowledge, but distance itself from, politics. In the North, community archaeology projects are often employed as opportunities for contemporary cross-community relationship-building in which the subject is the backdrop, and very rarely will it directly reference the divisive nature of the past that continues to shape the present. Paul Mullan (2021) has recently written about the relationships between community archaeology and the Heritage Lottery Fund (the major funding body for community archaeology). It is notable in his retelling how reticent archaeologists have been to complete work with local communities if the subject of the excavation may confront contemporary identities. For example, Mullan discussed the Lough Neagh Landscape Partnership in which the archaeologists involved had "initial concerns" regarding engaging a perceived CNR (Catholic Nationalist Republican) community with an archaeological site associated with a battle in which the English army emerged victorious during the Nine Years' War (1593–1603) in their townland. They were worried the subject "may not have gone down well among a community who might instinctively have sided with the defeated Gaelic confederates" (Mullan 2021: 251). Such concerns illustrate that while community archaeology operates in both political jurisdictions in Ireland in similar ways—the legislation that governs archaeology in Northern Ireland has more in common with the Republic of Ireland than anywhere else in the United Kingdom (Mullan 2021: 247)—it exists in different (a)political contexts. There are very different understandings as to what a politically sensitive topic is, the idea of community differs considerably, and there are different funding apparatus and modes of operation (see Kiddey, this volume: Chapter 7). Overall, there are very different understandings of what is political and what is apolitical in the contemporary context, and while the politics of archaeology remains largely unarticulated—or best avoided—in both contexts, it makes it very difficult across the board to address how politics might impact on community archaeology.

I present two brief case studies to dissect a little further the issues of completing "community" archaeology in Ireland. Both are atypical forms of "community" archaeology in terms of neither being funded, excavation-based projects, but they are presented to consider the potential roles for archaeology in engaging with marginalized and vulnerable communities. The aims of these case studies are to consider how we might creatively engage with communities in processes outside of traditional "community archaeology" forums in our contemporary world that avoid traps of reactionary populism.

Irish Statue Toppling on Social Media

The first case study reflects on the discussions and debates that have arisen from Black Lives Matter on Irish Twitter (now named X) and their ramifications in the real world since the spring of 2020. As already noted, Ireland has a complex colonial history due to it being colonized at an early stage by its nearest neighbor—England, later Britain—to the extent it was considered a "laboratory for Empire" (Ohlmeyer 2005). But the proximity of colonizer/colonized also allowed for certain Irish individuals and groups to bypass structural oppression and benefit from, and exploit, colonial opportunities. It is not a straightforward oppressor/oppressed situation, and likewise one can trace ambivalence in examining the fate of Ireland's once extensive colonial monuments and memorials since independence in the early 1920s. Obviously, there are different permeations of these discussions in the Republic of Ireland

Figure 8.1. Statue of Queen Victoria at the Royal Victoria Hospital in Belfast. Photo by author.

and Northern Ireland—due to Ireland being partitioned in the 1920s with the North retained within the United Kingdom—and so the Republic of Ireland is the only entity that can truly be considered a "post"-colonial state. This case study explores a community angle related to the anachronism of enduring colonial remnants and the impacts of "Fallism" against a backdrop of online reactionary populism (see the introduction to this volume; González-Ruibal, this volume: Chapter 2).

While the newly independent "Ireland" of the 1920s had an abundance of colonial-era statues, many have since been removed or destroyed in the intervening 100 years. Statues of Queen Victoria (1837–1901) have had some of the most interesting postindependence trajectories including one example that was situated at University College Cork being buried in the grounds of the university in 1934 only to be excavated in time for the visit of Victoria's descendant, Queen Elizabeth II, in 2011 (Murphy 2011). The statue of Queen

Victoria situated at the seat of Irish government at Leinster House since 1908 was removed due to a carpark extension in 1948. By 1967 it was quietly residing in storage at Royal Hospital Kilmainham, an old British soldiers' hospital and retirement facility, alongside other colonial-era statues that had similarly fallen out of favor. The Leinster House Queen Victoria was not uncontroversially removed to Australia in 1986 and now sits in a square adjacent to the Irish Famine Memorial in Sydney (the Irish Famine Memorial was added after, and in response, to the famine and to honor Queen Victoria, known as "the Famine Queen"). In Belfast, a statue of Queen Victoria resided at one of the covered entrances to the Royal Victoria Hospital in Belfast, in the CNR area of the Falls Road (Figure 8.1). It remains in situ, but the hospital has been reconfigured in such a way that the entrance is no longer in use, so the statue is virtually unseen (which may have been a response to a frequent activity of passersby to place used cigarettes between her bronzed lips). Many other imperial statues were helped to their final resting place by sticks of dynamite planted under cover of darkness, including, most famously, Nelson's Pillar on O'Connell Street in 1966 (Fleming 2016; RTÉ 1967).

While there are still a small number of contentious, colonial-era statues in situ, they tend not to be the focus of debates of historic colonialism or contemporary experiences of racism. One reason for the lack of focus on statues is that Ireland was colonized so extensively and for so long that decolonizing place and space has been a long and partial process that also recognizes the ambivalence of entangled colonial relationships. The most egregious examples of its colonial past have been altered or hidden—only significant place names changed, including Queenstown (Cobh), Kingstown (Dún Laoghaire), Queens County (Laois), and Kings County (Offaly)—and the rest are largely ignored. In Northern Ireland a number of contentious statues remain in place—the slavery-supporting John Mitchel in Newry (Corr 2020), and there are at least two statues to Capt. John Nicholson (Iqbal 2020) commemorating his murderous exploits in India that are still situated in Lisburn and Dungannon. There have been very little online or other discussions about their potential removal since BLM, and there are a number of reasons for this lack of engagement with Fallism. First, regarding Mitchel, he was best known as an Irish nationalist leader, and his statue is in an enduringly nationalist town, which eclipses any problematic opinions he espoused outside of Ireland. This tendency toward partial memory of Irish nationalist heroes is also shared, for different purposes, with the online activities of the Far Right in Ireland, who often decontextualize the quotes of historic Irish nationalists for their own exclusionary purposes in the present (Molloy 2023). Second, Nicholson was a British colonial "hero," and for unionist communities there is no real desire

Figure 8.2. One of the Shelbourne statues, situated at the entrance to the Shelbourne hotel in Dublin. Photo by author.

to critique British colonialism. Third, Northern Ireland remains an unstable postconflict society, and an enduringly homogeneous society, and while there have been some changes to its demography in the last 25 years, they are not sufficient to turn public attention from its more recent sectarian conflict to wider historical injustices.

In the wake of the antiracist protests sparked by BLM in Ireland in 2020, there were some wider discussions about Ireland's colonial legacies alongside—but often separate from—Black Irish people's contemporary experiences of racism and how that may or may not relate to archaeological/heritage issues. One especially telling example was a collection of decorative statues of Nubian princesses and their two torch-bearing slaves that lit the front of the exclusive Shelbourne hotel in Dublin (Figure 8.2). They suddenly became the focus of a Fallism debate in July 2020 (Heyward 2020) due to their

preemptive removal by the hotel's (American) owners. These objets d'art / colonial statuary have been in place since the nineteenth century (Colla 2007),
and in the intervening years they had receded into the background of the hotel's entrance as decorative features that were barely noticed before they were
swiftly removed on July 27, 2020. The general manager's official statement
on their removal indicated it "had been coming for a number of weeks given
what has been happening in the world" (McGreevy 2020), clearly referencing
the BLM protests as an initiating point for the hotel's alteration. The removal
sparked a significant mainstream and social media debate despite the fact "no
one seemed to notice them until they were gone" (Heyward 2020), and heritage and archaeology were central to how this debate unfolded. Online conversations included some of the well-worn tropes of right-wing populist "culture wars"—that removal was erasure, an attack on Irish cultural heritage, and
evidence that BLM debates were being imported to Ireland (Linehan 2020)—
but there were also nuanced and measured discussions about how statues of
enslaved women (even if not referencing the transatlantic slave trade) may or
may not be relevant to contemporary Black Irish women's experiences today.

Academics took a prominent position in the online debates, and it was
notable how different disciplinary perspectives, claims of expertise, and lived
experience were used to center their perspectives that were subsequently amplified (or ignored) by social and mainstream media. This was an interesting case in the early months of lockdown in which the mainstream media
followed social media discussions—and newspapers frequently used Twitter
soundbites and online commentators to support their arguments—rather
than leading and directing the discussions. From an archaeology perspective,
it was clear that archaeologists played a niche role in the discussion that occupied a more managerial and traditional materialist perspective. Those who
commented tended to be heritage managers who focused on the "factual"
historical origins and intentions of the manufacturer of the statues. These interpretations came into conflict with more constructivist heritage approaches
that often came from Black Irish women who voiced their thoughts on the
contemporary relevance of the discussion. Historians and art historians such
as Kyle Leyden took the lead in academic interventions. Leyden presented a
highly detailed historical background for the statues, including the dates of
their manufacture in France and journey to Ireland, which were used to argue
that the statues were unrelated to the transatlantic slave trade and therefore
were irrelevant to issues connected to BLM (McGrath 2020). Irish heritage
agencies, including the Dublin City Council archaeology planning office
and the Irish Georgian Society, followed this materialist interpretation of the
statues and were swift to bypass any contemporary political context, instead

demanding the restoration of the statues to the facade of the hotel due to a lack of planning application to remove them, which was ultimately completed in December 2020 (McGreevy and Kelly 2020). In contrast, constructivist perspectives were provided by some Black Irish commentators such as Dr. Ebun Joseph, a lecturer in Black Studies at University College Dublin, who articulated the view that restoring the statues was a "missed opportunity" for Ireland to engage with the statues and their impact on Black Irish women as a contemporary issue (O'Donnell 2020). My perspective, as a critical heritage scholar, was presented in a number of Twitter threads that emphasized the need to expand our understandings of colonialism beyond the transatlantic slave trade and to engage with material culture having an evolving contemporary context. I emphasized the need to listen to Black Irish women in dealing with this issue. Due to my Twitter activity, I was contacted by *Atlas Obscura*, who wanted to explore the potential connection of these statues to contemporary experiences of racism in Ireland. In the resultant article I was quoted: "Black Lives Matters is seen as an American problem, not our problem. . . . But once it's about an object—here in Dublin, instead of there—suddenly Irish people don't think these statues are racist, and that we don't have these issues" (Heyward 2020).

Ultimately, I thought this debate was a missed opportunity for Irish archaeologists to engage with Black Irish communities, who are largely absent from community engagement. Instead the debate (unintentionally) allowed Far Right perspectives on Ireland's history to take precedence over the opinions of Ireland's increasingly diverse population (Molloy 2023). It was clear in professional archaeology's stilted and limited reactions that there was a lack of imagination and training in working with such political issues in contemporary society. Watching and contributing to this debate, I realized that social media had a potential role to play in these emerging conversations, especially in the heightened context of national lockdowns. While I was surprised and disappointed by the lack of constructivist perspectives displayed by heritage organizations in Ireland—and that many Irish academics followed narrow, materialist reading of the statues—the conversations also indicated how insular and apolitical they remained. In responses to this debate, it was evident how little contemporary archaeology and critical heritage studies had impacted Irish archaeology and ultimately how many people could be aghast at racism "over there" but downplay discussions of racism in Ireland. The biggest challenge for me was to listen to the many varied perspectives of Black Irish women. In contrast to Dr. Joseph's arguments, the broadcaster and author Dr. Emma Dabiri reiterated through various Twitter conversations that she thought the focus on the Shelbourne statues was a distraction from dealing with the everyday experiences of contemporary racism in Ireland. While I can understand her point of view, it seemed to me that archaeology had a potential role to play in engaging with a marginalized community but rather played into Far Right exclusions by not being able to do so.

Working with Survivors of Ireland's Magdalene Laundries through Contract Archaeology

The second case study is political in a distinctly Irish context and relates to deficiencies in how archaeologists work with the remnants of institutions, especially Magdalene Laundries, in the aftermath of abuse scandals. Recent government reports have revealed that extensive abuse occurred since independence in religious-run, government-mandated social institutions (Ryan Report 2009; McAleese Report 2013). While this is not uncommon in places with colonial histories, what is unusual is how long these institutions persisted in Ireland. The last Magdalene Laundry—which were institutions that incarcerated tens of thousands of girls and women in Ireland to launder and repair clothes, often against their will (O'Donnell et al. 2022)—ceased operation in 1996. At the request of the activist group Justice for Magdalenes Research (JFMR), I became involved in archaeological consultation related to a derelict Magdalene Laundry in Dublin in 2018. The traditional archaeological role in such a process is based on the legal obligation on the developer of any site in Ireland to mitigate the impact of construction on the "environment" (archaeology is included in this definition in the Irish context). Up to this point a number of archaeological and architectural contractors had worked with the site at Donnybrook as one would engage with any unexceptional industrial site. They dated the walls and looked for evidence of older remains as well as scanned and excavated looking for potential unmarked graves. Their reports noted that the site had a significant social history due to its use as a Magdalene Laundry, but they seemed unsure how to translate that significance into a holistic archaeological approach to the site beyond recommending that the industrial machinery be recorded. Having submitted these initial reports with the planning application in 2016, the planning office rejected the application due to archaeological deficiencies and especially "the potential for burials to be uncovered" (Kelly 2017). This decision was undoubtedly influenced by recent public scandals surrounding the discovery of unconsecrated and unmarked mass graves at both the former Magdalene Laundry of High Park in Dublin in 1993 (Humphreys 2003) and, more infamously, the Bon Secours Mother and Baby Home at Tuam in County Galway (Barry 2017; see Montgomery, this volume: Chapter 3, for discussion of similar finds at former so-called residential schools in Canada). However, legislation has not changed to systematically deal with the social relevance of these sites, so decisions as to how they should be archaeologically assessed did not consider how the communities who had been placed within them might be involved. I was asked to be an adviser in this process due to the developers requiring more creative and people-centered approaches to deal with such sites that were operational in the recent past.

My approach to this project was to engage with the politics of this site but also explicitly consider how relevant communities could be involved in the mandated archaeological recording. I wanted to acknowledge that archaeology had a privileged role to play in determining how the extant sites from Ireland's recent dreadful history of gendered institutionalization manifest, and we should not disavow it. By 2022 only three of the 10 original postindependence Magdalene Laundries in the Republic of Ireland survived to some degree (all partially), with the rest having been demolished or redeveloped (despite the last laundry only closing in 1996). While Magdalene Laundries would not usually be considered "archaeology" in the Irish planning process, it was notable that, due to a wider societal reckoning, some council planning departments have been reluctant to allow their redevelopment without first conducting extensive archaeological work, but there is little specific expertise in the sector to approach such recent remnants.

In working with the former Donnybrook Magdalene Laundry as an archaeological site, I decided to be directed by the social justice imperatives of the case, that is, by explicitly engaging with Donnybrook as a place of forced incarceration of girls and women, with many victims and survivors who were able to speak of their experiences. I was conscious that to focus solely on the material world of the Magdalene Laundry—as is the norm in contract archaeology—would skew the investigations to recording it primarily as an industrial site. Rather, I wanted to ensure that while the archaeological methodologies would include traditional excavation and recording techniques—expected for planning applications—it would be supplemented by more creative and responsive approaches that would bring together memory and material to provide people-oriented outputs.

I was also inspired by the work of Lucas Lixinski, who has convincingly argued for the inclusion of cultural heritage as a facet of transitional justice due to the need to consider how we can "write and rewrite history in the nomination and selection of heritage items" (Lixinski 2015: 279) in the aftermath of major societal traumas. I wanted to consider how a selective sample of the material world of Donnybrook could be transitioned to national heritage. To do all this, there was a need to consider community as multifaceted—

involving a community of archaeologists working in various ways with the site as well as including a community of victims and survivors. At a very early point in the consultation process, I contacted my colleague Franc Myles of Archaeology and Built Heritage to request that he complete an inventory of the artifactual remains of the site, and I also contacted Brenda Malone, curator at the National Museum of Ireland, and asked her to visit the site with me to determine whether some of the material world of the Magdalene Laundry could be added to the national collection. My own contribution to the archaeological work was to complete a standing brief, which entailed monitoring and recording what was being disposed from the site by contractors to ensure nothing of social significance was removed, and to complete small-scale and experimental site-responsive oral testimonies. The latter would allow a small number of victims and survivors to record their memories of, and reactions to, the site in its current postoperative and predevelopment state. My two contributions were conceived as being appropriate, contemporary archaeology responses as they were engaging with the site in what Rodney Harrison has called a "surface-survey" (2011: 157) approach that views the site as an active assemblage in the present and explicitly includes survivors as central to the recording exercise.

All my contemporary archaeology projects have considered people a significant part of the methodological process of recording material places, and I have always done so with a focus on how we connect people with their material environment in a meaningful way. These projects have never been consciously articulated as "community"; rather, they have always included the perspectives of the community members most intimately connected to the place. For me this means working with people *as* they are engaging with the materiality of the site. Ideally this has been on site, as I have found that being physically immersed in the buildings and landscapes better enables community members to be more reactive to the experience and less practiced or self-conscious in what they are communicating. But there are clear issues in following such an immersive process when working with victims and survivors of institutions who are vulnerable to such processes. To complete this exercise, a small number of women who were previously incarcerated at Donnybrook Magdalene Laundry were approached by JFMR. Two women who had spent short periods at the site many decades ago agreed to contribute, and I worked with them over the summer of 2018.

The first change from my usual process was that I had ongoing prior contact with both of the women to answer any questions and talk through the process of what we were going to do. I met both women on two separate occasions in a neutral space before we went to the site, so we were able to talk about what would happen. I showed them some pictures of the site as it currently looked (as I knew the dereliction might be shocking to them otherwise) and we talked about the consent forms and resources for counseling for after the process. Both women also brought a companion—one brought her husband; the other brought a female friend—and we went to the site together. I told both women that we would walk around the site and I would be taping our conversation and taking photographs of anything in particular that the women pointed out, but otherwise they would not be visually recorded. When they asked what I wanted them to talk about, I indicated that I did not want to direct their responses; they were to say whatever thoughts came into their head as we walked around the complex. It was emphasized that there was no detail too large or too small, and they were under no pressure to talk about anything that made them uncomfortable. It was reiterated that we could stop at any stage and leave the site when they wished. In theory, I did not want to direct our discussion but rather follow the ethics of Cahal McLaughlin's Prison Memory Archive project, wherein "leading questions were eschewed in order to return more agency to the participants" (McLaughlin 2015).

In practice, this process was much more complicated than I had previously experienced with ex-political prisoners at Long Kesh / Maze prison (McAtackney 2014); the participants were physically much older than the men I had previously worked with and at times were clearly more physically and mentally vulnerable in responding to institutions in which they had been indoctrinated with shame while they were forced to inhabit them. While my experiences with the two women were also quite different, I felt on both occasions that I needed to direct, in various ways, how we moved around the complex and what we discussed more than I had anticipated. This decision to be more actively involved in the process was made spontaneously soon after we entered the site as I reacted to the variations in the women's responses to the openness of the process. I was also concerned about how retraumatizing the experience might be if they had little support to navigate the site. I had to reaffirm the aim of this oral testimony process: first to complete site-responsive testimonies so victims and survivors could add their narratives rather than the process be dominated by the machines and infrastructure of the industrial laundry. Of secondary importance was their potential ability to identify the meanings of objects that otherwise would did not be communicated by their physical form (primarily so they could be included in our inventories and for the National Museum). In essence, this process was what Homi Bhabha has called a "right of narration" (2003). In contrast to the flawed reports related to Ireland's institutional past, this process was not about playing "gotcha"—to

Figure 8.3. The sorting room of the former Donnybrook Magdalene Laundry, Dublin. Photo by author.

locate some objective, some irrefutable truth—but about allowing their memories and lived experiences to be the focal point of the recording exercise.

In practice, the women had different approaches to how they began and proceeded with their testimonies. One of the women wished to start outside the gates of the site and wanted to provide information about herself to frame her introduction to the site rather than allow for a fully site-responsive experience. I felt it was important that she was able to control how we engaged with the site, so I did not intervene to direct her back to the site. The second woman waited until we entered the site for the recording to start, and she followed the process of responding to her physical reintroduction to the laundry. What was not expected was quite how much the contemporary state of the site—and especially its tangible ruination—would shape and determine the initial responses. The active nature of the site's ruination made it an uncanny site to encounter, and this was exacerbated by our entrance to the site. As we moved through the public entrance to the large sorting area—both areas the women would not have encountered before as these were later additions to the laundry—they entered a large space derelict of previous furniture, filled with a variety of dirt and debris—including graffitied walls—and the floors were punctuated with large holes from recent archaeological excavations

Figure 8.4. Laundry machines in the former laundry at Donnybrook Madgalene Laundry. Photo by author.

(Figure 8.3). The oral recording from the first woman picks up her audible intake of breath—involuntary shock—at the disturbed state of the room. Such an entry to the site clearly disorientated the women to the extent that the site-responsive intention of the oral testimonies quickly derailed as they silently tried to make sense of the material disruption in front of them. To enable some form of reconnection to the site, and to support them as they tried to make sense of it, I deviated from this being a solely site-responsive exercise. Rather, I proceeded to guide them to some of the oldest and most complete areas—where the large industrial laundry machines still remained—to allow them to refamiliarize themselves with the site (Figure 8.4).

Being reacquainted with the laundry machines brought back memories to the women of where they had worked and how they had used the machines and associated infrastructure. Short discussions about how one would use the machines were often means—for me and for them—to reset the conversations or insert some form of control back into the site-responsive engagement when it became difficult for them to remember or verbalize reactions. But these deviations were also useful inclusions. The first woman was of small stature, and she indicated how difficult it was for someone her size to navigate the industrial space by pointing out an otherwise anonymous blue pallet that she and others would have stood on to allow them to reach into the back of the industrial washing machine. She was also able to discuss the more intangible nature of her experiences as we stood at a sorting station, and she explained to me and my colleague, Franc Myles, that the nuns would use the repetition of prayer and enforced silence to ensure the women were not verbally communicating with each other while sorting laundry. In contrast, the other woman punctuated her testimony with anxious exclamations about how little she could remember of the site due to how much it had changed and how little she could make sense of it. She could indicate how machines were used when requested, but her strongest memories were of an intangible nature—of the heat, steam, and noise of the busy laundry when it was operational. Although less factually informative, this oral testimony was also important in indicating how specific memory can be as well as its frailties in reconnecting with these uncanny spaces. What stuck in my mind after we had finished was how much being at the site prompted the second woman to reflect on her time in the laundry as a fracture point in her life—the memories she articulated were more often focused on how her life led her to it and how it was shaped afterward—rather than focus on her experiences *of* and *in* the laundry. This felt like an important insight into how her traumatized memory reacted to the disorientation of the site; rather than focus on the material world around her, she abstracted to the impact of the laundry on her. For various reasons, all these insights were useful in understanding not only the place but its enduring traumatic impact on lives and that community of marginalized women. I hoped that such an intervention could give inspiration to other contract archaeologists in the future so they may engage with meaningful places in ways that include communities. It has been important to us to give agency back to victims and survivors, as we are entering a period when their numbers dwindle, the material remains disappear, and minimization occurs.

Conclusion

The political nature of archaeology is largely unacknowledged in Ireland despite the contemporary political context being a significant factor in not only how we engage with communities but also what aspects of the past are remembered and examined or sidelined and forgotten. The aim of this chapter has been to consider how we reconceptualize what community archaeology can be in an era in which community is promoted against a backdrop of reactionary populism. Part of this process is to recognize that communities take various forms, and our engagement with them does not need to be through an organized, consciously public-focused excavation. One medium that has become increasingly important is through engaging with social media, which I have shown through the first case study has many opportunities to engage but also can be an exclusionary place, especially if we are not careful to avoid replicating Far Right appropriations of belonging. I aimed to show that archaeology can have a more dispersed and meaningful presence in our discussions and debates about how we form identity and make meaning in our contemporary world, which can acknowledge how the materiality of the past is constituted in the present in many evolving ways.

The second aim of this chapter has been to consider how we envision community archaeology projects in ways that are appropriate to the exercise and to think about the role of specific communities in working with us to understand them, and the sites we work with, better. For both case studies, this meant including the perspectives of affected communities by allowing them to narrate their understandings of material and place (which may differ from an "objective" recording of the material form). This does not mean that, as archaeologists, we should be in thrall to any and all community opinions and record every word people tell us as "truth," but we should consider how we include marginalized voices. We must recognize that in certain contexts, community members have a right of narration (Bhabha 2003) that help us understand contested places better, and they should be included in how we write up our archaeology reports, especially as they may determine how they are remembered moving forward.

Acknowledgments

I would like to acknowledge the bravery and resilience of various marginalized and vulnerable people and communities in Ireland and their openness to sharing their experiences and working with heritage researchers and organizations regardless of the pushback they often receive (especially on social media). With special thanks to the two women who walked with me through the former Donnybrook Magdalene Laundry and recounted their experience, and to my colleagues Brenda Malone, National Museum of Ireland; Franc Myles, Archaeology and Built Heritage; and Justice for Magdalenes Research.

References Cited

ArchaeoBalt. 2020. ArchaeoTourism and Social Media Round Table, YouTube, January 21, 2021, 1:07:30. https://www.youtube.com/watch?v=pPDZsq__KnY, accessed February 5, 2022.

Baker, Christine, Finola O'Carroll, Paul Duffy, Denis Shine, Steve Mandal, and Michael Mongey. 2019. Creating Opportunities and Managing Expectations: Evaluation Community Archaeology in Ireland. In *Transforming Heritage Practice in the 21st Century,* edited by John H. Jameson, Sergiu Musteată, pp. 15–28. One World Archaeology, New York.

Barry, Dan. 2017. The Lost Children of Tuam. *New York Times,* October 28. https://www.nytimes.com/interactive/2017/10/28/world/europe/tuam-ireland-babies-children.html.

Bhabha, Homi. 2003. Democracy De-Realized. *Diogenes* 50: 27–35.

Brown Centre on Education Policy. 2021. From COVID-19 to Culture Wars: The Growing Hostility of Education Politics, December 9. Video presentation available online. https://www.brookings.edu/events/from-covid-to-culture-wars-the-growing-hostility-of-education-politics/, accessed November 3, 2023.

Buckley, Cara. 2021. The Sinking of a Bust Surfaces a Debate over Denmark's Past. *New York Times,* February 9. https://www.nytimes.com/2021/02/09/arts/design/frederik-v-bust-denmark.html.

Colla, Elliott. 2007. *Conflicted Antiquities: Egyptology, Egyptomania, Egyptian Modernity.* London: Duke University Press.

Cooney, Gabriel. 1996. Building the Future on the Past: Archaeology and the Construction of National Identity in Ireland. In *Nationalism and Archaeology in Europe,* edited by Margarita Díaz-Andreu and Timothy Champion, pp. 146–163. Routledge, London.

Corr, Shauna. 2020. Statue of Slavery Supporter John Mitchel in Newry Should be Pulled Down, Say Campaigners. Belfast Live. June 10, 2020. https://www.belfastlive.co.uk/news/belfast-news/john-mitchel-statue-newry-should-18392253.

Day, Madi, and Bronwyn Carlson. 2021. White Supremacists and Far Right Ideology Underpin Anti-Vax Movements. *Conversation,* November 22. https://theconversation.com/white-supremacist-and-far-right-ideology-underpin-anti-vax-movements-172289.

Doward, Jamie. 2020. I've Been Unfairly Targeted, Says Academic at Heart of National Trust "Woke" Row. *Guardian,* December 20. https://www.theguardian.com/uk-news/2020/dec/20/ive-been-unfairly-targeted-says-academic-at-heart-of-national-trust-woke-row.

Doyle, Ian W. 2018. Community Archaeology in Ireland: Less Mitigator, More Mediator? In *Shared Knowledge, Shared Power: Engaging Local and Indigenous Heritage,* edited by Veysel Apaydin, pp. 45–59. Springer Briefs in Archaeology, New York.

Fleming, Diarmaid. 2016. The Man Who Blew up Nelson. *BBC,* March 12. https://www.bbc.com/news/magazine-35787116.

Friis, Rasmus, and Jakob Legarth Sandorff. 2021. Researchers: Political Offensive against "Pseudoresearch" Is Prejudiced and Dangerous. *Uniavisen,* March 22. https://uniavisen.dk/en/researchers-political-offensive-against-pseudoresearch-is-prejudiced-and-dangerous/.

Guest, Kate. 2021. Heritage and the Pandemic: An Early Response to the Restriction of COVID-19 by the Heritage Sector in England. *The Historic Environment: Policy and Practice* 12: 4–18.

Harris, Gareth. 2021. Fuelling Culture War, UK Government Forms New "Retain and Explain" Board for Controversial Monuments. *Art Newspaper.* May 17. https://www.theartnewspaper.com/news/uk-culture-secretary-fuels-culture-war.

Harrison, Rodney. 2011. Surface Assemblages. Towards an Archaeology *in* and *of* the Present. *Archaeological Dialogues* 18: 141–161.

Hassett, Dónal, Hussein Omar, and Laura McAtackney. 2021. The Case for Rethinking Ireland and Empire. *RTÉ Brainstorm,* April 19. https://www.rte.ie/brainstorm/2021/0419/1210712-case-rethinking-ireland-empire/.

Heyward, Guilia. 2020. A Dublin Hotel Removed Four Statues and Sparked a Historical Debate. *Atlas Obscura,* August 31, 2020. https://www.atlasobscura.com/articles/shelbourne-hotel-statues-dublin.

Holland, Kitty. 2023. Far Right in Ireland; Gaining A Foothold Like Never Before. *Irish Times,* February 3. https://www.irishtimes.com/ireland/2023/02/03/far-right-in-ireland-gaining-a-foothold-like-never-before.

Humphreys, Joe. 2023. Magdalen Plot Had Remains of 155 Women. *Irish Times,* August 21. https://www.irishtimes.com/news/magdalen-plot-had-remains-of-155-women-1.370279.

Hutchinson, John. 2001. Archaeology and the Irish Rediscovery of the Celtic Past. *Nations and Nationalism* 7(4): 505–519.

Iqbal, Sajid. 2020. It's Time That Nicholson's Statue Was Also Pulled Down. *Naya Daur,* June 21. https://nayadaur.tv/2020/06/when-will-nicholsons-statue-be-pulled-down/.

Kelly, Olivia. 2017. Donnybrook Magdalene Laundry Demolition Proposal Scrapped. *Irish Times,* April 8, 2017. https://www.irishtimes.com/culture/heritage/donnybrook-magdalene-laundry-demolition-proposal-scrapped-1.3041047.

Kennedy, Rebecca, and Barbara Minguez Garcia. 2020. Heritage in Crisis: COVID Adverse Economic Impacts. ICCROM. April 9. https://www.iccrom.org/heritage-times-covid, accessed August 12, 2024.

Linehan, Hugh. 2020. The Shelbourne Statues: Will We Ever See Them on St Stephen's Green Again? *Irish Times,* August 1, 2020. https://www.irishtimes.com/culture/heritage/shelbourne-statues-will-we-ever-see-them-on-st-stephen-s-green-again-1.4317789

Lixinski, Lucas. 2015. Cultural Heritage Law and Transitional Justice: Lessons from South Africa. *International Journal of Transitional Justice* 9: 278–296.

McAtackney, Laura. 2014. *An Archaeology of the Troubles: The Dark Heritage of Long Kesh / Maze Prison.* Oxford University Press, Oxford.

McGrath, Dominic. 2020. Art Historian Says Sculptures Removed from Shelbourne Hotel Did Not Depict Slaves. *The Journal,* July 31, 2020. https://www.thejournal.ie/shelbourne-dublin-sculpture-statue-slaves-5165686-Jul2020/.

McGreevy, Ronan. 2020. Shelbourne Hotel Removes 153-Year-Old Statues of Slave Girls from Its Plinth. *Irish Times,* July 28, 2020. https://www.irishtimes.com/news/ireland/irish-news/shelbourne-hotel-removes-153-year-old-statues-of-slave-girls-from-its-plinth-1.4315733.

McGreevy, Ronan, and Olivia Kelly. 2020. Dublin City Council Begins Action Against Shelbourne Hotel for Removing Statues. *Irish Times,* August 6, 2020. https://www.irishtimes.com/culture/heritage/dublin-city-council-begins-action-against-shelbourne-hotel-for-removing-statues-1.4323697.

McLaughlin, Cahal. 2015. A Documentary Archive of Prison Experience: Introduction to the PMA. *Prison Memory Archive.* https://www.prisonsmemoryarchive.com/illustrated

_essay/a-documentary-archive-of-prison-experience-introduction-to-the-pma/, accessed November 3, 2023.

Molloy, Joshua. 2023. From British Imperialism to "Globohomo": Analysing the Irish Far-Right's Engagement with Irish Nationalism on Telegram. *Global Network on Extremism & Technology,* September 22. https://gnet-research.org/2023/09/22/from-british-imperialism-to-globohomo-analysing-the-irish-far-rights-engagement-with-irish-nationalism-on-telegram/.

Monbiot, George. 2021. It's Shocking to See So Many Leftwingers Lured to the Far Right by Conspiracy Theories. *Guardian,* September 22. https://www.theguardian.com/commentisfree/2021/sep/22/leftwingers-far-right-conspiracy-theories-anti-vaxxers-power.

Moshenska, Gabriel, Sarah Dhanjal, and Don Cooper. 2011. Building Sustainability in Community Archaeology: The Hendon School Archaeology Project. *Archaeology International,* no. 13/14: 94–100. https://dx.doi.org/10.5334/ai.1317.

Mullan, Paul. 2021. Community Archaeology and the Heritage Fund in Northern Ireland. *Journal of Community Archaeology and Heritage* 8: 245–255.

Murphy, John A. 2011. The Story of Queen's Victoria's Statue at University College Cork. UCCIreland, *YouTube,* May 20, 2011. https://www.youtube.com/watch?v=vnIdp2d7brA.

Nakhaie, Reza, and F. S. Nakhaie. 2020. Black Lives Matter Movement Finds New Urgency and Allies Because of COVID-19. *Conversation,* July 5. https://theconversation.com/black-lives-matter-movement-finds-new-urgency-and-allies-because-of-covid-19-141500.

O'Donnell, Dimitri. 2020. Historic Statues to Be Restored to Front of Shelbourne Hotel. *RTÉ,* September 24. https://www.rte.ie/news/dublin/2020/0924/1167307-shelbourne-statues/.

O'Donnell, Katherine, Maeve O'Rourke, and James Smith (editors). 2022. *REDRESS: Ireland and Justice in Transition.* University College Dublin Press, Dublin.

Ohlmeyer, Jane. 2005. A Laboratory for Empire? Early Modern Ireland and English Imperialism. In *Ireland and the British Empire,* edited by Kevin Kenny. Oxford: Oxford University Press.

Raidió Teilifís Éireann (RTE). 1967. Queen Turns Green at Royal Hospital. RTE Archives. Accessed July 2021. https://www.rte.ie/archives/2017/0110/843928-queen-victoria-in-kilmainham/.

Report of the Commission to Inquire into Child Abuse (Ryan Report). Dublin, Department of Justice, 2009. https://www.gov.ie/en/publication/3c76d0-the-report-of-the-commission-to-inquire-into-child-abuse-the-ryan-re/.

Report of the Inter-Departmental Committee to Establish the Facts of State Involvement with the Magdalen Laundries (McAleese Report). Dublin: Department of Justice, 2013. www.gov.ie/en/collection/a69a14-report-of-the-inter-departmental-committee-to-establish-the-facts-of/?referrer=www.justice.ie/en/JELR/Pages/MagdalenRpt2013.

Selvin, Claire. 2021. Toppled Statue of Slave Trader Goes on View in Bristol, Generating Controversy. *Art News,* June 8. https://www.artnews.com/art-news/news/edward-colston-statue-m-shed-museum-bristol-1234595170/.

Shu-Feng, Tsao, Helen Chen, Therese Tisseverasinghe, Yang Yang, Lianghusa Li, and Zahid A Butt. 2021. What Social Media Told Us in the Time of COVID-19: A Scoping Review. *Lancet Digital Health* (3): e175–194.

Simpson, Faye, and Howard Williams. 2008. Evaluating Community Archaeology in the UK. *Public Archaeology* 7: 69–90.

Thomas, Suzie, Carol McDavid, and Adam Gutteridge. 2014. Editorial. *Journal of Community Archaeology and Heritage* 1: 1–4.

Trigger, Bruce. 2006. *A History of Archaeological Thought.* Cambridge University Press, Cambridge.

Waddell, John. 2005. *Foundation Myths: The Beginnings of Irish Archaeology.* Wordwell, Dublin.

Wilkins, Brendon. 2011. When the Celtic Tiger Roared: The Golden Years of Commercial Archaeology in Ireland. *Current Archaeology,* January 25. https://archaeology.co.uk/articles/features/when-the-celtic-tiger-roared-the-golden-years-of-commercial-archaeology-in-ireland.htm.

9

Contending with Colonial Heritage as a Transnational Activist Network

The Museum of British Colonialism

Gabriel Moshenska, Anthony Maina, Hannah McLean, Andrea Potts, Beth Rebisz, and Chao Tayiana Maina

Against Colonial Heritage Narratives

British colonial heritage is riddled with lies, omissions, erasures, half-truths, and whole-cloth fabrications, yet challenges to its legitimacy are met with an almost unhinged viciousness and rage. From the 1940s onward, Britain's colonies began to win their independence in often blood-soaked freedom struggles. The archives of the colonial state, stuffed with damning records of exploitation and brutality, should by convention have passed to the newly independent nations. But in practice, the British government sanctioned a covert campaign of destruction and wholesale theft of these archives (Cobain 2016). It is these attempts at official erasure and the literal theft of the archival heritage of newly independent nations and peoples that provide the context and necessity for an interdisciplinary historical-archaeological approach to British colonial violence.

Today the whitewashing of brutal colonial history by reactionary populists in government, cultural institutions, and higher education is part of a "culture war" in Britain and in other colonial and formerly colonial nations (Cammaerts 2022). This artificial nostalgia for a mythical imperial glory is grounded in part in the mass erasure of archives described above. Thus, a poll conducted in 2014 found that most of the British public regard the British Empire as a source of pride. One-half of those surveyed believed that the impacts on colonized nations were positive, and more than one-third wished that the British Empire still existed (Jasanoff 2020). In the mainstreams of British culture these imperial fantasies are deemed "common sense," in the Gramscian sense of "the ensemble of opinions that have become collective and a powerful factor in society" (Crehan 2016: ix). Amid the current worldwide reemergence of reactionary populism, we have seen a weaponization of "common sense" in the form of national myths: triumphant, sovereign pasts to be reclaimed, often violently. In contemporary Britain, that commonsense order of things is unapologetically imperialist (Mitchell 2021; Traverso 2019).

Aligned against these forces of reaction in Britain is a lively and deep-rooted body of scholarship and activism that seeks to critically examine the heritage of the empire. This includes academic initiatives such as the data-focused Legacies of British Slave-Ownership Project (Hall et al. 2014) and Corinne Fowler's Colonial Countryside Project (Fowler 2020). The history of empire and its traces in contemporary British society have been the subject of searing scholarship by writers such as Priyamvada Gopal (2019) and Kehinde Andrews (2021). In response, UK government ministers have demanded that funding be cut to these projects and have instructed leading museums and heritage bodies to "defend our culture and history from the noisy minority of activists constantly trying to do Britain down" (Massing 2021). This is a common theme in reactionary populist responses to radical history, as seen in the United States with attacks on the *New York Times*'s 1619 project (see González-Ruibal and McGuire, this volume: Chapter 1).

In the face of widespread disinformation and state-sanctioned censorship of academics and heritage organizations, there is a clear and growing need for civil society organizations to shine a light on the history of the British Empire. The youth-led activist group Fill in the Blanks (2020) focused on the lack of imperial history in formal education, while Rhodes Must Fall in Oxford aims to remove the statue of Cecil Rhodes from Oriel College as part of a wider set of demands by students to decolonize and diversify the university (Kwoba et al. 2018).

The aim of this chapter is to describe and discuss an activist response to British colonial erasure and its roots in reactionary populism. It focuses on the work of the Museum of British Colonialism (MBC), a UK–Kenyan heritage activist collective focused on the legacies of British colonial violence, and in particular the Mau Mau rebellion in 1950s Kenya and the counterinsurgency campaign. Through a description of this interdisciplinary work, ranging from archaeological fieldwork to digital mapping and public outreach, our aim is to illuminate some of the potential impacts and uses of transnational activist networks to intervene in contested heritage narratives. The values of a networked approach include flexibility, informality, nonhierarchical structure, and the ability to work fast and respond to events (Pieck 2013). Our key argument is that as reactionary populist governments across the world are increasingly restricting academic freedom, corrupting cultural institutions, and seeking to control official heritage narratives, the relative freedom of transnational civil society organizations to organize and operate outside of these restrictions is all the more valuable and significant.

The Mau Mau Rebellion: Context and Heritage

One of the main activities of the MBC to date has been fieldwork and digital heritage work around the internment camps created by the British colonial authorities as part of their counterinsurgency strategy against the Mau Mau rebellion. The rebellion itself was the culmination of decades of anticolonial organizing and activism. British colonization of Kenya began in the late nineteenth century, and it became a formal colony in 1920. Throughout the history of the colony there were protests and violent resistance, mostly focused on land. Colonists were attracted to Kenya by the extremely fertile land in the temperate central region, and the laws of the colony provided favorable land rights to Europeans while preventing Africans from growing cash crops. To create a captive labor force, laws were introduced to restrict movement, punitive levels of taxation further impoverished the African population, and the continual seizure of land disrupted long-established patterns of inheritance and kin-group dynamics (Anderson 2005; Kanogo 1987).

There were small-scale rebellions before, during, and after the Second World War, but the emergence of the Mau Mau as armed resistance in the early 1950s was also based on the experiences of many Kenyan men in the King's African Rifles during the Second World War, who returned to Kenya to find even more punitive land theft, labor restrictions, and a refusal to engage with demands for democracy (Edgerton 1990; Furedi 1989).

The suppression of Kenyan political parties and campaigns for democracy in the 1940s and 1950s led to the reemergence of traditional Gĩkũyũ "oathing" practices for the formation of secret societies (Blunt 2013). These, together with the stockpiling of weapons, are seen as the point of emergence of Mau Mau as a semiorganized, semicoherent ideology: only toward the end of its existence as a grouping of guerrilla units did Mau Mau become a nearly unified, cohesive military force. The violent struggle began with the murders of white settlers and leading African supporters of the colonial regime, and with a series of massacres on both sides that led the colonial government to declare a state of emergency (Bennett 2013).

The Mau Mau rebellion was primarily a guerrilla conflict conducted between British-led forces and Mau Mau units mostly based in the forests of central Kenya. Much of the conflict was fought between the Mau Mau and so-called Home Guard units of Kenyan loyalist militias, most of them armed, paid, and led by British settlers or colonial officers (Bennett 2013). To crush the rebellion, the British forces—drawing on counterinsurgency strategies developed in the Malaya Emergency—sought to capture or kill Mau Mau guerrillas hiding among the wider population while working to separate Mau Mau from their support base in rural villages. For both of these problematic populations, the colonists' solution was mass internment.

The state of emergency gave the British authorities the power to detain people without trial, and this power was abused to an astonishing level during the uprising. The tens of thousands of detainees from military sweeps of Nairobi and other towns quickly filled Kenya's prisons, and new internment camps were constructed for the large numbers of suspects being detained indefinitely, few of whom ever faced trial. At any one time there were approximately 50–60 detention camps in operation across Kenya, many of them deliberately located in remote and inhospitable areas including deserts in the north and west, and swamps and islands in the east. Prisoners in these camps were systematically underfed, and violence was routine. Detainees were forced to work on farms and in large infrastructure projects, including road building and canal digging. Thousands of prisoners were worked to death in these projects, alongside thousands more who died in the camps (Elkins 2005).

Meanwhile, to control the rural populations suspected of supplying Mau Mau with food, weapons, and ammunition, hundreds of thousands of Gĩkũyũ were forced into "barbed-wire villages"—settlements surrounded by wire fences and ditches full of spikes. In some of these villages the population were only allowed to leave for one hour per day to farm their land under armed guard, which resulted in widespread starvation, sexual violence, and very high infant mortality (Rebisz 2021). Around 800 of these "villages" were constructed across Kenya during the uprising. Both sets of camps—those for Mau Mau suspects and those for civilians—were modeled on the camps and villages used by the British in Malaya in their 12-year-long fight against communist forces (Elkins 2005).

Toward the end of the Mau Mau uprising in the late 1950s, there was an effort to empty the camps and return prisoners to their communities. At this time the inflexible policy of forcing prisoners to confess and retract their Mau Mau oaths before release led to an upsurge in violent interrogation, torture,

Figure 9.1. Interviewing Wambugu Wa Nyingi in 2018. Photo by Gabriel Moshenska.

mutilation, and murder. What had previously been isolated episodes of brutality became widespread policy, leading to heightened international attention and strong criticism from left-wing politicians in Britain (Anderson 2005).

In March 1959, 11 prisoners at Hola Camp in southeastern Kenya were beaten to death by guards in cold blood as a warning to other prisoners who refused to work (Anderson 2005). A twelfth man, Wambugu Wa Nyingi, survived the beating and awoke from a coma in the camp mortuary three days later—he was one of the group of six men and women who sued the British government in 2006, and we interviewed him during our fieldwork in 2018 (Figure 9.1). Sadly, he passed away in 2020. In the aftermath of this massacre there was a failed cover-up, and in the resulting scandal the rest of the camps in Kenya were closed and the prisoners released.

Echoes of the Mau Mau Rebellion

The heritage and representation of the Mau Mau rebellion has been a source of controversy in both Kenya and the United Kingdom since well before the conflict ended, and this is reflected in history writing and studies of commemoration (e.g., Hughes 2011, 2017). There is also a rich literature written by Mau Mau veterans and others interned during the conflict (e.g., Clough 1998; Kariuki 1963). In 2005 two books were published that brought global attention to the atrocities committed by the British authorities in late-colonial Kenya, which became independent from Britain in 1963. The first of these, Caroline Elkins' *Imperial Reckoning* (also published as *Britain's Gulag*) is a sensational and engaging work of historical reporting based on hundreds of interviews and extensive archival research that focuses primarily on the system of camps used to hold Mau Mau suspects. The second, David Anderson's *Histories of the Hanged,* examines the brutal and often corrupt legal processes that the British employed in the fight against the Mau Mau, including the use of mass detention and the execution of more than 1,000 Gĩkũyũ for a variety of often very minor crimes. These books drew and built upon earlier work by Kenyan historians and scholars.

These books led to a renewed interest in Britain's post-1945 imperial history and its wider receptions and representations. In 2006 a group of Kenyan men and women who had been tortured by British colonial forces brought a legal claim for compensation against the UK government. Both Elkins and Anderson were involved in this case as expert witnesses. The court case was ultimately successful, and in 2013 the government issued an official apology and paid compensation (Anderson 2011, 2015).

In 2011, amid the court case, the UK Foreign Office was forced to reveal the existence of a secret archive of documents relating to a number of former colonies including Kenya. They revealed widespread official knowledge of the tortures and murders conducted in the camps. More significantly, they revealed a systematic process of destroying and concealing official documents from former colonies: many were burned, some were dumped at sea (at safe distances from the shore), and yet more were repatriated to the secret archive in the United Kingdom, their existence officially denied for decades (Anderson 2011, 2015; Duffy 2015).

In the aftermath of the Second World War, Britain and other European colonial powers had scrambled to regain control of overseas territories, including those that had been occupied by Japanese imperial forces. British troops sought to assist the French in regaining control of Vietnam, and the Dutch of Indonesia. Over the next two decades British forces violently suppressed independence movements in territories including Malaya, Kenya, Oman, Cyprus, Aden, and Northern Ireland. British police, military, and security services personnel moved between these conflicts, sharing practices and expertise in mass internment, torture, execution, and other counterinsurgency tactics (French 2012). As former colonies gained independence, British colonial officers were reluctant to hand over their archives—including records of these acts of violence—to the new rulers of the independent nations. Against all proper processes and laws, they stole or destroyed the archives (Cobain 2016).

The Museum of British Colonialism: Beginnings

The Museum of British Colonialism was founded in 2018 by a group of Kenyan and British women. The museum described itself as "a network and platform for facilitating global conversations about British colonialism and its legacies . . . a repository for digital resources that highlight lived experiences of British colonialism" (all quotes from MBC are from its website[1]). As such, it is part of a growing phenomenon within the heritage sector of museums without walls or a physical collection, and instead a focus on digital resources. Partly, this is a practical matter, but it also reflects a tension with the colonial legacy of the European notion of "the museum" and its historical development (Moshenska 2020). The membership of MBC has grown and evolved, as is natural with a wholly volunteer team. As a digital platform it has hosted and promoted the work of other small heritage projects with allied aims: this flexibility and mobility is one of the advantages of a networked approach, as this chapter demonstrates. To date, most research on activist networks focuses on transnational advocacy networks operating on a much larger scale than MBC (see Castells 2015; Keck and Sikkink 1998). However, many of the features of transnational advocacy networks also apply to MBC, including the aim to amplify marginalized voices.

One of the group's first projects was a documentary film, *Operation Legacy*, produced in collaboration with the online history documentary channel HistoryHit TV. The film focuses on the history of the stolen archives and the court case in which they were forcibly made public and aims to challenge audiences' conceptions of state archives as pristine and reliable sources of information. As well as being made available online, public viewings of the documentary with panel discussions have been held in Kenya and the United Kingdom, including in Northern Ireland in collaboration with the Pat Finucane Centre.

Activism implies activity—there is insufficient space here to list all of the work that the MBC has carried out in the first years of its existence, but there is a value in highlighting those actions that have directly addressed the museum's stated aims to raise awareness and understanding of British colonial heritage, and to foster discussion about its legacies. The Paper Trails research network is a part of MBC's work to promote colonial histories. It began as a series of interviews with scholars posted on the MBC website and has expanded into a network of researchers and practitioners working on the history and legacies of colonialism. This includes early career scholars and those outside the Global North. The MBC website hosts interviews with these researchers alongside a member directory and publications list to enhance exposure and aid network-building.

One of the functions of digital activist networks is mutual amplification, sharing social media and publicity connections to reach larger audiences (see McAtackney, this volume: Chapter 8). The MBC has been active in building these connections as part of an informal network of heritage activist groups working on anticolonial radical history. A good example of this is *A History of Everyone Else,* a video series aiming to share neglected narratives from the history of British colonialism: "resistance movements, stigmatized social groups, artists, young people and more." The MBC partnered with *A History of Everyone Else* to host their videos. To learn more about the MBC's work, the website provides a comprehensive set of resources and information.

Fieldwork

Our fieldwork in 2018 and 2019 aimed to explore (1) what traces remained of the network of detention camps and associated sites, and (2) how the camps are regarded and managed as heritage in contemporary Kenya. The fieldwork was supported by a grant from the UCL-Gothenburg Centre for Critical Heritage Studies and by crowdfunding run by the MBC. In Kenya we worked with the state heritage body, National Museums of Kenya, and their representative Anthony Maina, an expert on Mau Mau heritage sites. While several sources suggested that little or no traces of the camps remained, in discussion with Mr. Maina we identified several sites with surviving structures in Nyeri County, including two former detention camps—specifically forced-labor camps—that have been repurposed as schools.

Mweru Works Camp

Mweru High School sits on the site of what was Mweru Works Camp, a small detention camp that provided labor for a brick-making factory. During our fieldwork we identified two classrooms that had formerly served as cell blocks: the windows were clearly added at a later date, and the doors were heavy and barred. These and several other buildings had barbed wire filling the ventilation spaces between the tops of the walls and the overhanging roofs. In the center of the school site sits a small building that is marked as being the "tor-

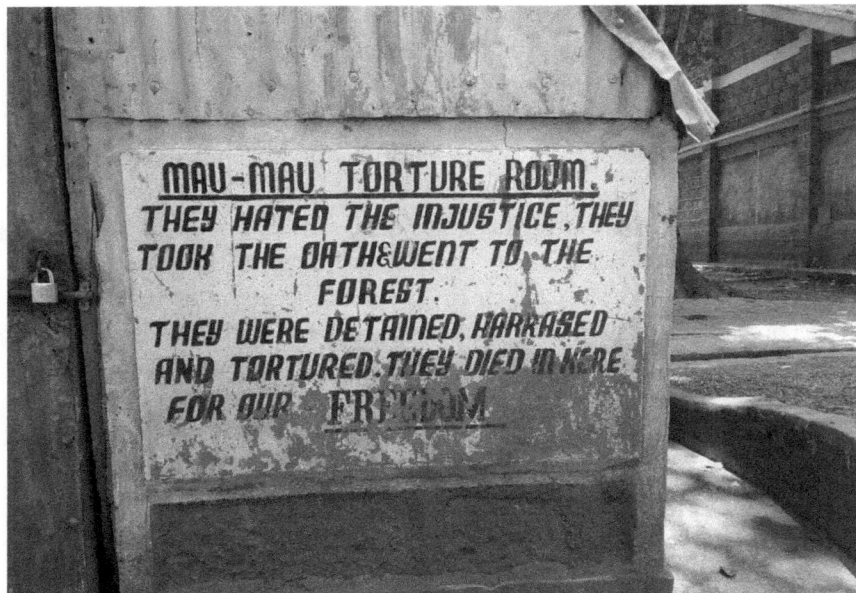

Figure 9.2. Information panel on the supposed "torture room" at Mweru High School. Photo by Gabriel Moshenska.

ture chamber" of the camp, preserved as a heritage site to teach students about the struggle for independence and the sacrifices it involved (Figure 9.2). The sign attached to the wall of this structure reads:

> Mau Mau torture room. They hated the injustice, they took the oath & went to the forest. They were detained, harassed and tortured. They died in here. For our freedom.

There is reason to doubt this interpretation. It is unlikely that a works camp would have a torture room as a distinct building: most torture took place in the context of interrogation in police stations and Home Guard stations. The structure is also very small, although it is possible that it was used as a solitary confinement cell for punishment. This is an interesting example of heritage interpretation but one that raises a number of issues about the context of our work. What would be the values and the consequences of challenging popular heritage narratives such as this, particularly as a joint Kenyan–British research team?

Within the school site we identified a communal washroom that was clearly converted from an older kitchen building with stoves and chimneys: in the walls of this building we found bricks marked MWC, for Mweru Works Camp (Figure 9.3).

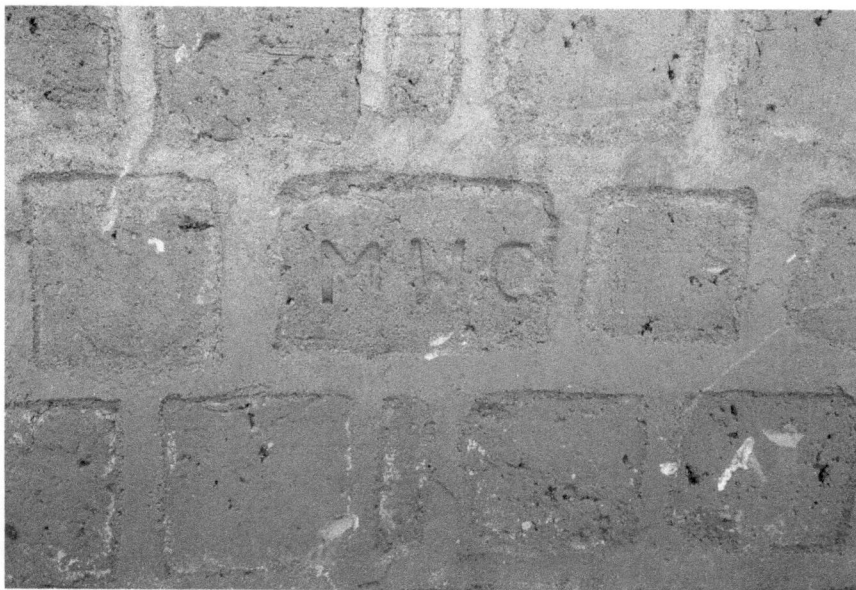

Figure 9.3. Brick stamped with "MWC" for Mweru Works Camp. Photo by Gabriel Moshenska.

Exploring the site further, we found several other buildings made of these bricks, including the headmaster's house, a classroom, and the remains of a small oven or kiln (Figures 9.4 and 9.5). Despite the use of the MWC bricks, we are uncertain at present whether these buildings were constructed during the period that the camp was in operation, but it seems very likely. In addition, the headmaster's house closely resembled the prison camp commanding officer's house at Aguthi Works Camp (see below), and it is likely that this was its original use.

We carried out a preliminary mapping and recording of the site, alongside extensive photography with the aim of photogrammetrical reconstruction of several of the structures. We intend to return to this site to conduct a survey and a full standing-buildings recording of all original camp buildings, as several of them are in poor states of preservation.

Aguthi Works Camp

Aguthi Works Camp is also a school now, known as Kangubiri Girls School. In December 1956 the population of Aguthi Works Camp was listed as 769 prisoners, almost double the 409 at Mweru at the same time. Aguthi was originally built as a "barbed-wire village" for civilian detention, either on the same site or just adjacent, but it later became one of the more brutal works

Figure 9.4. Camp building repurposed as a classroom at Mweru High School. Photo by Gabriel Moshenska.

Figure 9.5. Remains of an oven or kiln at Mweru High School. Photo by Gabriel Moshenska.

camps for Mau Mau suspects who were deemed too dangerous for release. At Aguthi there are substantial numbers of brick-built buildings surviving from the camp, both for prisoners and guards: many of the buildings had been rendered with cement following the site's acquisition by the school in the late 1960s, which had helped preserve them. Several of the larger cell-block buildings survive, some with eight and some with 16 cells. Two of these blocks are now dormitories for the pupils at the school, and two others are used as storage for tools and gardening supplies.

There are also two blocks of solitary confinement cells with sunken floors, which we were told by the school staff were filled with water to prevent detainees from sitting or lying down or sleeping—a form of torture. One of these buildings retained the original spy holes in the doors where guards could check on prisoners. From discussions with historians of the Mau Mau detention camps, we have come to be skeptical of claims relating to specific torture buildings.

Alongside the prisoner buildings is what had been the camp guards' dining and recreation hall, now used for storing furniture, and the camp administration block. The architecture of these "command" buildings is distinctive and includes the head teacher's house on the site, which closely resembles the one at Mweru.

One of the more unusual surviving features is part of the original perimeter ditch around the camp, which was originally more than five meters wide and two meters deep. Based on this location we were able to use old photographs to identify the site of the high wooden guard tower, which straddled the original gate to the camp. We also traced water pipes to locate the camp well and a swimming pool used by the guards.

As with Mweru, we got the sense of a site where extensive structures survived by virtue of being brick-built: most Mau Mau detention camps were based on wooden structures built quickly and to a low budget: one camp was reported to have cost just £40 to build, including labor and materials: the equivalent of roughly £1,000 today (Anderson 2005). Some used tents or prefabricated building elements made of wood, metal, or asbestos. These and the flimsy wood and wire fences and gates are unlikely to have endured as long as the brick buildings, although it is probable that traces of the deep ditches will survive at more sites.

Our guide around the camp was the school caretaker, who mentioned to us that on the edge of his village close to the school there was a mass grave. He did not know whether it was associated with the camp, with the barbed-wire village nearby, or with some other aspect of the Mau Mau rebellion. There is a growing acknowledgment that there are mass graves from the Mau Mau uprising scattered across Kenya, mostly forgotten or deliberately obscured (Anderson and Lane 2018). For many years it has been politically risky to commemorate Mau Mau, which was only removed from the list of illegal organizations in Kenya in 2003. They were not so straightforwardly regarded as national liberation heroes like other anticolonial movements such as the SWAPO party in Namibia and ZANU-PF party in Zimbabwe (Hughes 2017). For this reason, the mass graves, the camps, and other sites associated with Mau Mau are mostly unrecorded, unprotected, and increasingly erased. The dynamics of Mau Mau heritage and memory in Kenya remain complicated and contested (Coombes et al. 2014; Wahome et al. 2016).

"Emergency" and "Changing the Narrative"

The aim of MBC's work is to be public-facing and accessible, reaching new audiences, especially young people. During our fieldwork we recorded video diaries for YouTube and wrote reports for crowd-funding donors. In January 2020 the MBC held a public event in London in collaboration with the newspaper *Informer East Africa* and hosted by the London Africa Centre, a cultural hub for the African diaspora in the United Kingdom. The event included both a two-day program of talks and debates titled "Changing the Narrative" and an exhibition of MBC research and digital outputs titled "Emergency." It was funded in part by a grant from UCL/Gothenburg Centre for Critical Heritage Studies because one of the main purposes of the exhibition was to showcase the results of the fieldwork outlined above. "Changing the Narrative" was a set of themed panel debates on the subject of colonial heritage, with a focus on the following themes:

Archives, Libraries, and Collections—as contested possessions and knowledge spaces in colonial contexts.
Repatriation—of looted objects in Western museums but also of archives and records.
Decolonization—a critical examination beyond the buzzwords focusing on the intellectually impoverishing legacies of Western hegemony.
Reparations—if colonialism was a crime, what are the penalties and how will past injustices from slavery to exploitation and war be redressed? How can these movements create a radically fairer world?

The exhibition *Emergency: Sites and Stories of the Mau Mau Conflict* displayed the outcome of fieldwork, research, and digital heritage. The exhibition was split into three sections: Emergency Sites, presenting our initial fieldwork on two former detention camps; Emergency Stories, presenting three oral histories of elderly Mau Mau veterans who fought for independence from the

British; and a selection of 3-D digital maps and reconstructions of former detention camps developed in partnership with African Digital Heritage and using the results of our initial fieldwork and archival research.

Speakers and discussants included anthropologists, museum curators, African politicians, members of the MBC collective, archaeologists, filmmakers, researchers, and human rights activists. The audience of several hundred included young people from the African diaspora community in London. The impressive roster of speakers was itself a testimony to the MBC's networking success.

Discussion

The manipulation of history is a feature of reactionary populist governments everywhere: erasures, oversimplifications, and whole-cloth fabrications of the past sit alongside "just so" mythical narratives of ancient ethnogenesis, victimhood, and divine election (Gardner 2017; Traverso 2019). The Conservative government in the United Kingdom made the whitewashing of British imperial and colonial history a front in its contrived culture war, but this is only the most recent episode in a centuries-long process of violence, denial, and heritage-making. The news media and educational and cultural institutions are all complicit in these processes of censorship and gagging.

In contemporary Britain, Kenya, and elsewhere, these edifices of "common sense," built upon national and colonial myth, are crumbling in the face of antiracist and anticolonialist activism. In response, the forces of reaction are baring their teeth, issuing direct threats to scholars, teachers, and cultural and heritage institutions (Hofmann et al. 2021).

In this chapter we have made a case for a specific type of response to this threat: an agile, interdisciplinary, transnational heritage activist network that makes use of the opportunities presented by digital media as well as more traditional methods of historical and archaeological research and communication. Communities like the MBC are Manuel Castells' (2015) "networks of outrage and hope" on a micro scale, using technology to amplify our message and reach wide audiences.

Can this approach mount a real challenge to the "common sense" of colonial heritage in UK culture? We have sought to champion and celebrate an approach that is rooted in network-building, solidarity, and a degree of independence from "official" institutions and forums. But it is also important to recognize the ongoing challenges that we face. The MBC is entirely run by volunteers who contribute their labor when and how they can alongside their jobs, families, and so on. Burnout certainly occurs, and this kind of work undoubtedly remains inaccessible to many. It is important to avoid overly idealizing such conditions, and in the future we hope to become more sustainable and resilient in how we work. In the face of reactionary school curricula and national heritage narratives, activist networks are small fry.

However hard it tries to avoid it, Britain is experiencing a long-overdue reckoning with the heritage of empire. Like the postwar German struggles with the historical facts of the Third Reich, Britain's *Vergangenheitsbewälti-gung* can be seen as a petty squabble between historians or as a struggle for the conscience of a nation. One curious aspect of Britain's post-1945, pre-9/11 wars—most of them wars of empire—is their near-total invisibility within national culture. For a nation obsessed to the point of parody with the Second World War, there is a startling lack of literature or film devoted to its successors: no British equivalent of *M*A*S*H* or *The Battle of Algiers*.

How do we respond to this absence and to the broader dominance of imperial nostalgia? Our work embodies two distinct approaches. The first is what could be called a prefigurative approach to empire heritage (see Kiddey, this volume: Chapter 7), creating resources and records for a better future, embodying values of openness and polyvocality, and working to highlight hidden and erased pasts. The resources are there for students, educators, journalists, researchers, and curious members of the public to find and use: we create, curate, and promote them to the best of our abilities.

Our second approach challenges the premise of the problem, asking instead: who does the heritage of the British Empire belong to? And we answer: not solely or even primarily to Britain. The stories of Britain's colonial wars are alive and well in the national narratives and nationalist myths of formerly colonized nations across the world, in family histories and folk songs, in community museums, veterans' associations, memorial landscapes, and public art. A great deal of the value and power of our transnational activist network lies in decentering Britain from the narratives of its own empire. By focusing on Kenya and other formerly colonized nations, we are spinning and weaving strands of a truly global history of empire from the fragments of material that already exist in rich abundance.

Note

1 Museum of British Colonialism, https://www.museumofbritishcolonialism.org/.

References Cited

Anderson, David. 2005. *Histories of the Hanged: The Dirty War in Kenya and the End of Empire*. Norton, New York.

Anderson, David. 2011. Mau Mau in the High Court and the "Lost" British Empire Archives: Colonial Conspiracy or Bureaucratic Bungle? *Journal of Imperial and Commonwealth History* 39(5): 699–716.

Anderson, David. 2015. Guilty Secrets: Deceit, Denial, and the Discovery of Kenya's "Migrated Archive." *History Workshop Journal* 80(1): 142–160.

Anderson, David, and Paul Lane. 2018. The Unburied Victims of Kenya's Mau Mau Rebellion: Where and When does the Violence End? In *Human Remains in Society: Curation and Exhibition in the Aftermath of Genocide and Mass-Violence,* edited by Jean-Marc Dreyfus and Élisabeth Anstett, pp. 14–37. Manchester University Press, Manchester, England.

Andrews, Kehinde. 2021. *The New Age of Empire: How Racism and Colonialism Still Rule the World.* Penguin, London.

Bennett, Huw. 2013. *Fighting the Mau Mau: The British Army and Counter-Insurgency in the Kenya Emergency.* Cambridge University Press, Cambridge.

Blunt, Robert. 2013. Kenyatta's Lament: Oaths and the Transformation of Ritual Ideologies in Colonial Kenya. *HAU: Journal of Ethnographic Theory* 3(3): 167–193.

Cammaerts, Bart. 2022. The Abnormalisation of Social Justice: The "Anti-Woke Culture War" Discourse in the UK. *Discourse & Society* 33(6): 730–743.

Castells, Manuel. 2015.*Networks of Outrage and Hope: Social Movements in the Internet Age.* John Wiley & Sons, Oxford.

Clough, Marshall. 1998. *Mau Mau Memoirs: History, Memory, and Politics.* Lynne Rienner, Boulder, Colorado.

Cobain, Ian. 2016. *The History Thieves: Secrets, Lies and the Shaping of a Modern Nation.* Portobello Books, London.

Coombes, Annie E., Lotte Hughes, and Karega-Munene (editors). 2014. *Managing Heritage, Making Peace: History, Identity and Memory in Contemporary Kenya.* I.B. Tauris, London.

Crehan, Kate. 2016. *Gramsci's Common Sense.* Duke University Press, Durham, North Carolina.

Duffy, Aoife. 2015. Legacies of British Colonial Violence: Viewing Kenyan Detention Camps through the Hanslope Disclosure. *Law and History Review* 33(3): 489–542.

Edgerton, Robert. 1990. *Mau Mau: An African Crucible.* I.B. Tauris, London.

Elkins, Caroline. 2005. *Imperial Reckoning: The Untold Story of Britain's Gulag in Kenya.* Macmillan, London.

Fill in the Blanks. 2020. *South London Students Hack 5000 Newspapers to Call on the Government to Mandate the Teaching of Britain's Colonial History.* Fill in the Blanks, press release, January 9. https://medium.com/@fillintheblanksuk/south-london-students -hack-5000-newspapers-to-call-on-the-government-to-mandate-the-teaching-of -c2cb60b1c5e2, accessed November 1, 2022.

Fowler, Corinne. 2020. *Green Unpleasant Land: Creative Responses to Rural Britain's Colonial Connections.* Peepal Tree Press, Leeds, England.

French, David. 2012. Nasty Not Nice: British Counter-Insurgency Doctrine and Practice, 1945–1967. *Small Wars & Insurgencies* 23(4–5):744–761.

Furedi, Frank. 1989. *The Mau Mau War in Perspective.* Ohio University Press, Athens.

Gardner, Andrew. 2017. Brexit, Boundaries and Imperial Identities: A Comparative View. *Journal of Social Archaeology* 17(1): 3–26.

Gopal, Priyamvada. 2019. *Insurgent Empire: Anticolonial Resistance and British Dissent.* Verso, London.

Hall, Catherine, Nicholas Draper, Keith McClelland, Katie Donington, and Rachel Lang. 2014. *Legacies of British Slave-Ownership: Colonial Slavery and the Formation of Victorian Britain.* Cambridge University Press, Cambridge.

Hofmann, Daniela, Emily Hanscam, Martin Furholt, Martin Bača, Samantha Reiter, Alessandro Vanzetti, Kostas Kotsakis, et al. 2021. Populism, Identity Politics, and the Archaeology of Europe. *European Journal of Archaeology* 24(4): 519–555.

Hughes, Lotte. 2011. "Truth Be Told": Some Problems with Historical Revisionism in Kenya. *African Studies* 70(2): 182–201.

Hughes, Lotte. 2017. Memorialisation and Mau Mau: A critical review. In *Dedan Kimathi on Trial: Colonial Justice and Popular Memory in Kenya's Mau Mau Rebellion,* edited by Julie Macarthur, pp. 339–373. Ohio University Press, Athens.

Jasanoff, Maya. 2020. Misremembering the British Empire: How Did the British Become So Blinkered about Their Nation's Imperial History? *New Yorker,* October 26. https://www.newyorker.com/magazine/2020/11/02/misremembering-the-british-empire.

Kanogo, Tabitha. 1987. *Squatters and the Roots of Mau Mau, 1905–63.* Ohio University Press, Athens.

Kariuki, Josiah Mwangi. 1963. *Mau Mau Detainee: The Account by a Kenya African of His Experiences in Detention Camps, 1953–1960.* Oxford University Press, Oxford.

Keck, Margaret, and Kathryn Sikkink. 1998. *Activists beyond Borders: Advocacy Networks in International Politics.* Cornell University Press, Ithaca, New York.

Kwoba, Brian, Roseanne Chantiluke, and Athinagamso Nkopo (editors). 2018. *Rhodes Must Fall: The Struggle to Decolonise the Racist Heart of Empire.* Zed, London.

Massing, Katharina. 2021. Statues: The UK's Plan to "Retain and Explain" Problem Monuments Is a Backwards Step. *The Conversation,* March 9. https://theconversation.com/statues-the-uks-plan-to-retain-and-explain-problem-monuments-is-a-backwards-step-156430.

Mitchell, Peter. 2021. *Imperial Nostalgia: How the British Conquered Themselves.* Manchester University Press, Manchester, England.

Moshenska, Gabriel. 2020. Creating a Museum of British Colonialism. *New African,* September 16. https://newafricanmagazine.com/24035.

Pieck, Sonja. 2013. Transnational Activist Networks: Mobilization between Emotion and Bureaucracy. *Social Movement Studies* 12(2): 121–137.

Rebisz, Beth. 2021. Violent Reform: Gendered Experiences of Colonial Developmental Counter-Insurgency in Kenya, 1954–1960. PhD dissertation, Department of History, Bristol University, Bristol, England. https://doi.org/10.48683/1926.00115139.

Traverso, Enzo. 2019. *The New Faces of Fascism: Populism and the Far Right.* Verso, London.

Wahome, Ephraim, Felix Kiruthu, and Susan Mwangi. 2016. Tracing a Forgotten Heritage: The Place of Mau Mau Memory and Culture in Kenya. In *Conservation of Natural and Cultural Heritage in Kenya: A Cross-Disciplinary Approach,* edited by Anne-Marie Deisser and Mugwima Njuguna, pp. 212–226. UCL Press, London.

IV

Comparing and Contrasting
Archaeology's Study of Past Societies
with the Study of Contemporary
Material Worlds

10

Ancient Chaco, Historic Texas

A Self-Reflexive Tale

RUTH M. VAN DYKE

Community-based or collaborative archaeology is often portrayed as a force working in tandem with progressive social agendas, helping to empower people to learn about and protect their own pasts. Recently, however, Alfredo González-Ruibal and colleagues (2018) have pointed out that facile "heritage" archaeology can be deployed in reactionary populism, bolstering exclusionary narratives about national exceptionalism, for example. It does not therefore follow that all community-based archaeology supports a populist agenda. This critique should, however, impel archaeologists to think critically and self-reflexively about our community-based practices. Conversations around these issues were the impetus for this volume.

As González-Ruibal and Randall McGuire (this volume: Chapter 1) describe, there are many kinds of populisms, and many kinds of communities. Populisms share the perspective that political authority should rest with "the people," as opposed to elites. Reactionary populism refers to a right-wing brand of populism in which there is a desire to return to an imagined, simpler status quo characterized by homogeneous social identity and conservative morality. Reactionary populism tends to be xenophobic, racist, essentialist, patriarchal, and anti-intellectual. In the United States, reactionary populism is synonymous with the supporters of Donald Trump. These supporters tend to be white, religious, conservative, antieducation, antiscience, antifeminist, and anti-LGBTQ. They feel threatened by power in the hands of people who are not white; they want to militarize our borders to keep brown people out. In Florida, Texas, and some other states, they are banning books. As with most reactionary populist movements, note the strong focus on scapegoating.

Archaeologists tend not to adhere to reactionary populist agendas; nonetheless, our archaeological work can and has been deployed to support populist and even fascist ideas about the past (e.g., Hakenbeck 2019). This should give us pause. Is there a link between community-based archaeology and reactionary populism in the United States? This is the central question for the authors in this volume.

In the United States, most archaeologists doing community-based scholarship are either working to empower marginalized groups (e.g., Atalay 2012; Franklin and Lee 2020), or they are engaging local residents in the practice of archaeology (e.g., Miroff and Versaggi 2020). I am involved with both kinds of communities. In the pages that follow, I present two case studies. In the Chaco Canyon example, I am a settler-colonist scholar working to amplify the voices of marginalized Indigenous communities who have competing interests in the archaeological past. In the Texas case, I am an insider anthropologist working with a group of white, middle-class settler descendants seeking to celebrate an ethnic identity. I have very different kinds of roles and relationships to the communities in these two research areas. Both cases involve a great deal of self-reflexive thought. In neither case, I argue, does the archaeological work serve reactionary populism.

Ancient Chaco

At Chaco Canyon, in the Native American Southwest United States, I am a settler-colonist archaeologist working with Indigenous descendant communities, including the Pueblo and Diné (Navajo) peoples. As a scholar of the ancient Southwest, I am committed to advancing an Indigenous archaeology in which Native descendant communities control their own histories, materials, bodies, and intellectual property (Bernardini et al. 2021; Colwell 2017; Van Dyke 2020). This often entails ceding my archaeological authority to that of Indigenous experts. Indigenous peoples do not speak with one voice, however, and I navigate complex situations involving diverse factions and interests.

A millennium ago (ca. 850–1150 CE), Chaco Canyon was the center of life for Native peoples whose settlements spanned an area the size of Great Britain (some 100,000 sq. mi.) (Figure 10.1). Monumental architecture, roads, earthworks, rock art, and astronomical markers contributed to Chaco Canyon's designation as one of the United States' first national parks (1907), a UNESCO World Heritage Site (1987), and an International Dark Skies Park (2013). The surrounding Greater Chaco Landscape contains several hun-

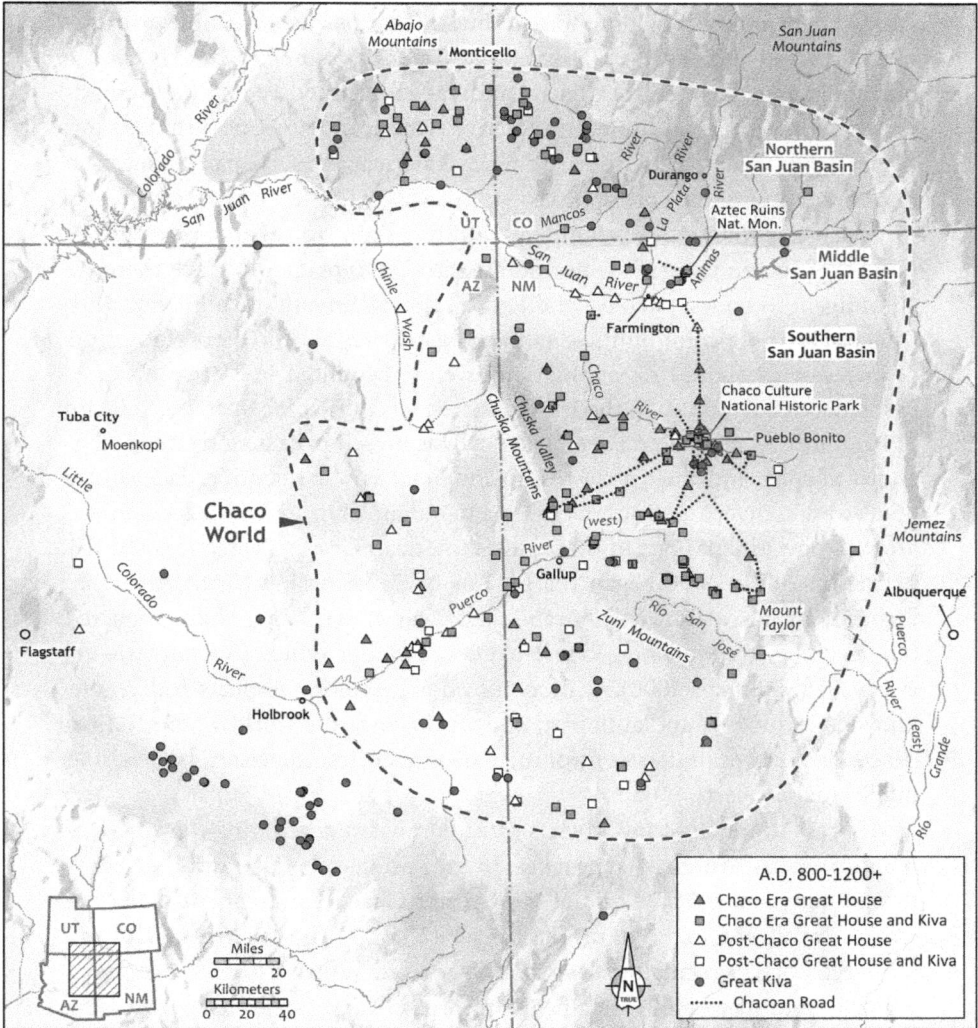

Figure 10.1. Map showing the known extent of Chacoan great houses and other features across the Greater Chaco Landscape, an area of some 100,000 square miles in northwest New Mexico, northeast Arizona, southeast Utah, and southwest Colorado, on the Colorado Plateau, in the southwestern United States. Catherine Gilman, courtesy of Archaeology Southwest.

dred associated Chacoan settlements, roads, agricultural fields, shrines, and rock art panels (Van Dyke and Heitman 2021). Most of the Greater Chaco Landscape is not part of a monument but includes territory administered by various private entities, the US Bureau of Land Management (BLM), and the Navajo Nation. The Greater Chaco Landscape is claimed by many stakeholders, including (but not limited to) Native American tribes, government bureaucrats, archaeologists, tourists, Euro-American and Hispano-American residents, and mining corporations.

Chaco Canyon figures prominently in the origin stories and sacred geographies of contemporary Pueblo and Navajo (Diné) peoples. In fact, there are 23 Indigenous tribes, pueblos, and nations that claim cultural affiliation with Chaco. For these communities, archaeological sites are the literal footprints of ancestors, honored monuments to events recounted in Native histories (Seowtewa et al. 2021). In the United States, a settler-colonist state (Veracini 2010), Euro-American archaeologists such as myself have long treated Indigenous peoples and their ancestors' belongings as our scientific data. Today Southwest archaeology is undergoing a paradigm shift toward a decolonized archaeology. The passage of the Native American Graves Protection and Repatriation Act in 1990 began the process of transforming North American archaeology into a more collaborative endeavor; these changes have impacted our teaching, our research, our practices, and our ethics (Kuwanwisiwma et al. 2018; Silliman 2008). A decolonized archaeology respects Indigenous knowledge, history, and authority, and works toward a world where Native-descendant communities control their own histories, materials, bodies, and intellectual property.

At present, much of my work is directed toward amplifying the voices of my Indigenous American colleagues. In the past decade this work has veered toward activism, as the fabric of the Greater Chaco Landscape is being destroyed by oil, gas, and coal mining (Figure 10.2). Without going too far into the weeds of US regulatory laws and processes, suffice it to say that existing legislation is woefully insufficient to protect Chacoan archaeology at the landscape level, let alone the qualitative aspects of this fragile area such as viewscapes, soundscapes, and night skies. The BLM, which oversees much oil and gas mining on the Greater Chaco Landscape, is supposed to solicit input from all stakeholders prior to granting mineral extraction leases. In practice, however, Native concerns have been largely ignored. I have been working as part of a coalition of archaeological and environmental nonprofits who seek to convince the BLM to listen seriously to Native concerns before granting mineral leases. I recently codirected an open-access, hybrid book project that features videos of Hopi, Zuni, Acoma, and Diné cultural experts explaining,

Figure 10.2. An oil well located on Navajo Nation land 750 m from Pierre's Chacoan community. The well is one of 14 that are visible and audible from the Chacoan community. Photo by author.

in their own words, the importance of the Greater Chaco Landscape to their peoples (Van Dyke and Heitman 2021).

I would argue that, in this context, I am allying myself with Indigenous peoples in direct opposition to the forces of reactionary populism in the United States. Oil, gas, and coal corporations are vocally supported by the antiscience climate deniers in the Trump camp. Since climate change is an illusion, the populists argue, we might as well continue to mine and burn oil, gas, and coal (never mind the astronomical profits made by the mineral extraction corporations). Furthermore, reactionary populists in the United States see white European domination over the physical landscape as a God-given right. This view is grounded in the history of the development of the BLM itself. In the early nineteenth century, the Doctrine of Discovery, part of a US Supreme Court ruling, was used to justify seizure of Indigenous territories on the grounds that these lands were vacant and undeveloped—hence, the creation of a General Land Office (which in 1946 became the BLM) to mete out and administrate the proper use and "management" of "vacant" lands within US borders. I do not mean to argue that the BLM is run by reactionary populists; rather, I argue that aspects of reactionary populist ideology (climate change denial, antiscience, pro-white domination) find support within the settler-colonist-created apparatus of the US government. So, on several fronts, my work with Indigenous communities to fight against oil and gas development near Chaco Canyon can be seen as an instance of community-based archaeology *against* reactionary populism.

But the situation is not as straightforward as it might appear. Indigenous communities do not speak with one voice. In fact, Chacoan archaeology is a flashpoint for disputes over access, land use, and knowledge claims among Native groups with contradictory interests (Cordell and Kintigh 2010; Schillaci and Bustard 2010; Van Dyke 2017a). Tensions between Pueblo and Diné peoples, in particular, have long simmered. This is due in part to the US government's nineteenth-century implementation of reservation boundaries and laws that apportioned water, minerals, and other previously shared resources to one group rather than another. Today it is impossible for Chacoan archaeologists to work on this landscape without signaling political affiliations with one or more Native entities—we do this by the very language we use to describe the past. If we call ancient Chacoans "Anasazi," we are signaling to Pueblo peoples that we accept (or are open to) Diné interpretations that accord the Navajo a stake in Chacoan archaeology (and, by extension, a legitimate claim to the cultural and natural resources on the Greater Chaco Landscape). If we use the word "Ancestral Pueblo," we are seen by the Diné to be explicitly denying these claims. Attempts to circumvent the issue by using words like "the Chacoans" or "the inhabitants" may be met with mistrust or derision by both sides (Van Dyke 2017a).

In this context, it may not be surprising that the Navajo government is officially opposing recent legislation to help protect the Greater Chaco Landscape. In June 2023 the Joe Biden administration issued a twenty-year moratorium on new mineral leases within a "buffer zone" surrounding Chaco Culture National Historical Monument—the culmination of nearly a decade of work involving coalitions of Indigenous activists, archaeologists, and environmentalists (Figure 10.3). The "buffer zone" area contains Chacoan archaeological sites claimed by 23 pueblos, nations, and tribes, but the area lies within the contemporary political boundaries of the Navajo Nation. The current political leaders of the Navajo Nation are framing the issue as an example of settler-colonialist overreach on sovereign Navajo lands and are backing a bill that would rescind the protection. Despite the official stance of their government, many local Diné residents oppose continued oil and gas mining, citing noise and chemical and light pollution (Denetclaw 2023). The All-Pueblo Governor's Council is outraged that the Navajo Nation is officially opposing a move that would protect Pueblo heritage.

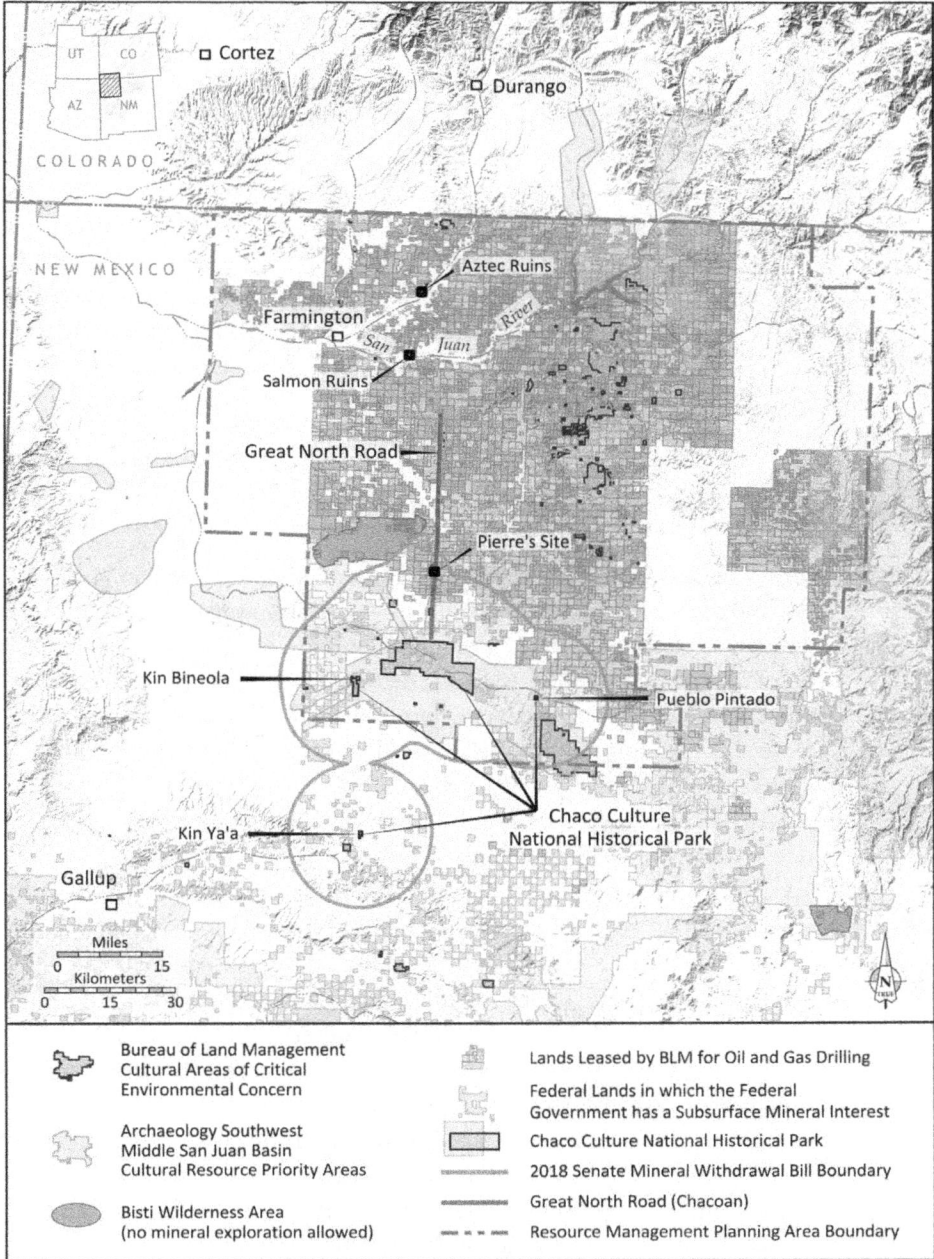

Figure 10.3. Map showing the 10-mile-wide "buffer zone" surrounding Chaco Culture National Historical Park. The buffer zone boundary is outlined at the bottom of the map. Shaded areas to the north have already been leased for mineral extraction. Catherine Gilman, courtesy of Archaeology Southwest.

In my life as a Chaco scholar, I am in the thick of these struggles, working with both Pueblo and Diné cultural experts in Chaco. I must always keep in mind my position as a Euro-American archaeologist working with Native communities whose trust must be earned, whose priorities are not necessarily congruent with my own, and who by rights should have control over the production of knowledge about the Chacoan past. Owning my own positionality, I am attempting to thread the needle, allying with Indigenous cultural leaders who, like me, want to protect the archaeology at the expense of the mining. I have unpacked this situation here to demonstrate some of the complexities of working with Indigenous communities (plural!) and to illustrate that Chacoan community-based archaeology is not simply about amplifying Indigenous community voices in opposition to white, reactionary, populist aims.

Historic Texas

I am working in Texas with a very different, yet equally fascinating community. Here I am an "insider anthropologist"—a white, seventh-generation Texan descended from Alsatian immigrants who arrived in Castroville, southwest of San Antonio, in the 1840s. A decade ago I began a partnership with the Castro Colonies Heritage Association (CCHA), a group promoting the history of Alsatian migrants to the area in the 1840s. I have found that the political landscape of Castroville is no less complicated than that of Chaco (Van Dyke 2017b). Before describing the community with whom I work, let me provide some historical background.

Official Texan identity today can look very white and Euro-American, grounded in a familiar colonial narrative featuring hardy white pioneers valiantly braving difficulties to carving out a country in virgin territory. However, Texas has a long and multifaceted Indigenous, Hispanic, and Black history (Clemons 2008). The arrival of white, southern US culture in Texas dates back two centuries, to a time when Comanche, Lipan Apache, and other Indigenous groups held most of a territory formally controlled by Mexico (Mexico gained independence from Spain in 1821). Mexican settlers moving north into Texas were plagued by Indigenous raids, so the Mexican government invited southern US white farmers and planters (mostly of Irish and English descent) to settle in the territory. The white southerners brought enslaved Africans. Slavery, however, was illegal in Mexico—a key but rarely acknowledged factor that drove Texas to break away from Mexico in 1836 and form an independent republic. The white southern founders of the newly formed Republic of Texas needed to stave off the Mexicans to the south and the Comanche and Apache everywhere else. They solved this problem by inviting empresarios—businessmen and speculators—to bring white European settlers to Texas with promises of free land. The Alsatian immigrants were part of this process (Weaver 1985), as were Czechs, Poles, and thousands of German immigrants from Bavaria (Jordan 1966).

Between 1842 and 1844, a Portuguese empresario named Henri di Castro financed the immigration of over 2,000 Alsatians to Texas, including my great-great-great-grandparents. On September 2, 1844, Castro led 27 colonists west from San Antonio to break ground on his first colony—Castroville, on the banks of the Medina River. Although Castroville was founded as an Alsatian colony, the Alsatians were by no means the only group in the area. An established Hispanic population had been in residence in San Antonio for 150 years. A southern white population had been present since the 1820s, together with their enslaved Black workers. And there was an increasingly oppressed and angry Indigenous population. The Alsatian immigrants were mostly peasant farmers who had been lured to Texas under false pretenses to serve the interests of the monied classes who controlled the state government; once they arrived and fully grasped the difficulties of their situation as settler-colonists in a hostile territory, many who had the means to do so returned to Europe. CCHA ancestors were those who stayed and persevered, creating an insular community that has retained elements of Alsatian language, music, and cuisine to the present day.

The CCHA, founded in the 1980s, actively promotes the area's historic connections to Alsace. The CCHA is a vibrant center of community life for a core group of about 50 well-educated, middle- and upper-class residents who identify as Alsatian descendants and who have the leisure and means to support research into their own heritage. The CCHA sponsors activities including genealogical research, lectures by local historians, and an annual trip to Alsace. This revitalization of Alsatian heritage has accelerated over the past decade. There is a local troupe of Alsatian dancers, a new Alsatian Festival, and the town has established cultural exchanges with their villages of origin in contemporary Alsace (Figure 10.4). In 2020 the CCHA hosted a delegation of Alsatian (French) schoolchildren in Castroville. In Blodelsheim, Alsace, on the banks of the Rhine, a French sister village hosts an annual Texas-style barbecue every year, where French residents wear cowboy hats, Texan visitors enjoy Alsatian Riesling, and everyone fraternizes in a polyglot mix of French, German, and English.

Recently the CCHA acquired a historic residence—the Biry/Ahr House—that they wished to turn into a "living history center" to celebrate and share the achievements of Alsatian pioneer forebears. The property contains a much-

Figure 10.4. Members of the Alsatian Dancers prepare to perform at the Alsatian Festival, Castroville, Texas, October 2021. Photo by author.

remodeled rock-built house and a "dog-trot"-style log cabin—both common nineteenth-century Texan vernacular constructions—as well as multiple privies, a well, and other domestic features. When I serendipitously arrived on the scene in 2012, CCHA leaders invited me to help them with the archaeology. Between 2013 and 2016, my students and I conducted four phases of testing and excavation at the Biry/Ahr House. The CCHA paid for the project and welcomed us into the community with famously friendly Texas hospitality. They housed us in their homes; cooked our meals; invited us to their weddings, barbecues, and funerals—in short, they integrated us into the local community of Alsatian descendants, and I had special credibility as a descendant of one of the founders.

Our excavations inside the rock structure proved to be fascinating. We peeled back four floors associated with specific occupations, and we found evidence of two earlier structures beneath the existing building, including datable evidence of construction events plausibly be associated with the original Alsatian settlers. By combining our archaeological data with historical narratives and census data, we can tell compelling stories about the material and social changes that took place over the long life of this house. Overall,

Figure 10.5. The Castro Colonies Living History Center (the Biry/Ahr house), after restoration by the CCHA, in August 2018. Photo by Patricia Markert.

the archaeological picture that emerged was one of people building in local architectural vernacular, eating and drinking the same things (beef and pork barbecue), wearing the same clothing, and using the same kinds of domestic materials as their Texan (Anglophile, German, and Hispanic) neighbors.

Meanwhile, the CCHA moved forward with their creation of a living history center at the site (Figure 10.5). The Castro Colonies Living History Center, recently opened to the public, focuses on a romanticized moment that has become part of local collective memory: the pioneer narrative of the original Alsatian settlers (Van Dyke 2017b). The house is decorated with a collection of local antiques to evoke a sense of nineteenth-century pioneer life as the CCHA members imagine it looked for their ancestors. Each spring CCHA members use the house to stage "They Came by Ship," a celebratory reenactment of the founding of Castroville.

On the surface, it may seem that our archaeological work in Castroville could be used to serve exactly the kind of reactionary populism cautioned against by González-Ruibal and others. Certainly, reactionary populism is strongly present in Texas. I probably do not need to elaborate on Texas' infamy in this regard, but here are a few facts. The state was carried by Republicans in the last 10 presidential elections; Electoral College votes went for Trump in 2016 and 2020. A growing list of books banned in Texas school districts includes titles by Dr. Seuss and Judy Blume. Under the leadership of Trump supporter and right-wing governor Greg Abbott, Texas has enacted one of the strictest antiabortion laws in the nation. Abbott has also instituted one of the most notoriously harsh border policies in the United States, filling the Rio Grande (the border between Texas and Mexico) with razor wire to maim and kill would-be crossers, caging and separating children from their families, and busing migrants to Vice President Kamala Harris' home in a cruel publicity stunt (Goodman 2023).

In Castroville, are our archaeological labors contributing to an uncomplicated celebration of European heritage in Texas, particularly one that leaves out the contributions of others who were and are on the scene? When the white Alsatian heritage of Castroville is celebrated, what happens to the Hispanic, Indigenous, and Black history of the community? My graduate students and I have contemplated this question. Black and Indigenous people are less visible in the local population today, but we note that approximately half of the current population of the area is Hispanic. In the twentieth century, families from Mexico were the primary work force employed by a local, Alsatian, and German-owned brick-making plant. Schools and Catholic churches were segregated "white" and Hispanic between the 1920s and 1950s. As late as the 1970s, children were forbidden from speaking Spanish in school, and "members only" policies at dance halls allowed doormen to reject people of Mexican descent at their discretion (Markert 2022).

But before jumping to the conclusion that our archaeological project is, indeed, serving populism, it is important to consider the motivations of the CCHA leaders in celebrating their Alsatian heritage. Although generally politically conservative, I would not characterize them as reactionary populists. Members of the community have sympathy for, and interest in the welfare of, marginalized groups. Aside from a sense of pride in their distinctive history, I can see at least two important reasons CCHA members are interested in Alsatian heritage. The first reason is economic. Neighboring communities in Texas have exploited aspects of European heritage to become very successful tourist destinations; Fredericksburg, Texas, for example, is locally famous for German food, antiques, beer, and (more recently) wine. Castroville, situated on a major highway 15 minutes southwest of San Antonio, is ideally positioned to capture some tourist dollars if it can position itself as a weekend destination, and Alsatian heritage is a good potential hook. The second reason is not unrelated. San Antonio is a fast-growing city of 1.5 million people that is experiencing suburban sprawl. For most of its existence, Castroville has been a village of just a few thousand people, many of whom know one another; interconnections and intermarriages among local families go back seven generations or more. Today, Castroville is in danger of beyond swallowed by the new subdivisions springing up around San Antonio, and there are many new and unfamiliar faces at the stores in town. Local inhabitants do not want to lose their connections to one another, and to this place; they do not want to become just one more in a series of hundreds of San Antonio "bedroom communities." Celebrating Alsatian heritage is one important way for locals to hold onto a sense of identity in a rapidly changing world.

Can archaeology be used to create a space for other narratives, dialogues, and heritages in the Castro Colonies? As an insider anthropologist with the authority and access that comes with that position, I have searched for ways to complicate the pioneer narrative, to try to use the archaeology to raise uncomfortable questions rather than reify pat answers. This work is ongoing, but there are promising indications that it can be successful. For example, we ensured that an exhibit on our archaeological work at the Biry/Ahr house includes Indigenous lithic tools we recovered during the excavation as well as links to a discussion of the Native presence in the area prior to and during colonization. Patricia Markert's (2022) dissertation research recorded Hispanic oral histories and instigated some painful conversations around the segregated Hispanic past. During my most recent visit to Castroville, I became aware of another potential site for archaeological excavation. An African American family lived on the outskirts of Castroville until the mid-twentieth century. They were accepted in the community and well-known locally as the "Black Alsatians"; their patriarch was a well-digger who reputedly spoke fluent Alsatian. Descendants today live in San Antonio, and the property is likely to soon fall under the developer's ax. When I raised the possibility of making this site the focus of a new local archaeological project and trying to involve Black heritage organizations in San Antonio, CCHA leaders enthusiastically embraced this possibility. Like me, they think it would be interesting and important to share the African American part of the Castroville story.

Conclusions

In the opening chapter of this volume, González-Ruibal and McGuire challenge archaeologists to think about the relationship between reactionary populism and community-based or collaborative archaeology. They cautioned that a turn toward populism may neuter archaeologists' ability to act as organic intellectuals or to work for positive changes in the world. In the context of my Chaco work, as a settler-colonist archaeologist, my primary job has been to cede archaeological authority or to use it to help bolster Native claims to power in a fight *against* the forces of reactionary populism. However, Native communities do not speak with one voice regarding Chaco, and I have had to make decisions about crafting allegiances with some groups at the expense of others. Concerns with reactionary populist agendas might feel more applicable in Texas, but such an analysis would be too simplistic. Here my students and I are using our scholarly positions to exert rather than cede authority. My position as an insider anthropologist has afforded me opportunities to challenge a monolithic narrative of Euro-American pioneer history and to help develop a more inclusive picture of the Texas past. In both situations, it has been important for me as an archaeologist to be self-reflexive and ever mindful of power relations and larger ethical goals.

In Chaco and in Texas, nothing is as simple as good versus bad community archaeology or challenging versus enabling populist perceptions about the past. Whether archaeologists become unwitting pawns of populism rests on the archaeologists themselves remaining self-reflexively aware of their identities as political actors and self-consciously staking out positions that fit with their own ethics.

Acknowledgments

My collaborative work on the Greater Chaco Landscape is funded by the National Park Service. The Greater Chaco Landscapes project involved a cast of over 20 contributors. I particularly want to thank my coeditor, Carrie Heitman, and co-organizer, Steve Lekson, as well as Indigenous collaborators Octavius Seowtewa, Curtis Quam, and Presley Haskie (A:shiwi); Ernest Vallo Jr. (Acoma); and Will Tsosie and Davina Two Bears (Diné). In Texas my collaborative work is funded by the Castro Colonies Heritage Association; fieldwork and laboratory analysis has been carried out by a legion of Binghamton University student volunteers. I particularly appreciate PhD student Patricia Markert's intellectual and substantive contributions to the Texas project.

References Cited

Atalay, S. 2012. *Community-Based Archaeology: Research with, by, and for Indigenous and Local Communities.* University of California Press, Berkeley.
Bernardini, Wesley, Stewart Koyiyumptewa, Greg Schachner, and Leigh J. Kuwanwisiwma (editors). 2021. *Becoming Hopi: A History.* University of Arizona Press, Tucson.
Clemons, Leigh. 2008. *Branding Texas: Performing Culture in the Lone Star State.* University of Texas Press, Austin.

Colwell, Chip. 2017. *Plundered Skulls and Stolen Spirits: Inside the Fight to Reclaim Native America's Culture.* University of Chicago Press, Chicago.

Cordell, Linda S., and Keith W. Kintigh. 2010. Reply to Schillaci and Bustard. *PoLAR: Political and Legal Anthropology Review* 33(2): 378–383.

Denetclaw, Pauly. 2023. Navajo Nation Opposes Any Chaco Canyon Buffer Zone. *Source NM,* July 17, 2023. https://sourcenm.com/2023/07/17/navajo-nation-opposes-any -chaco-canyon-buffer-zone/.

Franklin, Maria, and Nedra Lee. 2020. African American Descendants, Community Outreach, and the Ransom and Sarah Williams Farmstead Project. *Journal of Community Archaeology & Heritage* 7(2): 135–148.

González-Ruibal, Alfredo, Pablo Alonso González, and Felipe Criado-Boado. 2018. Against Reactionary Populism: Towards a New Public Archaeology. *Antiquity* 92(362): 507–515, 525–527.

Goodman, J. David. 2023. Gov. Abbott's Policing of Texas Border Pushes Limits of State Power. *New York Times,* July 26, 2023. https://www.nytimes.com/2023/07/26/us/texas -greg-abbott-border-migrants.html.

Hakenbeck, Susanne. 2019. Genetics, Archaeology, and the Far Right: An Unholy Trinity. *World Archaeology* 51(4): 517–527.

Jordan, Terry G. 1966. *German Seed in Texas Soil: Immigrant Farmers in Nineteenth-century Texas.* University of Texas Press, Austin.

Kuwanwisiwma, Leigh J., T. J. Ferguson, and Chip Colwell (editors). 2018. *Footprints of Hopi History: Hopihiniwtiput Kukveni'at.* University of Arizona Press, Tucson.

Markert, Patricia G. 2022. Making Alsatian Texas: An Archaeological, Linguistic, and Ethnographic Study of Place and Migration in Castroville and D'Hanis, Texas. PhD dissertation, Anthropology Department, Binghamton University–SUNY, Binghamton, New York.

Miroff, Laurie E., and Nina M. Versaggi. 2020. Community Archaeology at the Trowel's Edge. *Advances in Archaeological Practice* 8(4):398–408.

Schillaci, Michael A., and J. Wendy Bustard. 2010. Controversy and Conflict: NAGPRA and the Role of Biological Anthropology in Determining Cultural Affiliation. *PoLAR: Political and Legal Anthropology Review* 33(2): 352–373.

Seowtewa, Octavius. 2021. A:shiwi (Zuni) Perspectives (video only). In *The Greater Chaco Landscape: Ancestors, Scholarship, and Advocacy,* edited by Ruth M. Van Dyke, and Carrie C. Heitman, pp. 188–189. University Press of Colorado, Boulder.

Silliman, Stephen W. (editor). 2008. *Collaborating at the Trowel's Edge: Teaching and Learning in Indigenous Archaeology.* University of Arizona Press, Tucson.

Van Dyke, Ruth M. 2017a. Chaco Canyon: A Contested Memory Anchor in the North American Southwest. In *Between Memory Sites and Memory Networks: New Archaeological and Historical Perspectives,* edited by Kerstin P. Hofmann, Reinhard Bernbeck, and Ulrike Sommer, pp. 195–221. Freien Universität Berlin und der Humboldt-Universität zu Berlin, Berlin Studies of the Ancient World 45, Edition Topoi, Berlin.

Van Dyke, Ruth M. 2017b. Durable Stones, Mutable Pasts: Bundled Memory in the Alsatian Community of Castroville, Texas. In "Webs of Memory, Frames of Power: Collective Remembering in the Archaeological Record," edited by David W. Mixter and

Edward R. Henry. Special issue, *Journal of Archaeological Method and Theory* 24(1): 10–27.

Van Dyke, Ruth M. 2020. Indigenous Archaeology in a Settler-Colonist State: A View from the North American Southwest. *Norwegian Archaeological Review* 53(1):41–58.

Van Dyke, Ruth M., and Carrie C. Heitman (editors). 2021. *The Greater Chaco Landscape: Ancestors, Scholarship, and Advocacy.* University Press of Colorado, Boulder.

Veracini, Lorenzo 2010. *Settler Colonialism: A Theoretical Overview.* Palgrave Macmillan, London.

Weaver, Bobby. 1985. *Castro's Colony: Empresario Development in Texas, 1845–1865.* Texas A&M University Press, College Station.

11

Hurtful Heritage

Materializing a Past to Sediment/Unsettle Exclusionary Practices

Patricia A. McAnany

Racist monuments are killing us.
—Chelsey R. Carter (2018)

Such are the words of a young academic who presented the many ways in which the valorization of Southern Confederate soldiers from the US Civil War has adversely impacted the biological health and well-being of African Americans. As a professor at a southern university, I witnessed firsthand the nature of that harm and entrained violence. In a quad called McCorkle Place located directed outside my office, a bronze statue of an infantryman (rumored to have been cast in New England with a Boston policeman serving as a model) stood on a high pedestal for over 100 years. It was erected by the Daughters of the Confederacy, dedicated on June 2, 1913 (Figure 11.1). When I joined the faculty at the University of North Carolina–Chapel Hill in 2008, the statue (nicknamed "Silent Sam") was described to me as a commemoration of UNC students (white males) who fought for the Confederacy. At first the statue seemed relatively harmless, but then a more critical gaze began to crystallize. The explicitly racist content of the 1913 dedication speech delivered by local mill owner Julian S. Carr (1913) began to circulate. Its toxic rhetoric—nostalgic for the more "genteel" antebellum days of violent enslavement and unquestioned white supremacy—was indicative of a reactionary populist and racist credo that is regaining increasing visibility in the twenty-first century.

Across campus, African American students began to relate how their parents—apprehensive of racial attacks on their children—had instructed them to stay clear of the Confederate monument. Students, faculty, and staff

Figure 11.1. Front image on a postcard showing the dedication of a Confederate statue on the University of North Carolina campus, June 2, 1913. "Unveiling of the Confederate Monument, June 2, 1913," in Orange County, North Carolina Postcard Collection [P052], courtesy of North Carolina Collection Photographic Archives, Wilson Library, UNC–Chapel Hill.

called for the removal of the statue, but university leadership feared alienating financially generous alumni and were genuinely constrained by the dictates of an ultraconservative Board of Governors. Clashes between students and right-wing militias occurred around the monument, and a student spilled her blood mixed with red paint on its dedication plaque. Finally, on August 20, 2018, one year after the deadly events in Charlottesville, Virginia, students and activists managed to divert the campus police long enough to tie a rope around the statue and pull it down. Carol Folt, UNC chancellor at the time, was exhausted from trying to reason with a Board of Governors opposed to monument removal. She ordered the pedestal to be dismantled and the lawn replanted. In a final act, Chancellor Folt resigned before the board could vote to fire her.

My personal accounting of this monument—and its toppling—introduces a kind of tangible heritage that is resonant of pain and denigration to some while evoking celebratory triumphalism and continued relations of domination for others—a version of what Viviane Saleh-Hanna (2015) calls Black hauntology. My account drills to the heart of this exploration of hurtful heritage—a kind of remembrance that bolsters group identity at the expense of inflicting pain on those who are excluded. In my participatory research in Maya archaeology, we are forever asking "Who benefits from our activities?" Much of my heritage work in the Maya region and southeastern United States has been focused on amplifying the voices of peoples excluded from nationalist and archaeological narratives (e.g., McAnany 2016, 2020). Here I turn the question around to ask, "Who is hurt by heritage-making activities?" Such "makings" entail identity-enhancing acts and practices that exclude some to benefit others (Harrison 2018).

I concern myself with political narratives—particularly those of domination—that can evoke violence and constrain future action, constituting what Charles Cobb (2021: 90) has called "landscapes of forgetting." Such landscapes can encode what Hannah Arendt (2006) called the banality of evil—a point to which I return throughout this chapter. Insofar as archaeologists are forever involved with establishing the cultural identity of past peoples, our research can feed directly into tangible practices of societal exclusion (Hofmann and Frieman 2021). The way in which the politics of identity can morph into the "thin ideology of populism" (Stanley 2008) or become what Kwame Appiah (2018) calls the ethnic/nationalist "lies that bind" should give archaeologists pause—particularly in the realm of heritage conservation. Traditional ethics of heritage management dictate a democracy of values and transparency in presentation of identity-linked monuments. By drilling deeper into case studies, however, questions arise regarding what should be displayed and how. Why are some monuments and buildings removed from public places, forgotten, or reflexively repurposed without violence while others remain stubbornly entrenched and wedded to the mythology that monument removal is a violation of history?

In the pages to follow, I investigate how domination and exclusion are written onto landscapes via monumental constructions, which can then inflict harm on those who are excluded, as the opening epigram by Chelsey Carter indicates. This inquiry proceeds by comparing contentious manifestations of tangible heritage in the southeastern United States, on the one hand, with the Maya region, on the other. In the latter case, monuments dedicated before and after Spanish colonialism reveal very different approaches to the politics of identity and inclusion. Attention to precolonial monument enshrinement and removal in the Maya region provides insight to the distinction between monument construction and the crafting of history, while contemporary heritage tourism arguably represents a kind of heritage warping. Before examining these cases, I consider some of the broader issues surrounding heritage, memory, and monuments.

Memory and Hurtful Heritage

"It's just a statue" is a comment that one hears about inert masses of stone or metal placed in conspicuous public locales. "It can't hurt anyone" often follows. The turn toward object agency within philosophy and the social sciences casts doubt on assertions regarding the agency-free status of objects (Bennett 2010; Brown 2001; Hodder 2012; Latour 2007; Olsen 2012). But as Lori Khatchadourian (2020) has argued, linking objects with causation does not absolve humans of culpability. In other words, while statues may be capable of eliciting strong associations with racism and memories of enslavement or even genocide, it is humans and not material things that are accountable for creating such memories. By according affordance to nonhumans, moreover, one cannot overlook the unsettling irony of why certain monuments are capable of eliciting painful and corrosive memories. It is because they encode in one form or another a denial or degradation of the humanity of those who were subjugated (Stoler 2008: 193). That this denial can be encapsulated in a casual observation such as "It's just a statue" drills to the heart of Arendt's (2006) statement—evil, indeed, can be entirely banal.

I use the term "hurtful heritage" to describe this materialization of relations of domination because it avoids the colorism of the phrase "dark heritage" or "dark tourism" (Foley and Lennon 1996; Thomas et al. 2019). Hurtful heritage differs from negative heritage, a concept that involves the creation of a new monument designed to evoke painful memories of human tragedy—to cement a collective memory (Meskill 2002). The New York City memorial to the victims of the 9/11 destruction of the World Trade Towers is a prime example of negative heritage, which also differs from the memorialization of Second World War concentration camps. The latter were designed to be places of great pain and death but now have been transformed into sites of conscience (Foley and Lennon 1996; see also Bernbeck, this volume: Chapter 12; Moshenka et al., this volume: Chapter 9; and McAtackney, this volume: Chapter 8). In the context of forced-labor camps, putting hurtful heritage on display is linked to reckoning with the past generally to avoid repetition of an atrocity in the future—to keep the wounds of past atrocities open, as Reinhard Bernbeck (this volume: Chapter 12) proposes. But can all sites of hurtful heritage be transformed into sites of conscience, or do some resist reflexive repurposing? James Young (1993: 6) points out that sites of conscience require societies proximate to such a place to bear the emotional burden of difficult memories—a burden that may be rejected as reactionary populist (and nonapologetic) movements surge to the forefront of national or sectarian politics.

In reference to futurities, Lindsay Martel Montgomery (this volume: Chapter 3) notes the difficulty of building a future upon an enhanced understanding of past pain and suffering—places and memories of hurtful heritage. Likewise, Kailey Rocker (2022) observes how reckoning with the hurtful heritage of a Soviet-era prison camp in Albania is not easily incorporated into the national imaginary of a forward-looking and democratic country. Although these issues cannot be resolved in the limited space of this chapter, the ultimate disposition of sites of hurtful heritage evokes compelling questions. What should be buried for the sake of societal healing or at least repair, and what should be kept in the public eye no matter how painful to avoid repeating cycles of domination and violence? I return to this question first in reference to Confederate monuments and then by way of monuments to colonialism in the Maya region.

In a broader sense, heritage is about memory-making, which need not be materialized at all. Distinct from history or archaeology, heritage entails a group-focused memory of a thing, place, or practice. Powerful in shaping identity, it exists in tension with the disciplines of history and archaeology precisely because it "inevitably involves some identity project" (Wertsch and Roediger 2008: 320). Notably, Pierre Nora (1989) examined the distinction between history and memory and the way in which *lieux de mémoire* (places of remembrance) are created by the interplay of the two. Alfredo González-Ruibal and colleagues (2018) argue that archaeologists—especially those undertaking critical heritage studies—tend to overlook this tension to embrace an epistemic populism. Here I explore how populisms—based on race or nation—are expressed, resisted, and sometimes reshaped.

Veysel Apaydin (2020: 17) discusses the popularity of material culture in heritage studies and how its tangible properties aid cultural memory. Heritage monuments embody memory and are vital for creating a sense of belonging—a collective identity. Thus, heritage and memory are tightly interlinked in the work of both societal inclusion and exclusion—the latter a hallmark of reactionary populism. Maurice Halbwachs (1992), pioneer of memory studies, pointed to membership in a social group as a key referent for fixing collective memory. The link between a shared memory and place, further developed by Nora (1989), Paul Connerton (1989), and many archaeologists (Van Dyke 2019), is directly relevant to this consideration of monuments.

Consider the group gathered by the Daughters of the Confederacy at the 1913 dedication of the Civil War monument on the Chapel Hill campus. In this case, memory-making around the privately funded statue erected on a public campus was so intentional that a postcard featuring a photo of the gathering was available to those who attended the event. A note written on the reverse side of the postcard (Figure 11.2) reveals the staged activities that

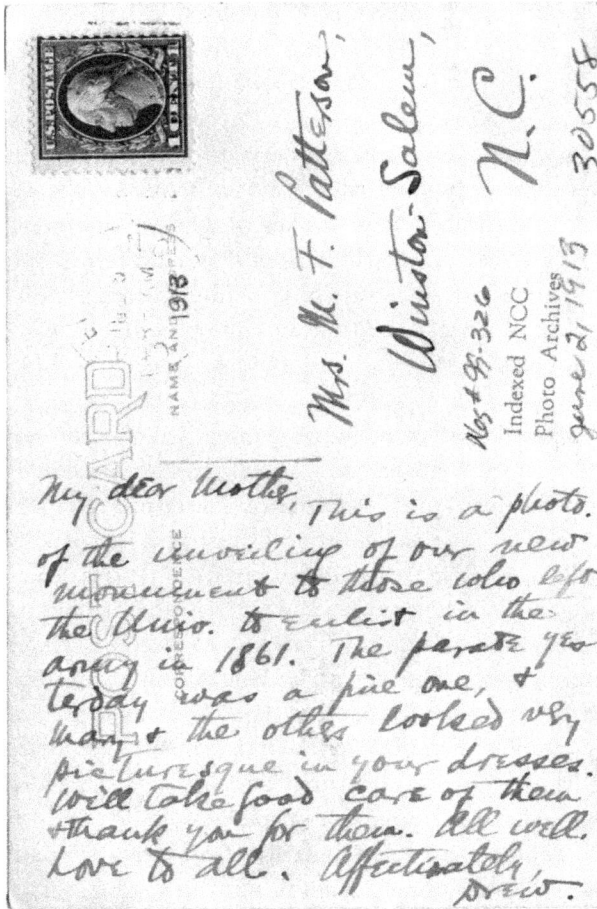

Figure 11.2. Back of postcard. Text reads "My dear Mother, This is a photo of the unveiling of our new monument to those who left the Univ. to enlist in the army in 1861. The parade yesterday was a fine one, & Mary and the others looked very picturesque in your dresses. We'll take good care of them and thank you for them. All well. Love to all. Affectionately, Drew." "Unveiling of the Confederate Monument, June 2, 1913," in Orange County, North Carolina Postcard Collection [P052], courtesy of North Carolina Collection Photographic Archives, Wilson Library, UNC–Chapel Hill.

created an image of Southern white women of the Old South wearing long, white dresses that evoke purity and perhaps vulnerability to alleged predations of Northern industrialists.

The staged postcard illustrates that, as Connerton has argued, collective memory is not virtuous, and neither is forgetting a failure. He distinguishes seven types of forgetting—three of which are relevant here: repressive erasure; prescriptive forgetting; and forgetting that is constitutive in the formation of a new identity (Connerton 2008). Monument removal is a type of prescriptive forgetting that—depending on one's perspective—could represent repressive erasure as echoed in contemporary cries of "cancel culture" in reference to the removal of Confederate monuments (Hanson 2017) or, conversely, the formation of a new and more inclusive identity.

Salient Cases of Hurtful Heritage

The cases of hurtful heritage under consideration here do not represent a systematic sample. Rather, they are examples of which I have gained familiarity experientially or through research. These selected *lieux de mémoire* highlight the distinctives ways in which prescriptive forgetting might be invoked (or resisted) for a heritage locale or monument that has ceased to represent a desired collective memory. Examples indicate the specific contexts in which social memory (that is, not forgetting) and continued interaction with a monument that evokes painful collective memories can affect a form of reckoning or what Deborah Thomas (2019) calls "repair." In other contexts, wounds cannot begin to heal unless interaction with a monument is dramatically reshaped or the monument is removed from all social interaction, such as UNC's Silent Sam Confederate statue. Examples from the Maya region highlight the impact of colonialism in effecting prescriptive forgetting that morphed into hurtful heritage as descendant peoples were excluded from or stereotyped by the commodification of their heritage. This last point may seem counterintuitive to the reader. How can people be hurt by a valorization of their own heritage? Simply put, a community's heritage can be weaponized by excluding them from decisions about heritage presentation, by glorifying an ancestral past while subjecting descendants to a racialized hierarchy, or by representing descendants in a stereotypical and fossilized manner for the purpose of commodification. We return to these points below.

A Civil War General Dismounted

In Charlottesville, Virginia, home to the University of Virginia, an equestrian statue of Confederate general Robert E. Lee was dedicated in 1924 on a small square surrounded by residences. After learning that the removal of the statue was being considered by the town council, I traveled to Charlottesville in May of 2017 to visit the square. Upon arrival, a local tour of Confederate monuments was under way. As the tour group approached the square, a homeless African American woman who had sought shelter overnight under a tree with low-hanging branches quietly moved away. Three months later, neo-Nazis marched through the University of Virginia campus chanting racist slogans and threats; after two days of protest, one counterprotestor was killed and several injured. For those of us teaching on southern campuses, this event forced a reckoning with the dangerous underbelly of southern heritage.

Regardless of the many threats issued by those involved in the "Unite the Right" rally, the town council later voted to remove the statue, and it finally came down on July 10, 2021—about four years later. This slow rate of change—but nonetheless a transition away from the display of hurtful heritage—is not atypical. For this reason, the geological term "sedimentation" (invoked in the title of this chapter) is a particularly accurate descriptor of the sluggish rate of change and of transitional justice for African American peoples in the United States.

As Paul Shackel (2001) and others have noted, Confederate monuments erected throughout the South are remarkable for several reasons: (1) there are hundreds if not thousands of them; (2) most were dedicated 50 years or more after the end of the Civil War and thus represent memory-making of a martial event fought one to two generations earlier, and (3) in the aftermath of a civil war the losing side rarely erects monuments commemorating a lost cause. But in the South, crafting a "Lost Cause" narrative became a much-celebrated vocation and was subsequently taught in schools and celebrated at civic events. This narrative, which emphasizes the courage and gentility of Confederate soldiers, sought to maintain a race-based hierarchy without directly referencing it. The dedication of monuments to the Confederacy—no matter how distant from the event—provided a touchstone for a version of Southern heritage that supported Jim Crow segregation laws (Cox 2021). Although these monuments invoke hurtful heritage, seldom if ever are they converted into sites of conscience. The social imaginary that they support—of an aristocratic white class that enslaved Africans and created a caste of subordinated workers—may simply be too toxic to repurpose into a site of conscience. Plans to bring the monuments into a critical conversation about human rights or to contextualize them with additional signage repeatedly founder on what Ann Stoler (2008) alludes to as the nostalgia of empire.

The Long Arc of Hurtful Heritage in the Maya Region

When I first became a student of Maya archaeology, I was awed by the beauty and naturalism of Classic Maya stone sculpture and hieroglyphic texts. I also wondered why so many carvings of rulers and associated texts extolling their fine pedigree had been "erased" (the term "defaced" is also used, and quite accurately since the face and head are frequent sites of erasure). For instance, if you visit the Classic Maya royal court of Yax Mutal (known today as the archaeological site of Tikal in Guatemala), you will travel around the site on raised causeways built 1,500 years ago. Alongside one of these causeways, the carved two-dimensional figure of an Early Classic (275–600 CE) Maya ruler was discovered (Martin and Grube 2008: 39). Rather than standing tall in its typical place of prominence in the main plaza of Yax Mutal, the stela had been uprooted, the carved face erased by grinding, and the monument

Figure 11.3. Piedras Negras Panel 3 (Late Classic Maya); note that faces and upper torsos of figures have been chiseled away. Courtesy of the Penn Museum, image no. 21137.

dumped by the side of a causeway. This case is not an isolated example—it took place across Mesoamerica (Pool and Loughlin 2017). Often archaeologists can only guess at the circumstances that provoked monument erasure, although regime change seems a likely suspect. Another famous example is a carved panel from Piedras Negras (Figure 11.3) depicting a 749 CE visitation scene in a throne room with seven subordinates sitting at the feet of ruler Itzam K'an Ahk IV (Martin 2020: 134). At some point after the panel was carved, the faces and upper torsos of most of the figures were chopped away. Classic Maya royals exhibited little tolerance for the continued display of personalized monuments created by predecessors who could not be claimed as ancestors.

In contrast to this orchestrated forgetting, ancestralizing related forebearers was the coin-of-the-realm in the southern lowlands. I was deeply impressed by the presence of ancestor veneration—particularly as expressed in mortuary practices. Only later did I begin to comprehend the conservatism of ancestor veneration and its power to maintain a status quo within a dominant kin line (see McAnany 2013). Ancestor veneration resonates with our understanding of heritage-making activities as crucial to group identity and, conversely, to exclusion from a group.

"Monument dumping" practices—while seemingly contrary to the preservation of ancestral burial sites and shrines—can accomplish many of the same goals as does ancestralizing a landscape. Both align with memory communities and acts of creation and erasure. Maya royals, it seems, harbored no illusions that stelae or royal tombs represented a historical record that could

Figure 11.4. Rosalila Temple (Classic Maya), dedicated to the dynastic founder of Copán, K'inich Yax K'uk' Mo' and buried intact within Structure 16. Created by and courtesy of Christopher Klein; also courtesy of National Geographic Society.

not be expunged. These elaborate monuments arguably were perceived as instruments of political power rather than embodiments of historical information. As such, a shift in power required their disposal or, perhaps more to the point, neutralization of the powerful animacy that resided within and emanated from their material properties. A belief in the continued vitality of monuments—particularly those depicting rulers—mandated neutralization through destruction rather than conservation. Chelsey Carter's (2018) statement about the lethal danger of monuments accords well with Classic Maya ontology.

On the memorialization end of the spectrum, great effort might be expended to preserve a shrine to a deceased ruler if the dynastic line prevailed through perilous intergenerational transmissions of power. Many years ago I had the privilege of visiting one of the most famous funerary shrines of the Classic period—that of K'inich Janaab Pakal I of Palenque. After descending 25 meters down an airless stairway within the pyramid, I encountered the massive sarcophagus of the deceased ruler buried deep inside the Temple of the Inscriptions. When archaeologist Alberto Ruz Lhuillier found the tomb of Pakal in 1952, it had not been looted, although the stairway to Pakal's mortuary chamber had been filled with stone rubble—perhaps to avoid such erasure.

Rosalila Temple at Copán (Figure 11.4)—discovered through extensive tunneling inside Structure 16—provides another example of the situational ethics of Maya monument preservation. (We return to the tunnels inside the Copán acropolis shortly.) Dedicated to dynastic founder K'inich Yax K'uk' Mo,' whose body was interred elsewhere, the shrine was entombed intact within Structure 16 with meticulous attention given to preserving the delicate stucco masks that adorned its exterior. These archaeological examples indicate that monument preservation was linked to dynastic politics and designed to sediment relations of power and the authority of a particular ruling line. Who was remembered and who was forgotten created a hurtful heritage for excluded political factions that no doubt conspired to be (re)instated as those who would be remembered. Here the salient point is that monuments preserve or sediment political domination rather than embody historical facts.

Colonialism and Heritage Warping in the Maya Region

Spanish colonization of the Americas—from the sixteenth century onward—involved slave-raiding as well as "slaving in place" via missionization and *encomienda*. The triumphalism of Spanish colonization—even when and where its success came be questioned—was imprinted dramatically on the landscape by way of colonial architecture—both secular and ecclesiastical. In Yucatán, the colonial capital of Mérida was built on top of T'hó—a large precolonial political capital (Barba et al. 2019; Restall 1998). During the nineteenth century, barons of the henequen haciendas built lavish town houses in Mérida along Paseo Montejo, a wide avenue featuring conspicuous statues of the Montejos—conquistadors of Yucatán.

Dismantling T'hó and overprinting it with a Spanish colonial capital surely represents repressive erasure and sedimentation of a new regime. Nonetheless, bus drivers from rural Yucatec–Mayan towns headed for Mérida are known to describe their destination as T'hó, signaling a memory that persists over 400 years. Reference to T'hó indicates a failure to forget or, to extend the work of Connerton (2008), a failure of colonialists to create a kind of forgetting that is constitutive of a new identity. A widely acknowledged characteristic of Spanish colonialism in the Maya region is the subjugation of Indigenous peoples and formation of a political/economic/social caste system that survives to this day as a racialized hierarchy. Mérida is a destination for rural Mayan peoples to shop but more frequently to perform childcare and housekeeping services or work in other low-wage jobs. Such stratification serves as a constant reminder of the failure of colonialism and of the republic that followed to create an inclusive society despite the official Mexican mantra of *mestizaje* (Bonfil Batalla 1996). Erasure that is constitutive to the formation of a new identity did not completely occur. A bus driver's reference to a deep-history place name can be interpreted as an act of resistance to the repressive erasures of colonialism and contemporary exclusionary politics.

In my cultural heritage work with descendant communities, I have been criticized for suggesting that there is link between contemporary Mayan peoples and the remains of a past that literally cover landscapes of the Maya region. It is the case that many ethnolinguistic Mayan groups disavow a direct connection to the past. In rural villages near Classic period archaeological sites, one can hear fascinating stories about giants who lived in the past and are said to have built the stone palaces and temples that are now collapsing and, according to some, in need of architectural conservation and restoration to attract tourists.

As part of heritage programming throughout the Maya region, we conducted surveys in rural communities and began to detect important trends (see McAnany 2016 for additional details). First, we learned that descendant communities are repeatedly told they are not related to those who built the palaces and temples upon which a mega-million-dollar tourism industry is based. Second, we discovered that school children learn nothing about their deep history or about the literary traditions of their ancestors (Landry Montes et al. 2021). Instead, students are taught about the glories of Spanish colonization. One student understood the ninth-century implosion of Classic Maya dynastic centers as immediately followed by the arrival of Spanish conquistadors who saved civilization. In this case, forgetting was externally imposed. Through repressive erasure, a new narrative was fashioned that disassociated people from their past and denigrated their forebearers as failures or prone to violence and warfare (McAnany and Parks 2012; Wilcox 2010). Heritage can become a hurtful weapon when warped by forces of domination. While a relationship to their past was actively discouraged—which curtailed significant economic benefit from tourism and authority over the representation and narrative content of their past—Maya peoples also were portrayed as out of time (Fabian 1983; Thomas 1996) or frozen in the past for the benefit of the touristic gaze.

In a classic piece of scholarship titled "The Ruin," Georg Simmel (1965: 260) philosophizes about the decay of a building during which

a new meaning seizes on this incident, comprehending it and its spiritual form in a unity which is no longer grounded in human purposiveness but in that depth where human purposiveness and the working of non-conscious natural forces grow from their common root.

Epitomizing the Western aesthetic, Simmel (1965: 265) characterizes the "ruin as past . . . a site of life from which life has departed." Beyond the nostalgia of this sentiment—which feeds the romantic tragedy often envisioned for the end of the Classic Maya period (and engenders tourism revenue entrained by that sentiment)—is the fact that it is completely at odds with how many ethnolinguistic Mayan peoples relate to Classic period "ruins." As Markus Eberl and Santiago Cho Choc (2024, personal communication) have noted, Q'eqchi' peoples view old structures—especially when pyramidal in form—as embodiments of great power and animacy in the present rather than dead things of the past. Regardless of whether local communities propose a direct linkage biologically or culturally with those who built these monumental structures over 500 years ago, they sense their power in the present, which makes a very clear statement about relational ontology (for more on this topic, see Kosiba et al. 2020). Thus, the recognized importance of large archaeological sites throughout Guatemala as places of offering and healing signified by the firepits constructed in the plazas at the base of pyramids at sites such as Kaminaljuyu, Tikal, Iximché, and many more.

Regardless, Western nostalgia and attachment to the idea that anything not preserved in tip-top condition is redolent of tragic abandonment has become the dominant narrative in reference to Maya political capitals of precolonial times. The principle of *terra nullius* has been aggressively used by nation-states throughout the Maya region to claim these places "for the state" and to "protect" them to accrue profit from their development as sites of heritage tourism. Continued use of these powerful old places as sites of pilgrimage, healing, and offerings by descendant communities is overlooked or purposefully thwarted as entrance gates and ticket booths are constructed. Since the Maya region is split into five nation-states (Mexico, Guatemala, Belize, Honduras, and El Salvador), the situation via access and co-management is highly variable from country to country (for more discussion, see McAnany 2016).

In southern Belize, Q'eqchi' and Mopan peoples requested permission from the director of the Institute of Archaeology to conduct ceremonies or sell handicrafts within the plazas of reconstructed tourist sites such as Lubaantun and Nim Li Punit. In Honduras, Ch'orti' activists occupied the entrance to the World Heritage site of Copán several times between 1998 and 2009 in hopes of being recognized as rightful stakeholders and with the goal of receiving a portion of ticket revenues in order to address problems of endemic poverty and land disenfranchisement (McAnany and Parks 2012). In Guatemala, after a brutal civil war (1960–1996) in which the killing of Mayan peoples reached genocidal proportions (Manz 2004; Menchú 1984), a peace accord was reached in 1996. Finally in 2002, the minister of culture granted Mayan spiritual guides and their followers the right to be present—to be seen—at heritage locales under the jurisdiction of the Ministry of Culture (Ivic de Monterroso 2004). The meaning of such access—hard won and with a steep price in human lives—to Indigenous peoples of Guatemala is reflected in the fact that rarely are the firepits at which prayers and offerings are made unattended.

The editors of this book pose the question: archaeology for whom? In the Maya region, archaeology most frequently is conducted either for the purpose of developing international tourism or for the professional development of archaeologists from wealthy nation-states. Project directors often view local communities as a source of cheap labor to excavate dangerously deep trenches and tunnels. While running an educational program in primary schools attended by Ch'orti' children living within 20 kilometers of Copán in western Honduras, we learned that most children had never visited the archaeological site. But they had heard of the tunnels into which archaeologists and local workers descended each day and were very curious about them. These are the same tunnels that revealed the beautifully intact buried temple called Rosalila, discussed earlier. Local students did not know about this discovery and its significance for understanding the dynastic history of Copán and their own ancestry.

Dario Euraque (1998) has written about the problematic relationship between ethnic identity and the heritage branding of Honduras as a place of Maya mysteries. In fact, most Indigenous peoples of Honduras do not identify ethnically as Mayan. For tourism, however, heritage was weaponized, misrepresented, and used to deny the existence of other Indigenous peoples. At the same time, the exclusionary way in which nationalized archaeological sites are managed and commodified for tourism (in Honduras and elsewhere) means that, in many cases, ancestral places have become sites of hurtful heritage to descendants because they must struggle for access and management rights and must resist being stereotyped as ossified window dressing—an enhancement of the touristic experience (Ardren 2004).

Significantly, all five nation-states within the Maya region are signatories to the United Nations Declaration on the Rights of Indigenous Peoples (UNDRIP) passed in 2007. Two articles within this declaration (11.1 and 12.1) assert the rights of Indigenous peoples over archaeological and historical sites as well as religious and cultural sites. In most cases these place-based rights are at odds with the reality of the situation. Although UNDRIP asserts lofty principles, it is not tied to an international tribunal or any means of enforcement or adjudication but rather relies on signatory nations to operationalize UNDRIP via legislative action, which has been slow to materialize across the Maya region. Thus, relations of domination and exclusionary practices have yet to be reshaped.

In the Maya region, European colonial relations of domination pose an inflection point that casts a long shadow over Indigenous heritage practices. While it is true that during precolonial times repressive erasure happened in the form of monument erasure and dumping, it occurred within the political cycles of a sovereign people. Colonial and more recent forms of forgetting—such as the erasure of T'hó and alienation of descendants from their past—occur within the context of centuries-long ethnic domination and racial hierarchizing that warped Maya cultural heritage. Contemporary ritual practices conducted in front of precolonial monuments unsettle the Western mystique of a past that is long dead, that belongs to no one, and that therefore can be freely commoditized for heritage tourism (Picas 2022).

In a broader sense, these instances of hurtful heritage are embodied within monuments that evoke memories of military defeat, colonization, enslavement, genocide, disenfranchisement, and loss of autonomy over place. In a very real and affective sense, statues and buildings can promote or erode a sense of well-being, as Chelsey Carter (2018) so aptly stated. While statues can be removed from public viewing and places converted to sites of conscience, the arc of societal change remains excruciatingly slow.

Discussion

Whether expressed in the increasing frustration and exhaustion of African Americans or through Mayan peoples struggling for the right to be seen as active participants in the management of their heritage, unsettling exclusionary practices that create moments and monuments of hurtful heritage is painfully slow. The geological term "sedimentation" refers to an (often slow) accumulation of matter over time and thus is an apt descriptor of how exclusionary practices form, erode, and can reconstitute. The current resurgence within the United States of exclusionary populist sentiment regarding immigration and the rights of women and nonwhite people provides a powerful example of hurtful heritage. When populism is founded on exclusion rather than an inclusive and liberating ideology, it provides powerful fodder for virulent racism. Hurtful heritage can be opaque and difficult to pinpoint because it is baked into structural inequalities that have been naturalized. As such, relations of exclusion behind hurtful heritage can display painful durability and challenge destabilization.

Relations of exclusion resist transformation despite the creation in the United States of legal structures that support desegregation and the dismantling of racial hierarchies or the United Nations' passage of a declaration supporting the rights of Indigenous peoples. The transition to a more just union within the United States is endlessly ongoing and slow to mature. Resistance to removing Confederate monuments and the seeming impossibility of transforming such monuments into sites of conscience signals the embeddedness of white supremacy. Impatience with the deep structural armature of racism gave rise to the 1619 Project, in which Nikole Hannah-Jones (2021) documents the willful forgetting of the heritage of enslavement that undergirds US prosperity. Failure to transform race-based domination into a newer and more inclusive social fabric—whether in the United States or Yucatán, Mexico—appears tied to many factors, including a perceived loss of privileged access to resources. Racism in both the United States and the Maya region share these characteristics, which are hallmarks of twenty-first-century reactionary populism.

Concluding Thoughts

Types of forgetting codified by Connerton (2008)—namely, repressive erasure, prescriptive forgetting, and forgetting that is constitutive in the formation of a new identity—have proven useful to unpacking the concept of hurtful heritage. By examining what is (and is not) forgotten and how forgetting occurs, we move closer to "the demystification of collective entities and meanings" (Funkenstein 1989: 22). During a time when reactionary populism is on the rise, demystification is badly needed.

Examples provided in this study aim to provide greater context around which to understand both societal transitions and durabilities in the formation of collective entities that purport to share memories and forward-looking purpose. As Nora (1989: 23) observed: "*lieux de mémoire* have no reference in reality; or, rather, they are their own referent: pure, exclusively self-referential signs." Although I doubt that Nora had Confederate statues or Maya stelae in mind when he penned this thought, it is an apt descriptor of how statues can embody hierarchy and domination. For the US Southeast, these relations persist well beyond the dismantling of Jim Crow laws and the civil rights struggles of the 1960s. The statues were *lieux de mémoire* grounded in the durability of white supremacy rather than the reality of mid-twentieth-century legal reforms. In the Maya region, stelae and funerary shrines from

Classic period times help to clarify the political message of monuments and dispel notions of monuments as neutral conveyors of history.

Heritage—as a group-focused project that crafts memory and reinforces community—comes in many shapes and sizes. Here we have cast a critical eye on heritage-making through tangible monuments that served to sediment practices that are/were exclusionary or worse. In the process, we confront the pain and suffering associated with monuments that valorized Confederate soldiers, precolonial Maya rulers, Spanish conquistadors, and an intrusive Spanish colonial capital. But unpacking hurtful heritage needs to occur within a reflexive rather than voyeuristic framework. Concern with futurities requires us to do more than analyze inflicted damage to better understand it (Tuck and Yang 2014; Montgomery, this volume: Chapter 3). By witnessing and supporting the dismantling or transformation of monuments that embody hurtful heritage, archaeologists can quicken the unsettling of narratives of domination and exclusion. In doing so, we promote the well-being of those who have been affected by the monuments of hurtful heritage referenced by Chelsey Carter, and we can diminish the material dimension of evil discussed by Hannah Arendt.

References Cited

Apaydin, Veysel. 2020. The Interlinkage of Cultural Memory, Heritage, and Discourses of Construction, Transformation and Destruction. In *Critical Perspectives in Cultural Memory and Heritage: Construction, Transformation and Destruction,* edited by Veysel Apaydin, pp. 13–29. UCL Press, London.

Appiah, Kwame Anthony. 2018. *The Lies That Bind: Rethinking Identity.* Liveright, New York.

Ardren, Traci. 2004. Where Are the Maya in Ancient Maya Archaeological Tourism? Advertising and the Appropriation of Culture. In *Marketing Heritage,* edited by Y. Rowan and U. Baram, pp. 103–113. AltaMira, Walnut Creek, California.

Arendt, Hannah. 2006. *Eichmann in Jerusalem: A Report on the Banality of Evil.* Originally published 1963. Penguin Classics, New York.

Barba, Luis, Josep Ligorred, Jorge Blancas, and Agustín Ortiz. 2019. Searching with Georadar Ancient T'hó, a Mayan City Underneath the Modern Merida, Yucatan. *STAR: Science and Technology of Archaeological Research* 5(2): 247–256.

Bennett, Jane. 2010. *Vibrant Matter: A Political Ecology of Things.* Duke University Press, Durham, North Carolina.

Bonfil Batalla, Guillermo. 1996. *México Profundo: Reclaiming a Civilization.* Translated by Philip A. Dennis. University of Texas Press, Austin.

Brown, Bill. 2001. Thing Theory. *Critical Inquiry* 28(1): 1–22.

Carr, Julian S. 1913. Julian Shakespeare Carr Papers #141. Southern Historical Collection. The Wilson Library, University of North Carolina, Chapel Hill.

Carter, Chelsey. 2018. Racist Monuments Are Killing Us. *Museum Anthropology* 41(2): 139–141.

Cobb, Charles R. 2021. Landscapes of Forgetting and Structural Silence in the American Southeast. *American Anthropologist* 124: 90–103.

Connerton, Paul. 1989. *How Societies Remember.* Cambridge University Press, Cambridge.

Connerton, Paul. 2008. Seven Types of Forgetting. *Memory Studies* 1(1): 59–71.

Cox, Karen L. 2021. *No Common Ground: Confederate Monuments and the Ongoing Fight for Racial Justice.* University of North Carolina Press, Chapel Hill.

Euraque, Dario. 1998. Antropólogos, Arqueólogos, Imperialismo y La Mayanizacion de Honduras, 1890–1940. *Yaxkin* 17: 85–101.

Fabian, Johannes. 1983. *Time and the Other: How Anthropology Makes Its Object.* Columbia University Press, New York.

Foley, Malcolm, and J. J. Lennon. 1996. JFK and Dark Tourism: A Fascination with Assassination. *International Journal of Heritage Studies* 2(4): 198–211.

Funkenstein, Amos. 1989. Collective Memory and Historical Consciousness. *History and Memory* 1(1): 5–26.

González-Ruibal, Alfredo, Pablo A. González, and Felipe Criado-Boado. 2018. Against Reactionary Populism: Towards a New Public Archaeology. *Antiquity* 92(362): 507–515.

Halbwachs, Maurice. 1992. *On Collective Memory.* University of Chicago Press, Chicago.

Hannah-Jones, Nikole. 2021. *A New Origin Story: The 1619 Project.* Random House, New York.

Hanson, V. D. 2017. Our War against Memory. *National Review,* August 22. https://www.nationalreview.com/2017/08/erasing-history-censoring-confederate-past-rewriting-memory-mob-vengeance/.

Harrison, Rodney. 2018. Critical Heritage Studies Beyond Epistemic Populism. *Antiquity* 92(365): 1–3.

Hodder, Ian. 2012. *Entangled: An Archaeology of the Relationships between Humans and Things.* Wiley-Blackwell, Malden, Massachusetts.

Hofmann, Daniela, and Catherine J. Frieman. 2021. Introduction: Archaeology and Populism. *European Journal of Archaeology* 24(4): 519–523.

Ivic de Monterroso, M. 2004. The Sacred Place in the Development of Archaeology in Guatemala: An Analysis. In *Continuities and Change in Maya Archaeology: Perspectives at the Millennium,* edited by Charles W. Golden and G. Borgstede, pp. 295–307. Routledge, New York.

Khatchadourian, Lori. 2020. False Dilemmas? Or What COVID-19 Can Teach Us about Material Theory, Responsibility and "Hard Power." *Antiquity* 94(378): 1649–1652.

Kosiba, Steve, Thomas B. F. Cummins, and John Wayne Janusek (editors). 2020. *Sacred Matters: Animacy and Authority in Pre-Columbian America.* Dumbarton Oaks Research Library and Collection, Washington, D.C.

Landry Montes, Khristin N., Patricia A. McAnany, and Iván Batún Alpuche. 2021. Decolonizing the Classroom and Centering the Biocultural Heritage of Cenotes in Yucatán, México. *Mayanist* 3(1): 19–38.

Latour, Bruno. 2007. *Reassembling the Social: An Introduction to Actor-Network Theory.* Oxford University Press, Oxford.

Manz, Beatriz. 2004. *Paradise in Ashes: A Guatemalan Journey of Courage, Terror, and Hope.* University of California Press, Berkeley.

Martin, Simon. 2020. *Ancient Maya Politics: A Political Anthropology of the Classic Period 150–900 CE.* Cambridge University Press, Cambridge.

Martin, Simon, and Nikolai Grube. 2008. *Chronicle of the Maya Kings and Queens.* Thames & Hudson, London.

McAnany, Patricia A. 2013. *Living with the Ancestors: Kinship and Kingship in Ancient Maya Society.* Cambridge University Press, New York.

McAnany, Patricia A. 2016. *Maya Cultural Heritage: How Archaeologists and Indigenous Communities Engage the Past.* Rowman & Littlefield, Lanham, Maryland.

McAnany, Patricia A. 2020. Imagining a Maya Archaeology That Is Anthropological and Attuned to Indigenous Cultural Heritage. *Heritage* 3(2): 318–330.

McAnany, Patricia A., and Shoshaunna Parks. 2012. Casualties of Heritage Distancing: Children, Ch'orti' Indigeneity, and the Copan Archaeoscape. *Current Anthropology* 53(1): 80–107.

Menchú, Rigaberta. 1984. *I, Rigoberta Menchú: An Indian Woman in Guatemala.* Verso, London.

Meskill, Lynn. 2002. Negative Heritage and Past Mastering in Archaeology. *Anthropological Quarterly* 75(3): 557–574.

Nora, Pierre. 1989. Between Memory and History: *Les Lieux de Mémoire: Representations* 26: 7–24.

Olsen, Bjørnar. 2012. Symmetrical Archaeology. In *Archaeological Theory Today,* edited by I. Hodder, pp. 208–228. 2nd ed. Polity Press, Cambridge.

Picas, Mathieu. 2022. (Re)significaciones patrimoniales en Tierra Mayas: Valores Sagrados de Sitios Arqueológicos en México y Guatemala. PhD dissertation, Society and Culture: History, Anthropology, Art and Heritage, Universitat de Barcelona.

Pool, Christopher A., and Michael J. Loughlin. 2017. Creating Memory and Negotiating Power in the Olmec Heartland. *Journal of Archaeological Method and Theory* 24(1): 229–260.

Restall, Matthew. 1998. *Maya Conquistador.* Beacon, Boston.

Rocker, Kailey A. 2022. Translational Justice: Facing the Past to Take on the Present in Albania. PhD dissertation, Department of Anthropology, University of North Carolina, Chapel Hill.

Saleh-Hanna, Viviane. 2015. Black Feminist Hauntology: Rememory the Ghosts of Abolition? *Champ pénal/Penal field* 12. https://doi.org/10.4000/champpenal.9168.

Shackel, Paul. 2001. Public Memory and the Search for Power in American Historical Archaeology. *American Anthropologist* 103(3): 655–670.

Simmel, Georg. 1965. The Ruin. In *Essays on Sociology, Philosophy and Aesthetics,* edited by Kurt H. Wolff, pp. 259–266. Harper & Row, New York.

Stanley, Ben. 2008. The Thin Ideology of populism. *Journal of Political Ideologies* 13(1): 95–110.

Stoler, Ann L. 2008. Imperial Debris: Reflections on Ruin and Ruination. *Cultural Anthropology* 23(2): 191–219.

Thomas, Deborah A. 2019. *Political Life in the Wake of the Plantation: Sovereignty, Witnessing, Repair.* Duke University Press, Durham, North Carolina.

Thomas, Suzie, Vesa-Pekka Herva, Oula Seitsonen, and Eerika Koskinen-Koivisto. 2019. Dark Heritage. In *Encyclopedia of Global Archaeology*, edited by C. Smith. Springer Nature, Switzerland. https://doi.org/10.1007/978-3-319-51726-1_3197-1.

Thomas, Nicholas. 1996. *Out of Time: History and Evolution in Anthropological Discourse.* 2nd ed. University of Michigan Press, Ann Arbor.

Tuck, Eve, and K. Wayne Yang. 2014. Unbecoming Claims: Pedagogies of Refusal in Qualitative Research. *Qualitative Inquiry* 20(6): 811–818.

Van Dyke, Ruth M. 2019. Archaeology and Social Memory. *Annual Review of Anthropology* 48: 207–225.

Wertsch, James V., and Henry L. Roediger III. 2008. Collective Memory: Conceptual Foundations and Theoretical Approaches. *Memory* 16(3): 318–326.

Wilcox, Michael. 2010. Marketing Conquest and the Vanishing Indian: An Indigenous Response to Jared Diamond's Archaeology of the American Southwest. In *Questioning Collapse: Human Resilience, Ecological Vulnerability, and the Aftermath of Empire*, edited by Patricia A. McAnany and Norman Yoffee, pp. 113–141. Cambridge University Press, New York.

Young, James E. 1993. *The Texture of Memory: Holocaust Memorials and Meaning.* Yale University Press, New Haven, Connecticut.

12

Archaeology against Right-Wing Extremism

Lessons from a Nazi Terror Site

REINHARD BERNBECK

I focus my contribution to this volume on the complexities of an archaeological project of the Nazi period in the middle of Germany's capital, Berlin, and the increasingly reactionary political context within which archaeologists carry out such research. I do so by considering present political conditions in Germany and my own entangled professional situation as a specialist in the archaeology of ancient Western Asia.

Anti-Semitism increases by the day in the current political climate in Germany, driven most visibly by an extremist, antidemocratic, right-wing party, the Alternative für Deutschland (AfD). The party's racist program is a return to a vaguely formulated German supremacy, with Germany understood as a "pure" nation, without immigrants, Jewish, or Muslim people. AfD sympathizers are responsible for a multitude of violent attacks on synagogues and other institutions as well as on individuals deemed "foreign."

The Hamas attacks on Israel on October 7, 2023, and their violent aftermath only exacerbate anti-Semitism, now coming also from groups with an immigrant background as well as many others. In this constellation, the AfD exploits its racist agenda by demanding the expulsion of large swaths of immigrant Muslims, particularly asylum-seekers. Paradoxically, the AfD's traditional anti-Semitism is increasingly supported by many of those whom they want to see deported.

This historical conjunction with the brutal particularity of Germany's Nazi past produces an extraordinarily complex situation for anyone who wants to engage at the same time with the archaeologies of both the Second World War in Germany and the archaeology of ancient societies in Western Asia.

In the following, I discuss the term "reactionary populism" and describe my own position as an archaeologist working in Western Asia and twentieth-century Germany. Thereafter, I review in some detail archaeological work I co-directed in the middle of Berlin in a Nazi forced-labor camp. Finally, I return to the issue of the relation between community archaeology and right-wing populism.

Reactionary Populism

At the core of this book is the notion of reactionary populism. I explore this political stance from an anthropological perspective that is influenced by German history and the European present. Populism includes two rhetorical elements found in both left- and right-wing positions: it is fundamentally anti-elite, and it involves a strong imagination of majoritarianism (Krastev 2017: 124). The anti-elite conviction expresses itself differently depending on the historical context because elites are defined variably: one such movement with emancipatory goals and deep historical roots is the Marxist struggle against property-owning classes.

The various reactionary populisms of today have other targets: educated elites and academics, immigrants, or ethnic or religious groups (see also the introduction to this volume). As a rule, populist movements are led by a charismatic figure (Pappas 2016). Internal differentiation is undesired; critique is used, if at all, as a euphemism for defaming those who do not belong. A tight symbiosis between leadership and followers emerges. Majoritarianism is the perfect principle for claiming a struggle for "democracy," the rule of an imagined—sometimes real—majority. "Drain the swamp" is a battle cry of the presumed masses against fantasized elites. Successful populist movements regularly flock around a seductive leader. Donald Trump is a typical case. Where such figures do not exist, populism does not flourish as well. Despite its successes in Germany, the right-wing AfD is a good case in point: so far, they have not been able to take over any major political responsibility, in contrast to the situation in Italy, the United States, Hungary, and other Western countries with prominent leading figures. More recently, however, the AfD has made significant advances in the elections in 2024.

The majoritarianist ideology of populism is not only directed against elites. Reactionary populism often targets marginalized people. Arjun Appadurai (2006) describes this graphically in his essay "Fear of Small Numbers." Minorities of various kinds are treated with disdain by the self-empowered majority: defined via ethnicity, like the Rohingya in Myanmar; via religion, like Muslims in India; or via foreignness in general, as in European countries.

What is initially located in the realm of discourse mutates into direct physical attacks but also seeps into public structures to the point that they metamorphose from a supportive balancing function to a threat. Populism can work its way into state institutions, as in the Hungarian and American judicial systems, seeking to make this apparatus subservient to the executive and abolish the separation of powers. The reason is simple: the judiciary is by definition a non-majoritarian institution that is only acceptable when its opinions converge with the so-called silent majority (Panov 2020: 257–258).

Interestingly, the concepts and praxis of community archaeology in our present crisis correspond to some extent to the preconceptions of right-wing movements. Community-oriented archaeologists generally have social justice in mind (Little 2023); structurally, they are an educated elite that allies itself with a minority to study the latter's past. This constellation fits the Manichaean worldview of reactionary populism. Right-wing movements see community archaeology as an unjustified appropriation and redistribution of resources to despised minorities and their past. Community archaeology considers exactly that to be its core program.

A further important issue for the discussions in this book is the concept of "community." Multiple attempts at definition and critique of this term can be found in the archaeological literature. We find a multiplicity of different opinions on community archaeology's main concepts, from participation, engagement, or cooperation to multiculturalism and decolonization. These opinions ultimately all point in the same direction: we should not carry out archaeological work separately from the social environment in which it takes place but rather should work toward an integrated practice. This is an uncontroversial demand (see the introduction to this volume). But what happens when such an integration-oriented archaeology encounters a community that is dominated by right-wing people? Any insistence on multivocality in community archaeology becomes extremely troublesome when reactionary groups drown out other local voices (González-Ruibal 2023).

Positionality and Epistemological Issues

I mentioned already the complex relations between post-Nazi Germany and the current rise of anti-Semitism. As an archaeologist who works in both Western Asia and Germany, I am forced to constantly reconsider my own position as a researcher, an idea that has a long intellectual history in feminist archaeology (Gero 1996; Wylie 2003). Several different ethical aspects situate me in a complex web of relations: my collective past as a German is closely tied to the end of the Second World War and the ensuing founding of the State of Israel in 1948—but also to its fallout, the Nakba, the expulsion of Palestinian inhabitants from their villages in Israeli territory. The horrendous nature of the twentieth-century German past leads its politicians to claim that Israel's security is Germany's raison d'état, with wide-ranging consequences when it comes to any possible public critique of the government of Israel.

My scholarly position is also influenced by more personal experiences. I grew up in small-town Germany where my school classes were riddled with Nazi rhetoric, where my family was—like many in those times—involved in the crimes of that period, and where racism toward "guest workers" from Turkey prevailed. I took part in emancipatory movements to free my generation from those ideas. Thus, I did not and do not need to be convinced of the danger of reactionary populism: it was the status quo in my youth. Racism, anti-Semitism, and xenophobia were part of everyday life.

My initial interest in archaeological research at Nazi-period sites derives from these cultural and individual origins. During fieldwork and interpretive research, I am constantly driven by the question of the identities of victims and perpetrators at such sites. On this level, archaeology is frustrating since results remain almost entirely on the level of anonymity. However, at the end of this chapter I show that this situation can also be an advantage under an increasing weight of right-wing public discourse.

Beyond my engagement in an archaeology of Nazi times, I am also specialized in Western Asian archaeology. For political reasons, this field of research finds itself in a somewhat absurd situation. The subdiscipline has largely suppressed any open talk about this absurdity, which is due to the hostile relations between Israel and surrounding nations: if one plans an archaeological project in the State of Israel, it is nearly impossible to also pursue such research in other states in the region. And the reverse: working in almost any other state in Western Asia automatically precludes archaeological fieldwork in Israel. While there are a few exceptions to this rule, Western scholars tacitly accept this situation.

My own work shows the same tendency. The closest I came to carrying out a project in an Israel-related context was fieldwork in the West Bank (Houdalieh et al. 2017). As I witnessed firsthand, such an undertaking significantly complicates an already complex academic-ethical position (Tillmanns 2012). Archaeological investigations with and among scholars considered inimical by many Israeli archaeologists put me as a German in an uneasy position, to say the least. Am I not helping to construct a collective past for a Palestinian population, one that has traditionally been intent on fighting Israel, even in some circles to eradicate it? Just as problematic: Do my research results potentially contribute to covert but widespread German anti-Semitism? It is not even the content of one's research, it is the simple choice of its location that turns into a highly politicized issue. Positions on both political sides tend to end in sweeping judgments, even among colleagues (Abu El-Haj 2002; Spielman 2019). Again, there are notable exceptions (Dodd and Boytner 2018; Scham and Yahya 2003).

My encounter with research in the conflictual situation of the Palestinian–Israeli context raised a fundamental epistemological issue that is also relevant for an archaeology conducted in conditions of reactionary abuse. In the Occupied Palestinian Territories, archaeology is taught in very few universities, while Israel has the most extensive university and research network in all of Western Asia. The hundreds of excavations in this small country have led to a highly detailed reconstruction of the past that focuses particularly on one period, the Iron Age, as the time of the presumed King David and the emergence of the Old Testament kingdoms of Judah and Samaria. Other periods are comparatively neglected, especially the Islamic era. Such constrained research agendas produce a particular narrative of a Jewish history (Silberman and Small 1997). Scholars in West Bank universities have long been precluded from studying Palestine's deep history since they do not have similar means with which to construct different, competing narratives. However, in addition to the few universities that have archaeological departments, some activists have tried to change this situation. Among them was Adel Yahya, a recently deceased Palestinian colleague who grew up in a refugee camp in the West Bank. He set up an organization, the Palestinian Association for Cultural Exchange, in Ramallah with the goal to construct and preserve a Palestinian past using archaeological means as well as oral history (Scham and Killebrew 2018; Yahya 2008). Yahya insisted that archaeological work in Palestine should be a community endeavor but should at the same time be conducted with scientific rigor to produce an "objective" Palestinian past that could be posited as a counterpart to an equally "objective" Israeli past. Palestinian archaeology and other social science research require, he argued, an empiricist-positivist approach (see also Greenberg 2018).

In contrast, theoretical discussions of community archaeology in the international realm are dominated by constructivism as the core intellectual attitude. Constructivism is based on the principle of giving Others a voice. Ideally, they play a role equal to archaeologists in a multivocal concert (e.g., Habu et al. 2008) and include Indigenous voices, perhaps lending them special weight (McGuire, this volume: Chapter 6). One main tenet of constructivism is its commitment to the Foucauldian claim of a historically changing but never disappearing relationship between power and knowledge. As Foucault (1981: 118) writes,

> Now I believe that the problem does not consist in drawing the line between that in a discourse which falls under the category of scientificity or truth, and that which comes under some other category, but in seeing historically how effects of truth are produced within discourses.

For Foucault, power is a structure underlying the production of truth.

Yahya's insistence on empirical research and scientific rigor flies in the face of multivocality as the basis for community archaeology, even though his work was an exceptionally successful example of such an integrative archaeology. Constructivism, Yahya taught me, is a luxury that one must first be able to afford. In my opinion, this is the most important link to our situation today. With the rise of reactionary populism, we have also lost that luxury. We can no longer simply pretend that an ideal multivocal endeavor opens a space where all voices count. Such an approach potentially plays into the hands of abusive, vilifying discourse, as we have seen it developing recently. Factuality is abandoned in the service of power, whether in Donald Trump's bizarre and dangerous comments on the Covid-19 pandemic, the anti-Semitic campaign against an imagined "Soros network" by Hungary's Fidesz party, or other cases. Such freewheeling rhetoric is a nightmarish realization of constructivism.

The current political and epistemological crisis leaves us with the question of what can replace constructivism as a paradigm. Instead of considering knowledge simply and entirely as a matter of power relations, it is more appropriate to conceptualize it as the result of negotiations around a real core. Generally, knowledge of the world is "about something." Such a representational notion of knowledge implies that truth is approachable via the mutual exchange of arguments—but truth is not reachable (Žižek 1994).

The outcome of this assessment of our current epistemological practices entails wide-ranging consequences. It amounts to a critique of ideology, a stance that cautiously claims a position of "knowing better" than those who are critiqued (Bernbeck and McGuire 2011; Moshenska 2023, this volume: Chapter 9). This position has ramifications for community archaeology: accounts by the communities that surround us in archaeological work may contradict our own specialist knowing. Under which conditions do we have the right or duty to claim that "we know better"? And where we do not voice our firm belief in a knowledge of the world that contradicts that of others, do we—to modify Spivak's (1985) term—adhere to a "strategic constructivism" that can be politically deleterious? Is our adherence to multivocality not sometimes hypocritical? In the following, I reflect on the complexities of positionality and epistemology in a rapidly changing political environment by giving a brief account of fieldwork carried out in the German capital, Berlin, at the Tempelhof airfield.

Tempelhof Airfield: Urban Community Archaeology

Archaeologists often narrow the concept of "community" by associating it with rural groups and villages (see the introduction and Ayán Vila, this volume: Chapter 5). This may be due to the complexity of urban communities. In abstract terms, the latter are best described as nodes in an overlapping set of networks without a coherent symbolic universe or a circumscribed geographic terrain. In this "jungle of cities," as Bertolt Brecht called it, almost everyone can, if they wish, remain below the radar of recognition. People from fringe groups—esoterics, squatters, the homeless, and the extremely wealthy—can live anonymously. But cities also offer occasions for attacks on others.

The urban network I briefly discuss here is Berlin. My concern are the complexities of an excavation project involving community archaeology in this urban setting. The place of archaeological investigation was a forced-labor camp from Nazi times on the Tempelhof airfield in Berlin, which I directed from 2012 to 2014 with Susan Pollock. Today the former airfield is an open area used for sports, gardening, and other leisure activities that cover a horrendous past (see also McAtackney, this volume: Chapter 8). Located next to it is Berlin's largest Muslim cemetery with a mosque and a cultural center. The mosque, which opened in 2003, was the target of four arson attacks in 2010 alone (Reißmann 2010).

Starting in 1940, the Nazis erected sprawling camps for foreign forced laborers, some civilian, some prisoners of war, on the edge of Tempelhof airfield, Berlin's main airport since the 1920s. With the Nazi assault on Poland on September 1, 1939, the premises were immediately converted into a factory to produce dive bombers, the feared Stuka JU87, and to repair damaged war planes, organized by Lufthansa (Budrass 2016; Wenz 2006). Forced laborers on the assembly line had to construct bombers that would potentially kill their families and friends.

In June 1945, shortly after the end of the Second World War in Europe, the US Air Force occupied the field. The site remained inaccessible to the city's population and to the West Berlin administration. Civilian flights were only allowed for airline companies of the Western Allies. Until the fall of the Berlin Wall in 1989, the airfield remained under control of the US Air Force. Another 20 years on, the airport was closed for air traffic altogether because of its location in the middle of the city. Immediately, citizen's initiatives tried to wrestle the huge expanse from the city government. After a major conflict between citizens and the police, the field was opened as an inner-city park. Yet, fears that urban planners would use the area for new buildings to house Berlin's growing population persisted. Organizers against the real estate mafia called for a referendum that was brought to a positive vote in 2014 (Hilbrandt 2016). Ever since, further construction on the field has stopped, and the park in the middle of the city is a site for grazing sheep, playing music, flying kites, racing bikes, and holding fashion shows. The citizens' group that launched the initiative to freeze further development of the field continues to meet as the "Field Forum" and determines which initiatives may be implemented on the former airport grounds. In 2016, 3,000 refugees from Syria and other countries were housed in containers at the edge of the area. After a temporary decline, the increasing number of refugees in 2022 and 2023 has led to the reuse of the containers.

Excavations

Another citizens' initiative with historical, antifascist interests, the Förderverein zum Gedenken an Nazi-Verbrechen um und auf dem Tempelhofer Flugfeld (cf. Förderverein Gedenken 2016) or THF 33–45 for short, approached Susan Pollock and me in 2011 to encourage us to conduct excavations at the Tempelhof airfield. Excavations were required by law because an international garden show was planned that would have potentially impacted archaeological remains. The impetus for our excavations was therefore not academic but a mix of civic interest and legal obligations. In this situation, we conducted an uninterrupted project from the summer of 2012 to the summer of 2014 and recovered an almost unmanageable quantity of 90,000 finds (Bernbeck and Pollock 2018; Hausmair 2019) from the "early concentration camp" Columbia and two forced-labor camps. The concentration camp in the middle of Berlin is largely unknown to Berliners. It consisted of a late-nineteenth-century prison and was not comparable to later camps as it served for short-term incarceration, and sometimes murder, of oppositional individuals within Berlin, with the goal of spreading an atmosphere of fear and terror in the city (Schilde and Tuchel 1990). While multiple witness accounts of this atrocious institution are available, our archaeological exploration revealed only a few material traces of the building's foundations (Bernbeck 2017).

In contrast, extremely scarce archival material of the forced-labor camps allowed us to enrich knowledge about the laborers' suffering in significant ways. Available documents and plans indicated that the camps had been erected by two companies, Weserflug and Lufthansa. The Weserflug section of the camp included 18 barracks, while the Lufthansa section consisted of at least four such buildings. From what is known, the Weserflug camp consisted

Figure 12.1. Excavation of barracks at the Tempelhof airfield, Berlin. © Landesdenk-malamt Berlin, Jessica Meyer.

of a barrack for French prisoners of war and two sections for "Russian" (i.e., Soviet) women and men (Bernbeck 2020).

Our excavations in the forced-labor camp revealed remains of barracks directly below the current green lawns. Burnt posts were the remains of wooden barracks with floor planks, boards for thin walls, and a slightly pitched roof. With a length of 52 meters and a width of 12 meters, the barracks housed 200–250 people, crammed into small rooms (Figure 12.1). At one end, a single bathroom had to suffice for all of the laborers. Infrastructural elements such as fence remnants and barbed wire divided the camp into different areas. The section for Soviet men also had a line of underground barbed wire, still in its original place. It may have been for Soviet prisoners of war, since it is known that they were inhumanely treated by the Nazis.

Two water reservoirs lined with concrete were intended to extinguish any fires emanating from burning barracks when British and later US air raids dropped incendiary bombs. Poorly constructed air-raid shelters (Figure 12.2) were meant to protect workers during the bombing attacks that increased massively toward the end of the war. The water reservoirs proved to be inadequate: In the winter of 1943 to 1944, one hit reduced the entire camp to charred remains (Bernbeck 2017).

Place and Memory

Although the repressive and inhumane history of the airfield has been known for some time, Tempelhof is dominated by the symbolism of its anticommu-

Figure 12.2. An air raid shelter next to a Lufthansa forced labor camp, destroyed by bombing and postwar bulldozing. © Landesdenkmalamt Berlin, Jan Trenner and Edward Collins.

nist role in the Berlin Airlift in 1948–1949, when Stalin attempted to integrate West Berlin into the Eastern Bloc by barring all access routes to the city. The ensuing airlift, carried out mainly by the US Air Force, led to a reorientation of remnant sympathies for the Nazis to staunchly pro-American attitudes in West Berlin—in the midst of the McCarthy era in the United States (Eisenhuth and Krause 2014).

In the present, with Germany's increasingly radical neo-Nazi movements, the question of how to deal with the history of the airfield has led to complex negotiations. Berlin's population is traditionally politically left-leaning despite a recent upheaval that brought a conservative party to power. However, the eastern and southeastern outskirts are inhabited by a substantial right-wing population. The more radical of them, mainly members of openly neo-Nazi groups, carry out attacks on memorials for Nazi victims in the city but also on people with a foreign background. The police take acts of sabotage by left-wing groups very seriously while turning a blind eye to right-wing extremists (Joswig 2023).

Due to the increasingly tense situation, many citizens' initiatives feel compelled to emphasize the memorialization of Nazi crimes and, above all, to redress the imbalance of material remains that enhance the visibility of perpetrators and makes victims almost invisible. Where are remains of the buildings that attest to the victims of the Nazis? Berlin had about 3,000 camps for the religious and political opposition, homosexuals, and particularly for prisoners of war and forced laborers. There were also transit camps, "Krankenlager" (camps for the sick), and even "Sterbelager" (camps for the dying). Almost no traces of these structures are visible anymore. In Tempelhof, the situation is particularly stark. The gigantic Nazi airport building, more than one kilometer long, dominates the district, while there is hardly any trace of the shabby barracks for the forced laborers. Taphonomy is political, and material culture turns into a vicious medium for silencing the oppressed.

The urge not to forget the Nazi atrocities led to the founding of the Association of Those Persecuted by the Nazi Regime (VVN[1]) right after the war, an association that has since been placed under observation by the Office for the Protection of the Constitution as infiltrated by communists. One of their members is Hans Coppi, who was born in a Berlin prison to two resistance fighters just before they were beheaded by the Nazis. The VVN as well as other groups campaign for a reorientation of commemoration at Tempelhof away from the overfocus on the postwar airlift to a "visibilization" of the forced-labor camps and the concentration camp that were once located there. Several groups and individuals share the goal of remembrance as an antidote to contemptuous attacks by right-wing extremists. However, they are far from an agreement about how to do so. A roundtable was established in 2012 where grassroots organizations interested in shaping the site's past have come together with members of the city administration to discuss issues of commemoration (Runder Tisch Tempelhof 2014).

As archaeologists, we are invited to the (still existent) roundtable but have no other role than to report our work. The intended downplaying of our input has not been a disadvantageous position. It has enabled us to intervene when retort was needed because specific claims did not adhere to "facts on the ground." We were not able to impose an agenda of our own, but we were listened to when presenting archaeological evidence. According to everyone's opinion, archaeologists are to be taken seriously because of the indisputable material results of their work: bricks, broken glass, or rusty nails. Our information does not help to speed up discussions that drag on over the years. Every step involving a new addition to information about the field's Nazi past is hotly debated, and the proclaimed attempt to devise a "general plan of remembrance" has yet to be realized.

The reactions to the roundtable's work in general, and our excavations in particular are not unanimously positive. In addition to the aforementioned neo-Nazis, we also encounter a more moderate opposition that condemns a perceived "surplus of commemoration" in Berlin (translations by the author):

> Isn't it enough with the memorials, commemorative plaques, days of mourning, memorial processions. . . . ? Doesn't German history have more to offer than these 12 years to remember?[2]

> Another memorial? Nowhere have so few voted for the NSDAP as in the constituency of Berlin. Nowhere are there so many memorials. Put one up in Munich—the capital of the movement—honestly. This over-memorializing in Berlin is sick. We want to live here, too![3]

Statements that align with this last one appear again and again in public debates: there are so many memorials, they impinge on everyday life. The past weighs too heavily on the present. My question for a community archaeology in Berlin under these circumstances is: Should this past not do so? In this instance, should community archaeology be guided by local desires for a respite from the past's burden? In my view, that would be entirely wrong. A glance at books written by those who live in Germany and whose families perished in Nazi times shows that silencing is still the dominant agenda, even if not uniformly (e.g., Ambros 2013). The AfD and other reactionary groups try to engender an ultranationalist counter-history of Germany's Nazi history by ridiculing Nazi atrocities and belittling its victims. Archaeologists must respond actively to this situation unless they risk reinforcing tendencies toward reactionary populism. The German right-wing scene has also developed a particularly perfidious strategy toward places of remembrance: they enter memorial sites at former concentration camps, leave swastikas on the ruins, and desecrate the material remains that are meant to keep the memory alive of those who were brutally murdered there (Knopke 2014). Not all preservation efforts of monuments are part of reactionary populism (contra Chapter 1, this volume).

Excavation as a Social Process

While the impetus for the excavation at Tempelhof came from a disparate assemblage of communities, the excavation itself also brought together people from a wide variety of social and ideological backgrounds. We were obliged to have an ordnance-clearing controller with us throughout the excavation to protect us from finds of unexploded ordnance. In this position, he was to be shown any potential bullets and remains of mines, bombs, and the like. Unfortunately, people who work in this realm often do so because of their interests in weapons rather than in the ethics of their use. This was also the case on our excavation. The "fireworker" turned out to be a young man with apparent far-right political leanings.

However, there were also other voices. Excavating remains of modern history in Europe provides multiple sites for reflection. I cite here some insights stemming from interviews with students who participated in the excavation. These interviews were conducted in 2015 and 2016, that is, not during the work but after some time had passed (Bernbeck 2017: 388–399).[4]

One student expressed a

> sense of duty to reveal the abuses of the time and a certain *schadenfreude* about the fact that we were able to expose the perpetrators with this. At least more people know now than before that Lufthansa does not have a clean slate.

Emotions on a personal level were not commonly expressed. For some, there was "never the feeling of directly digging up my own past." It was "actually curiosity and interest, rather than feelings of guilt, shame, sadness." But

> when personal items came to light, like a rosary in an air-raid shelter, and I thought about the owner(s), I had a moment of sadness. . . . But I have this attempt at empathy on other digs as well.

Another person commented:

> I was always very depressed when I held very personal objects like combs or parts of toys . . . in my hands. I tried to imagine the owners and wondered what meaning this object must have had for this person and for what reasons it now ended up where we found it.

Some students addressed their own background:

> My grandfather, for example, was a *partigiano* (partisan) during World War II and fought in Italy against the same regime that built the forced-labor camp on the Tempelhof Airfield. . . . I don't think that the temporal distance is of importance here, but rather the awareness that a time or an event which actively and strongly influenced my grandfather's life did so as well for the history of my family and myself.

In stark contrast, another student said:

> My great-grandfather was in the SS. . . . I had to think about how the Nazis acted during the war, knowing my own family was involved. . . . But to be honest, these thoughts were not really any different than for other epochs.

Students not only referred to the horrific past and the (lack of) emotions of revealing it but also to the contrast with the present surroundings within which they were working. This relation was perceived as tense and partly problematic:

> I came with my conception of a dark Nazi airport/aircraft labor camp but what I saw was a huge open park with an altered identity. I felt a strange insistence on changing the use of this area. . . . For me, it was an erasing of history. I was just shocked.

A further response observes a strong disconnect by referring to the times after the excavation:

> The more we uncovered, the stronger appeared the contrast with the softball field next door, the joggers, and the overall park atmosphere of Tempelhof Airfield today. After the excavation was finished and the trenches were backfilled, this contrast became even more powerful for me.

Students are part of a temporary, fluctuating network centered around an academic institution. The responses reported here show that they do not constitute a uniform community. Such work attracts a variety of participants who to some extent pursue a common goal. But the range of involvement went beyond the voices collected here. Some students simply wanted to take part in an excavation, no matter what kind of site it was. They were drawn to the practical and technical sides of the work rather than any historical interest. However, I do not think that we had anyone of reactionary persuasion with us, the employee of the ordnance-clearing company excluded. I must say that I did not know how to deal usefully with him other than asking him to remove advertisements with militaristic content he had hung up in our little contractor trailer.

Outlook: From Dispute Value to Indisputability

It is certain that reactionary attacks against memory sites of victims of the Nazi dictatorship will rapidly increase in the near future. This is not only due to a rapid shift in public discourse that is based on shallow or no factual knowledge, fed increasingly by right-wing social media; rather, economic resources for political and historical education change in direct relation to public opinion. German law distributes financial resources to political parties according to their proportion of votes in elections. The racist AfD's jump in the last federal elections from 4.7% in 2013 to 10.3% in 2021 fills their coffers; projections based on current polls predict 20 to 30% for the party. One of their foremost interests is to use these resources for the establishment of foundations such as the Desiderius-Erasmus-Stiftung that give history a sharp ideological twist toward nationalism, supremacist ideologies, and racism (Semsrott and Jakubowski 2021; introduction to this volume). The enormous success of their populist ideas is evident in endless posts. Growing awareness of these tendencies has yet to have a serious policy effect (Funke 2019).

What can archaeologists do to counter such developments, to prevent a threatening return to fascism that we can witness everywhere in Europe today? Gabi Dolff-Bonekämper (2000: 40) suggests that we need a new narrative about the past, and particularly of heritage, a narrative that must be committed to a "good popularization." Such a discourse should shy away from facile simplifications, the commodification of heritage, and a "progressive populism" (Ayán Vila, this volume: Chapter 5). Dolff-Bonekämper emphasizes the high value of public disputes over past materiality since they must resort to convincing arguments of facticity that include a concentration on detail. She summarizes this under the notion of the "dispute value" of sites and monuments, an effect that keeps collective memory alive.

This stands in contrast to the general concept of community archaeology as a process of negotiation between multiple actors, their voices, and interests. Instead of multivocality and a gradual process toward agreement and harmony, Dolff-Bonekämper (2021) advocates for sharp disagreements, open critique, and dissonance as a better path toward an indispensable reflexivity. Her stance radically rejects the ethical consequence of Foucault's idea of knowledge as power. Dolff-Bonekämper assumes—falsely—that communities and archaeologists have the possibility to argue on an equal footing. They do not. In the realm of archaeology, addressing a large, highly diverse, and anonymous audience is the privilege of public intellectuals rather than co-resident communities. Nevertheless, in the current political climate, it is wise to heed Dolff-Bonekämper's main message but with the proviso that the formalities of communication—dispute for the sake of differentiation—do not suffice.

The content of archaeology's projects is more important. In this realm, empiricism may take on a new weight, as Adel Yahya insisted. But the sheer materiality of the archaeological record is insufficient. It attests to forced-labor camps, Nazi architectural megalomania, ritual landscapes, and past or present sites of the poor. In almost all cases, the specific course of events at these places remains unknown, as do the people involved in it. I once thought of an archaeology of the Nazi period in terms of a "framed ambiguity" where historical knowledge and archives reveal general processes and smaller-scale practices and set the frame for the interpretation of highly ambiguous archaeological remains (Bernbeck 2015). With the rapid advance of reactionary ideas and the propagation of twisted historical discourse, the meaning of "framed ambiguity" needs to be reversed: archaeology provides the indisputable material frame for an increasingly disquieting discourse about the past.

Acknowledgments

I thank Randy and Alfredo for their invitation to contribute to this volume and their useful comments. Important input came also from Ruth Van Dyke, Katherine Hayes, and an anonymous reviewer. Susan Pollock and Barbara Hausmair discussed with me many of the issues raised here. I also thank Alfredo González-Ruibal and Felipe Criado-Boado for their hospitality at the Cidade da Cultura in Santiago de Compostela.

Notes

1 Verein der Verfolgten des Nazi-Regimes (VVN; https://berlin.vvn-bda.de/).
2 "Alexjacob" https://taz.de/Zwangsarbeiter-in-Tempelhof/!5140862/.
3 "Enzoaduro" https://taz.de/Berliner-Geschichte/!5096934/.
4 All quotes with permission of the interviewed; translated by the author.

References Cited

Abu El-Haj, Nadia. 2002. *Facts on the Ground: Archaeological Practice and Territorial Self-Fashioning in Israeli Society.* University of Chicago Press, Chicago.
Ambros, Peter. 2013. *Das wortreiche deutsche Schweigen.* Argument-Verlag, Hamburg.
Appadurai, Arjun. 2006. *Fear of Small Numbers: An Essay on the Geography of Anger.* Duke University Press, Durham, North Carolina.
Bernbeck, Reinhard. 2015. "Framed Ambiguity": Zum historiographischen Status der Dinge aus Grabungen in Konzentrationslagern und NS-Zwangsarbeitslagern. *Historische Anthropologie* 23(3): 413–430.
Bernbeck, Reinhard. 2017. *Materielle Spuren des nationalsozialistischen Terrors: Zu einer Archäologie der Zeitgeschichte.* Transcript, Bielefeld, Germany.
Bernbeck, Reinhard. 2020. The Archaeology of State Terror: The Example of Nazi Germany. In *Arqueología de la dictadura en latinoamérica y Europa occidental: Violencia, resistencia, resiliencia,* edited by Bruno Rosignoli, Carlos Marín Suárez, and Carlos Tejerizo-Garcia, pp. 210–224. British Archaeological Reports, Oxford.
Bernbeck, Reinhard, and Randall H. McGuire. 2011. A Conceptual History of Ideology and Its Place in Archaeology. In *Ideologies in Archaeology,* edited by Reinhard Bernbeck and Randall H. McGuire, pp. 15–59. University of Arizona Press, Tucson.
Bernbeck, Reinhard, and Susan Pollock. 2018. Quotidian and Transgressive Practices in

Nazi Forced Labor Camps: The Role of Objects. *International Journal of Historical Archaeology* 22(3): 454–471.

Budrass, Lutz. 2016. *Adler und Kranich: Die Lufthansa und ihre Geschichte 1926–1955.* Blessing, Munich.

Dodd, Lynn, and Ran Boytner. 2018. Archaeology and Bodies of Knowledge in the Israeli–Palestinian Conflict. In *Reclaiming the Past for the Future: Oral History, Craft, and Archaeology; Adel Yahya in Memoriam,* edited by Reinhard Bernbeck, Arwa Badran, and Susan Pollock, pp. 45–66. Ex Oriente, Berlin.

Dolff-Bonekämper, Gabi. 2000. Sites of Historical Significance and Sites of Discord: Historic Monuments as a Tool for Discussing Conflict in Europe. In *Forward Planning: The Function of Cultural Heritage in Changing Europe,* edited by Daniel Therond, pp. 53–58 Council of Europe, Strasbourg.

Dolff-Bonekämper, Gabi. 2021. *Der Streitwert der Denkmale.* Technical University, Berlin.

Eisenhuth, Stefanie, and Scott H. Krause. 2014. Inventing the "Outpost of Freedom": Transatlantic Narratives and the Historical Actors Crafting West Berlin's Postwar Culture. *Zeithistorische Forschungen / Studies in Contemporary History* 11(2): 188–211.

Förderverein Gedenken. 2016. Förderverein für ein Gedenken an die Nazi-Verbrechen auf dem und um das Tempelhofer Flugfeld e.V. *Förderverein für ein Gedenken an die Nazi-Verbrechen auf dem und um das Tempelhofer Flugfeld e.V.* http://thf33-45.de/, last accessed July 3, 2023.

Foucault, Michel. 1981. Truth and Power. In *Power/Knowledge: Selected Interviews and Other Writings, 1972–1977 by Michael Foucault,* edited by Colin Gordon, translated by Colin Gordon, pp. 109–133. Pantheon, New York.

Funke, Hajo. 2019. *Der Kampf um die Erinnerung.* VSA, Hamburg.

Gero, Joan M. 1996. Archaeological Practice and Gendered Encounters with Field Data. In *Gender and Archaeology,* edited by Rita P. Wright, pp. 251–280. University of Pennsylvania Press, Philadelphia.

González-Ruibal, Alfredo. 2023. Walking through the Darkest Valley: Heritage and Hatred in the Era of Reactionary Populism. In *Polarized Pasts: Heritage and Belonging in Times of Political Polarization,* edited by Elisabeth Niklasson, pp. 134–155. Berghahn, New York.

Greenberg, Raphael. 2018. The Jerusalem Heritage Zone: Two Proposals. In *Reclaiming the Past for the Future: Oral History Craft, and Archaeology; Adel Yahya in Memoriam,* edited by Reinhard Bernbeck, Arwa Badran, and Susan Pollock, pp. 21–44. Ex Oriente, Berlin.

Habu, Junko, Clare Fawcett, and John F. Matsunaga (editors). 2008. *Evaluating Multiple Narratives beyond Nationalist, Colonialist, Imperialist Archaeologies.* Springer, New York.

Hausmair, Barbara. 2019. *NS-Zwangsarbeit ausgraben: Archäologie auf dem Tempelhofer Feld.* 2nd ed. Landesdenkmalamt Berlin / Freie Universität Berlin, Berlin.

Hilbrandt, Hanna. 2016. Insurgent Participation: Consensus and Contestation in Planning the Redevelopment of Berlin-Tempelhof Airport. *Urban Geography* 38(4): 537–566.

Houdalieh, Saleh, Reinhard Bernbeck, and Susan Pollock. 2017. Palestinian Looted Tombs and Their Archaeological Investigation. *Journal of Eastern Mediterranean Archaeology and Heritage Studies* 5(2): 199–240.

Joswig, Gareth. 2023. 300 Straftaten rechts liegen gelassen. *tageszeitung* November 23, 2023. https://taz.de/Ermittlungen-gegen-Berliner-Polizisten/!5971521/.

Knopke, Christoph (editor). 2014. *Angriffe auf die Erinnerung an die nationalsozialistischen Verbrechen: Rechtsextremismus in Brandenburg und die Gedenkstätte Sachsenhausen.* Metropol, Berlin.

Krastev, Ivan. 2017. Auf dem Weg in eine Mehrheitsdiktatur? In *Die große Regression,* edited by Heinrich Geiselberger, pp. 117–134. Suhrkamp, Berlin.

Little, Barbara J. 2023. *Bending Archaeology Toward Social Justice.* University of Alabama Press, Tuscaloosa.

Moshenska, Gabriel. 2023. A Gloves-Off Activist Archaeology? *Forum Kritische Archäologie* 12: 49–52.

Panov, Stoyan. 2020. The Effect of Populism on the Rule of Law, Separation of Powers and Judicial Independence in Hungary and Poland. In *European Populism and Human Rights,* edited by Jure Vidmar, pp. 256–288. Brill, Leiden.

Pappas, Takis S. 2016. Are Populist Leaders "Charismatic"? The Evidence from Europe. *Constellations* 23(3): 378–390.

Reißmann, Ole. 2010. Moschee-Anschlagsserie schreckt Berlin auf. *Der Spiegel Online,* October 12, 2010.

Runder Tisch Tempelhof. 2014. Runder Tisch "Historische Markierung Tempelhofer Feld." Sachstandsbericht zur bisherigen Arbeit. https://tempelhofer-feld.berlin.de/documents/23/sachstandsbericht-rundertisch2014.pdf.

Scham, Sandra, and Ann E. Killebrew. 2018. Many More Rivers to Cross: Experiments in Shared Heritage. In *Reclaiming the Past for the Future: Oral History Craft, and Archaeology; Adel Yahya in Memoriam,* edited by Reinhard Bernbeck, Arwa Badran, and Susan Pollock, pp. 95–110. Ex Oriente, Berlin.

Scham, Sandra, and Adel Yahya. 2003. Heritage and Reconciliation. *Journal of Social Archaeology* 3(3): 399–416.

Schilde, Kurt, and Johannes Tuchel. 1990. *Columbia-Haus: Berliner Konzentrationslager 1933–1936.* Edition Hentrich, Berlin.

Semsrott, Arne, and Matthias Jakubowski. 2021. *Desiderius-Erasmus-Stiftung: Politische Bildung von Rechtsaußen.* Working Paper 51 of the Otto Benner Stiftung, Frankfurt/M.

Silberman, Neil A., and David B. Small (editors). 1997. *The Archaeology of Israel: Constructing the Past, Interpreting the Present.* Sheffield Academic Press, Sheffield, England.

Spielman, Doron. 2019. Israeli and American Dignitaries Unveil the Pilgrimage Road. *Times of Israel,* blog, June 30, 2019. https://blogs.timesofisrael.com/israeli-and-american-dignitaries-unveil-pilgrimage-road/.

Spivak, Gayatri Chakravorty. 1985. Subaltern Studies: Deconstructing Historiography. In *The Spivak Reader,* edited by Donna Landry and Gerald MacLean, pp. 203–235. Routledge, New York.

Tillmanns, Jenny. 2012. *Was heißt historische Verantwortung? Historisches Unrecht und seine Folgen für die Gegenwart.* Transcript, Bielefeld, Germany.

Wenz, F.-Herbert. 2006.*Flughafen Tempelhof: Chronik des Berliner Werkes der "Weser" Flugzeugbau GmbH—Bremen.* 2nd ed. Stedinger Verlag, Lemwerder.

Wylie, Alison. 2003. Why Standpoint Theory Matters: Feminist Standpoint Theory. In *Phil-*

osophical of Science, Technology, and Diversity, edited by Robert M. Figueria and Sandra Harding, pp. 26–48. Routledge, New York.

Yahya, Adel. 2008. Looting and "Salvaging": How the Wall, Illegal Digging and the Antiquities Trade are Ravaging Palestinian Cultural Heritage. *Jerusalem Quarterly* 33: 39–55.

Žižek, Slavoj. 1994. Introduction: The Spectre of Ideology. In *Mapping Ideology,* edited by Slavoj Žižek, pp. 1–33. Verso, London.

13

Commentary

CLAUDIA THEUNE

Alfredo González-Ruibal and Randall H. McGuire have asked me to write a commentary on the preceding chapters that also discusses forward-looking statements for community archaeology in times of populism or reactionary populism. The request caused me to reflect on the situation of archaeology and consider directions for the coming years to strengthen public interest and broad acceptance of profound archaeological interpretations and narratives among communities as well as to counter and limit reactionary populism and its influence on archaeology.

Fifteen contributions were planned for the conference, with the speakers coming from very different regions of the world: the United States (three contributions), Canada (one), Brazil (one), Argentina (one), Australia (one), Great Britain (three), Spain and Portugal (two), Ireland (one), Germany (one), and Austria (one). First, it should be noted that—and I am only referring to the current affiliations and educational backgrounds of the participants—a very broad field was covered, but not all global continents. Often, at least a temporary "Western" affiliation can be ascertained regarding training in archaeology or heritage studies. In the end 11 contributions are published, which still shows a broad internationality and thus diversity of the approaches to the conference topic. But if one takes a closer look at the authors' topics and their case studies, not all global regions are covered. For example, no colleague from the Eastern European region participated, and the Western Asian region is only mentioned in a few words by Reinhard Bernbeck. North and South American—admittedly in a large breadth—and Western and Central European examples predominate. This should not be understood as a criticism of the concept and the compilation of the contributions in this book. It may perhaps be related to the current political situation in many regions of the world or to the situation within archaeology that in some regions only a few archaeologists are addressing the impact of populism on our discipline.

We should consider including more regions of the world for future comparable conferences, even if it may happen to be uncomfortable so that other political positions are represented.

In this commentary I do not go into the chapters in detail. Instead, I provide a general commentary and discuss the main terms, such as "reactionary populism," "progressive populism," "community," and "neoliberalism," partly in response to the remarks of González-Ruibal and McGuire in the introduction. I also refer to the authors and their core theses. I perhaps do not always touch on the most important aspects for the authors, but I mention what is fundamental for me. I add my thoughts in order to make forward-looking statements that can possibly counter populism in general.

I think in this way the manifold impressions, the diverse approaches, and ways of proceeding toward a community archaeology can be commented upon, which develops and shares the archaeological (scientific) results together with the community. To anticipate, the presented suggestions and experiences regarding the most promising community archaeology are very different, as they depend on the regional framework conditions and the self-determined objectives. The variety of ways to do community archaeology that is presented is certainly one of the great added values of this book. It provides inspiration for other archaeologists around the world. But it also shows very clearly that there is no silver bullet for a widely accepted community archaeology; too many specific frameworks have to be considered.

In the introduction, Alfredo González-Ruibal and Randall McGuire give a very detailed and informative overview of the political developments of the last decades from a global perspective. They discuss in detail two main types of populism: reactionary (bad) populism and progressive (not quite so bad) populism. This is certainly true; we cannot and must not lump the different approaches together and must differentiate between them. The editors provide many examples of the distortion of history and archaeology by reactionary populists, but we should be aware that the progressive populists are also spreading populist narratives.

In the introduction, González-Ruibal and McGuire do not only address populist movements. Related developments that are fundamental for the current situation in society and politics are important to address, and thus also in archaeology. Nationalism, neoliberalism, and capitalism are just some of the other keywords that occur again and again in various chapters; these affect many regions of the world and, in turn, archaeology. In addition, Xurxo Ayán Vila cites Catholicism (Chapter 5). In some cases, tourism is mentioned by authors (e.g., Ayán Vila: Chapter 5; McAnany: Chapter 11), which, on the one hand, is certainly a source of income for the local population. On the other hand, tourism can lead to a high degree of commercialization and often damages the archaeological heritage as well as works against the positive multivoiced involvement of the communities.

Nationalism, which often bears colonial and hegemonic elements, was and still is widespread in many states (González-Ruibal: Chapter 2; Montgomery: Chapter 3; Moshenska et al.: Chapter 9). Often this is linked in archaeology—as rightly pointed out in several passages—to the formation of nation-states in the nineteenth and twentieth centuries, as well as the birth of archaeology in the nineteenth century. At that time archaeology was used to postulate apparently "ancient" traditions and origins of peoples and provided important arguments for the formation of nation-states. We know this approach from ancient times: here, too, people referred to older leading figures and heritage sites in order to construct their own heroic history. Often such narratives were and are also used in the twentieth and twenty-first centuries by people in power and politicians to postulate that archaeological findings can prove ancient (ethnic) traditions and justify territorial claims and other populist sentiments. Such nationalist narratives are still widespread or are experiencing a revival. The current wars in the world are exacerbating the ongoing growth of populism, with only the recent elections in Poland providing hope that democratic values are growing stronger again.

Apart from Spain, the United States, Hungary, and Poland are repeatedly cited as examples where nationalism is emerging, but similar developments can be observed in other countries of the world. The presented examples that can easily further be supplemented, for example, related to the AfD (Alternative für Deutschland) in Germany or developments in Austria. It is striking when official politicians, for example, in Hungary, associate archaeological cultures from the distant past with today's communities, ethnic groups, and then nations. Hungarian prime minister Viktor Orbán repeatedly advocates for a greater Hungary and displays nationalistic approaches when he offers Hungarian passports to people from Slovakia who can prove a "Hungarian ancestral line." Moreover, the inalienability of human rights is being called into question; for example, in 2019 the Austrian minister of the interior, Herbert Kickl, questioned fundamental rules such as those of the European Convention on Human Rights, and the former Carinthian governor Gerhard Dörfler put the protection of the (domestic/Austrian—whoever this is) population before human rights in relation to an asylum policy. The dangers of populism are clearly visible here.

Such apparent or constructed ethnic continuity often contributes to archaeological projects being accepted and being supported by the local population (Ayán Vila: Chapter 5). In Spain this is explicitly stated, and the reasons given are an "ancient" tradition; a unity based on a common language and faith and uniform customs; and the need for glory (González-Ruibal: Chapter 2). For Britain, too, it is stated that imperial grandeur continues to be propagated, but now a reckoning is taking place through community archaeology projects (Moshenska et al.: Chapter 9). Moreover, neocolonialist traits become evident when the sovereignty of Indigenous peoples and their rights to resources in their own territories are denied and government-backed capitalist goals are pursued or when claims of (white [bad]) settlers are supported and Indigenous claims and identity are erased (Montgomery: Chapter 3).

Allow me to add an example of archaeogenetic analysis, currently considered to be in vogue, that also promotes such nationalist thinking. The terminology used by scientists for the popular and widespread determination of the haplotypes is often associated with interpretations that include only a certain group of people and exclude others. This refers to the archaeogenetic DNA analyses of victims of the Holocaust currently being carried out, for example in Poland (Diepenbroek et al. 2021). Here haplogroups have been recognized that have been determined to be Ashkenazi Jews; these are distinguished from (Catholic?) Poles. This mixes religious and nation-state classifications. Even if the haplotype could be determined, this says nothing about the religious orientation of the victims. Written documents instead give the impression that the victims considered themselves to be Polish, Dutch, French, and German, and so on, in terms of their nationality. Whether they were practicing Jews, whether they regularly went to a synagogue and celebrated Jewish ceremonies or not cannot be determined by the DNA analyses. However, the distinction between Ashkenazi Jews and Poles suggests this. National Socialist classifications according to the Nuremberg Race Laws have been and are being adopted, possibly unconsciously, but they are repeated. Such interpretations are currently also purposefully promoted by other nations, both to argue inclusion in a national Jewish community or to portray exclusion, depending on the political objective (see also González-Ruibal: Chapter 2). To repeat, the current wars in Ukraine and the Gaza Strip support these developments.

It is important to state that archaeologists have always been involved in the process of linking archaeological/historical interpretations and political use (e.g., Montgomery: Chapter 3). Archaeology is never objective—as is sometimes still claimed—every archaeological interpretation is influenced by our sociopolitical background. It is questionable whether the often-cited ivory tower ever existed; archaeology (apart from detailed analyses) always took place in public. Citing the ivory tower is therefore possibly only as a retreat from the responsibility of interpretation. Too often "Western"—and certainly, although perhaps unconsciously, colonial—interpretations and those entrenched in old white patriarchal thought still play a role (Moshenska et al.: Chapter 9). This is particularly striking when state institutions explain their past to Indigenous populations (Gnecco: Chapter 4; Van Dyke: Chapter 10). Incidentally, this applies not only to the archaeology that is the focus of this volume but also, for example, to Egyptology (Köhler 2020) or classical archaeology. The constant critical examination of old and new archaeological interpretations and the questioning of common paradigms and narratives often reveal a remaining link to outdated patriarchal, colonialist mindsets. Only if we are aware of these mechanisms do we have the possibility of taking other positions and proposing alternative interpretations in the future.

I also regard the frequently expressed comments on terms like "neoliberalism," "capitalism," and the archaeology according to the polluter pays principle, which is now widespread in many countries, as quite elementary. These perspectives can only underline the argument that critical archaeology and engaged community archaeology will suffer as a result. Archaeologists are beholden to their clients if they want to compete in the tight market of bidding for commissions (Gnecco: Chapter 4). In such situations, it can be difficult to oppose the interests of funders who may, on behalf of governments, irreversibly destroy historic landscapes and heritage sites without regard to their significance. In such situations, promoting local communities, descendants, or other stakeholders and their interests is not the first objective. This undoubtedly addresses a global problem.

The term "community" is often mentioned in the chapters—a central part of community archaeology. One difficulty with the term is that it is rarely clearly defined. Apart from that, it is correctly emphasized that one cannot and should not speak of one community because there are always numerous communities. These are dynamic and can change regionally and over time. Communities can be compared to the sociological concept of groups, about which the cultural anthropologist Fredrik Barth wrote a groundbreaking essay nearly 60 years ago (Barth 1969). Barth emphasizes that it is boundaries and their constant negotiation that shape groups and make them dynamic; through boundaries, people can be included in and excluded from so-called we-groups (Elwert 1995). Populism has a lot to do with exclusion and inclusion. Exclusion is always possible when (ethnic) identity and territoriality are closely linked. Only if we decouple these two categories—especially also for archaeological heritage sites—and if we give up the dualities of us/them, native/foreign, and in/out does a tolerant, even prefigurative coexistence have a chance (Kiddey: Chapter 7). This approach has to be supported. González-Ruibal and McGuire write about it similarly in their introduction.

We must be aware that archaeology is always a political discipline. The entanglement of archaeology and politics (and populists) and communities is immense, each claiming the truth. It is important to note that truth is always about perception and that the same events and actions are perceived differently by different people and communities. This has to be understood first of all. Facts based on reality are facts; a distinction must be made between facts, perceptions, and interpretations. We need to emphasize this clearly in the future.

I am not sure that all archaeologists in the world heed this in their work. But in this volume, all the authors have taken a clear political perspective. All have highlighted the political developments of the last 10–20 years in the various countries and have shown the origins of the populist movements, their further courses, current movements, and effects. All have considered the role of archaeology. This is important if the reader is not so familiar with the regional social and political or archaeological background, and it helps to contextualize the case studies.

But we should not forget that not all of today's active archaeologists have the same political views as the authors of the present volume, among whom there is no follower of populism or someone who goes along with the (populist) governments (Gnecco: Chapter 4). Moreover, for India, populist archaeologists are referred to (González-Ruibal: Chapter 2). I could add examples from Russia in the context of Russia's war of aggression against Ukraine. It should therefore be emphasized once again that it is very important that the archaeologists in this volume take a clear and unambiguous political and social stand, that they stand up clearly and without restriction for democratic rights and for an approach to fellow human beings based on tolerance, and that they always place (their own) ethical and moral actions in the foreground, not the least also in the context of community archaeology.

In the following, I would like to briefly discuss some of the examples of working with communities presented in the chapters. And above all, the different communities do not have to be united in their respective goals, whether they are specific political goals or goals that concern archaeology (Gnecco: Chapter 4). That is certainly one of the very big challenges in community archaeology. The question is whether it is always possible to include different stakeholders or whether our tolerant, inclusive approach means that some groups are insufficiently involved. Nevertheless, we should always aim for a multiculturalist approach and a broad polyphony (e.g., Bernbeck: Chapter 12).

One point I noticed in the chapters of Reinhard Bernbeck and Ruth M. Van Dyke is that if community archaeology is essential to us, we must always redefine our role and engage differently in communities. For Reinhard Bernbeck, as a man socialized in the West German world, it is possible to involve different groups in the archaeological work on the National Socialist forced-labor camp in Berlin-Tempelhof. But he also says quite clearly that this is not possible in his projects in Afghanistan, Iran, and Iraq because he is a stranger there who does not have deep access to the local population. For the workers there, archaeological work on excavations is more about making money (as McAnany also says in Chapter 11 about excavations at sites of the Maya culture). Thus, even a great effort to achieve acceptance in the local community (or communities) can fail.

This volume emphasizes that archaeologists should hold the threads in their hands; should consciously not give up existing archaeological competences (Gnecco: Chapter 4; Ayán Vila: Chapter 5; Van Dyke: Chapter 10); should try to immerse themselves in the community and strive for affiliation, and yet should definitely dismantle (still-) existing academic (dominant) hierarchies and give up academic privileges.

Of great importance are the different, more or less successful approaches of community archaeology. About Ireland, it is stated that projects dealing with older prehistoric or medieval (nonpolitical) and local history are much more common than projects dealing with more recent history (McAtackney: Chapter 8). There is also the view that in many cases middle-class people are more likely to be addressed than working-class people (McGuire: Chapter 6). In Berlin-Tempelhof (Bernbeck: Chapter 12), participation and multi-participation was a goal of the work, even if some participants were politically oriented in a completely different way. In the 1990s, the archaeological investigations of the Colorado Coal Field project saw the intensive involvement of the local population (McGuire: Chapter 6). The project was supported and successful for two reasons: on the one hand, the solidarity of the miners was central. Although they were not biological descendants of the striking workers, the same profession brought solidarity into action. And on the other hand, the fact that two of the archaeologists (McGuire: Chapter 6) came from a working-class background and were socialists helped to build confidence in supporting the political aims of the miners. Today this would probably not work as the miners are now Trump supporters and would certainly be unlikely to show solidarity with the former strikers (McGuire: Chapter 6). The San Lourenzo hill fortification project in Galicia was also successful, despite a multitude of difficulties, because the archaeologist, Ayán Vila (see Chapter 5), was also a member of the local community and willing to make many compromises. The community archaeology projects in Chaco Canyon were also successful in the end—again, despite many challenges—because the archaeologist, Van Dyke (see Chapter 10) stepped back and intensively involved the various Indigenous groups in all processes. Conversely, she had to emphasize her archaeological competence in terms of broad and contextual interpretations so that the project in Texas could be pursued positively.

The concept of care is emphasized in Rachael Kiddey's description of the Made in Migration project (see Chapter 7). There is no doubt that caring and a strong focus on ethical and moral practices are key points of community archaeology for Lindsay Martel Montgomery (see Chapter 3), but the path is different: the academic discourse is not absolutely in the foreground; shared prefigurative practices in a collaboration with people of very different origins are. Whether everyone wants to follow (radical anarchist) prefigurative principles is open to question, but if it fits, why not? Gabriel Moshenska and colleagues repeatedly mention transnational activist networks as possible agents (see Chapter 9). People and archaeologists who still want to pull all the strings in community archaeology projects are less likely to follow this approach.

For Cristóbal Gnecco's example from Brazil, he describes "timid" multicultural approaches, and he also addresses the balancing act between a traditional academic archaeology and the demands for openness and tolerance (see Chapter 4). The strings should always be in the hands of archaeology, and Gnecco also mentions the possibility of playing the game of official institutions—if, as Ayán Vila points out, this can generate financial support (see Chapter 5).

Another aspect of nationalism is raised in the context of statues—or the destruction of statues (McAnany: Chapter 11; McAtackney: Chapter 8). The continued glorification of historical persons who harmed people, who murdered, who exploited and robbed, and who were responsible for crimes is aptly termed "hurtful heritage" (McAnany: Chapter 11) as opposed to perhaps more familiar terms such as "dark heritage" or "negative heritage." Such statues still follow old paternalistic, nationalistic, colonial, and racist attitudes, which can be painful for people. When we archaeologists criticize such national narratives entrenched in old power structures, when we expose oppression, exploitation, robbery, and exclusion, we (rightly) damage the traditional master narratives that have long been handed down, and we provide new narratives.

González-Ruibal's arguments on the moral superiority of the Spanish in the context of Spanish colonial power differ but are interesting in this context (see Chapter 2). Here the intermarriage of the Spanish with the Indigenous population and the creation of large mestizo populations is cited in praise of miscegenation; something similar is postulated for Italy.

The experience in Spain leads to the idea of asking new archaeological research questions, such as care and hospitality. In this way inclusion rather than exclusion can be emphasized: the local population could easily be involved in the discussion of such topics, as people can identify with these values (González-Ruibal: Chapter 2). The concept of solidarity and the aspect of shared experience would certainly also be such a future perspective (Gnecco: Chapter 4; McGuire: Chapter 6).

It thus becomes very clear that as archaeologists we have to cooperate situationally with one or multiple communities. There is no single, universally valid model for successful cooperation with local groups, descendants, or other communities. It depends on the conditions of the sociopolitical framework on both the small and large scales. I would also like to add the option of including art projects that bring together different stakeholders (and not only artists) and that could be applied to memory projects.

Laura McAtackney (Chapter 8) suggests social media as important vehicles for community archaeology in order to explicitly address a broad online audience. González-Ruibal and McGuire emphasize this point out as well in the introduction. On the one hand, this can provide positive information about community archaeology projects. But on the other hand, the same media are used by the opposing side in many ways, with truncated and simplistic representations, half-truths, untruths, and conspiracy theories widely disseminated.

Although great efforts are needed for alternative narratives to succeed, they should always be the final goal (Moshenska et al.: Chapter 9). Only open and tolerant societies are capable of confronting such new narratives or even allowing contested narratives and history. In some cases, this succeeds–for example, when Germany and Austria face up to their responsibility regarding the Holocaust and pursue an active remembrance policy, or when in Belgium the crimes of King Leopold are slowly being named as such. But too many atrocities in the former colonies continue to be insufficiently brought to light (Moshenska et al.: Chapter 9).

The editors suggest that great master narratives should also be created through archaeology, depicting essential lines of historical developments while emphasizing democratic and tolerant values. This is certainly a good idea. It is equally important to develop narratives that are significant for small regions in order to engage people in their local area and community with their history.

Not all community archaeology projects have positive developments. Exclusions, which can also be enforced by certain forms of repressive, prescriptive, or constitutive forgetting, are still present (McAnany: Chapter 11). Such forgetting is described in relation to the very one-sided heroization of (colonialist) people in power (McAnany: Chapter 11); the crimes committed in Ireland against countless children, young girls, and women in institutions run by nuns (McAtackney: Chapter 8); the attempts made to block plans to protected status of Indigenous landscapes (Montgomery: Chapter 3); and the negating or downplaying of colonial crimes and the exploitation and theft of cultural heritage (Ayán Vila: Chapter 5; Moshenska et al.: Chapter 9). Thus, it is our task to uncover the memories that have been buried in this way, to protect them from further forgetting, and to keep publicly pointing out the abuses in order to actively build new narratives with the help of an agile interdisciplinary and transnational activist network (Moshenska et al.: Chapter 9). This is also accompanied by the demand to pursue principled decolonizing and abolitionist approaches (Montgomery: Chapter 3), certainly an important one and one that we have to face anew every day. This should also include the return of looted cultural goods (Ayán Vila: Chapter 5).

Approaches in community archaeology also fail when imperial nostalgia (McAnany: Chapter 11) is too powerful to cause change, when old and new colonial narratives are to be powerfully preserved (Moshenska et al.: Chapter 9). In such cases, removing a statue, engaging in human rights critique, or adding further signage to contextualize such statues may not succeed. Obstacles to fruitful community archaeology also exist when economic (tourist) interests prevent the participation of the local population and when schools or general historiography do not teach connections with one's own cultural heritage but rather the glories of colonization as achievements (McAnany: Chapter 11; Moshenska et al.: Chapter 9). We should keep pointing out outdated views, and we may possibly succeed after some time of steady engagement.

This short overview of the contributions clearly shows that populism can have various and differently weighted causes that differ from region to region. Various strategies are needed to counter populism. To fully understand the effects of populism, it is important to note that populist (archaeological) interpretations are always driven by claims to power (Bernbeck: Chapter 12). Such interpretations simplify, certain aspects and narratives are omitted or added, and interpretations are manipulated or conspiracy theories spread according to the respective ideology. Therefore, we should always generate critical integration and thus also complex narratives (Ayán Vila: Chapter 5). That human societies are complex is not up for debate.

This is certainly one of the big challenges for the future. Not only archaeological contexts are simplified and claimed for certain narratives; in many other areas, complex facts are not only simplified by significant omissions but are also falsified. In many cases prejudices exist that we should expose as (unfounded) biases. To counteract this, we must therefore invest in education—at all levels. In archaeology, this means that we need to teach students to understand the entanglements of archaeology and politics. Students need to learn to make complex archaeological contexts fascinating, telling small and big narratives that are interesting to the community or communities, and involve them in the process of gaining knowledge.

Overall, I would like to emphasize once again that all the chapters are inspiring and diverse. This is what makes it so difficult to make forward-looking statements. It also becomes clear that there is no universal silver bullet for a successful community archaeology, certainly not in these times of growing populism, nationalism, neoliberalism, and neocolonialism as well as sprawling capitalism. Moreover, the regional political–social framework conditions are highly diverse, so hardly any successful strategy can be transferred without modifications to other regions. There is quite an overlap in the archaeological topics discussed, and some aspects crop up again and again. Nevertheless, the preconditions and options for action are different. Above all, the archaeologists involved are different. They have—despite a broad and deep consensus on a basic political stance—varying basic attitudes and approaches to goal-oriented community archaeology. This may seem limiting at first glance but is in fact the great benefit of this book. Readers can adopt or develop their own strategies for their projects from those employed in the variety of challenging and obstacle-laden projects in community archaeology in these times of populism described in this book. I believe archaeologists must face the dangers and challenges of their field in the current global political situation, take a (political) position, and look for good ways to involve diverse communities in their projects. That is an important aspect for the future.

One essential argument to counter populism is the constant advocacy of basic democratic values, human rights, and tolerance and acceptance of the diversity of communities. Another is community participation in archaeology as well as engagement in social and political processes to counter populism, misanthropy, and exclusion in order to expose prejudices and blanket statements. Education and awareness raising is essential in this regard. As a result, different perceptions and perspectives on history and, thus, different narratives can exist side by side; archaeology also plays a crucial role in this. Continuous engagement and tolerance are certainly the basic prerequisites for successful cooperation with communities.

Acknowledgments

I would like to express my sincere thanks to Niall Brady and Daniel McNaughton for their critical comments and support with the English translation.

References Cited

Barth, Fredrik. 1969. Introduction. In *Ethnic Groups and Boundaries: The Social Organisation of Culture Difference,* edited by Fredrik Barth, pp. 9–38. Universitetsforlaget, Bergen.

Diepenbroek, Marta, Christina Amory, Harald Niederstätter, Bettina Zimmermann, Maria Szargut, Grażyna Zielińska, Arne Dür, et al. 2021. Genetic and Phylogeographic Evidence for Jewish Holocaust Victims at the Sobibór Death Camp. *Genome Biology* 22: 200. https://doi.org/10.1186/s13059-021-02420-0#.

Elwert, Georg. 1995. Boundaries, Cohesion, and Switching. On We-Groups in Ethnic, National, and Religious Forms. *Bulletin l'APAD* 10: 1–16. https://doi.org/10.4000/apad.1111.

Köhler, E. Christiana. 2020. Of Culture Wars and the Clash of Civilizations in Prehistoric Egypt—An Epistemological Analysis. *Ägypten und Levante [Egypt and the Levant]* 30: 115–117.

CONTRIBUTORS

Xurxo Ayán Vila is the main researcher of the Portuguese Foundation for Science and Technology in the Institute of Contemporary History (NOVA University of Lisbon). He is the coauthor of *Arqueología: Una introducción a la materialidad del pasado* [Archaeology: An introduction to the Materiality of the past] (2019), and he is the author of the archaeological ethnography *San Lorenzo ven a nos: Memorias dun castro galego* [Saint Lawrence come to us: Memories of a Galician Hillfort] (2020).

Reinhard Bernbeck is a professor at Freie Universität Berlin [Free University Berlin], Germany. He is the author of *Materielle Spuren des nationalsozialistischen Terrors,* and he is the coeditor of *Ideologies in Archaeology* and *Subjects and Narratives in Archaeology.*

Felipe Criado-Boado is a professor of research at the CSIC (Spanish National Research Council). He is the director of its Institute of Heritage Sciences (INCIPIT), and he was recognized with the Spanish National Research Award 2024.

Cristóbal Gnecco is a professor of anthropology at the Universidad del Cauca, Colombia. His recent publications include *El tiempo de las ruinas, Políticas patrimoniales y procesos de despojo y violencia en Latinoamérica,* and *El Señuelo patrimonial: Pensamientos postarqueológicos en el Camino de los Incas.*

Alfredo González-Ruibal is a senior researcher at the Institute of Heritage Sciences of the Spanish National Research Council. He is the author of *An Archaeology of the Contemporary Era.*

Rachael Kiddey is a lecturer in heritage and museum studies at the School of Society and Culture, University of Plymouth, United Kingdom. She is the author of *Homeless Heritage: Collaborative Social Archaeology as Therapeutic Practice.*

Chao Tayiana Maina is the founder of African Digital Heritage and a cofounder of the Museum of British Colonialism. In 2023 she was awarded a Dan David Prize for her pioneering work in digital public history in Kenya.

Anthony Maina works with the National Museums of Kenya, based in Murang'a County. He is a leading expert on Mau Mau heritage and has consulted and collaborated on numerous research projects and media productions.

Patricia A. McAnany is a Kenan Eminent Professor of Anthropology at the University of North Carolina at Chapel Hill, and recipient of the A. V. Kidder Award. She is the author or coauthor of many books and articles, including most recently *Ciencia y Saberes de Cenotes Yucatecos*.

Laura McAtackney is a professor in archaeology and at the Radical Humanities Laboratory at University College Cork, Ireland, and she is a professor of heritage studies at Aarhus University, Denmark. She is the coeditor of the *Routledge Handbook of the Northern Ireland Conflict and Peace*.

Randall H. McGuire is a SUNY Distinguished Professor of Anthropology at Binghamton University. His latest edited volumes include *The Border and Its Bodies: The Embodiment of the Risk along the US–México Line* and *Walling In and Walling Out: Why Are We Building New Barriers to Divide Us?*

Hannah McLean is a postgraduate research student at the University of Glasgow studying memory and materiality in British colonial detention camps in Kenya.

Lindsay Martel Montgomery is an associate professor of anthropology and Indigenous studies at the University of Toronto. She is author of *A History of Mobility in New Mexico: Mobile Landscapes and Persistent Places,* and she is the coauthor of *Objects of Survivance: A Material History of the American Indian School Experience* and *Archaeological Theory in Dialogue: Situating Relationality, Ontology, Posthumanism, and Indigenous Paradigms*.

Gabriel Moshenska is an associate professor of public archaeology at the UCL Institute of Archaeology. He is the author of *Material Cultures of Childhood in Second World War Britain,* and he is the editor of *Teaching and Learning the Archaeology of the Contemporary Era* and *Key Concepts in Public Archaeology*.

Andrea Potts is a postgraduate research student at the University of Brighton. Her research focuses on representations and receptions of European colonialism in contemporary museums.

Beth Rebisz is a lecturer in history at the University of Bristol. Her research focuses on African history including studies of counterinsurgency, gender and women's history in Africa, and the heritage of British colonialism.

Claudia Theune is a professor of historical archaeology at the University of Vienna. An overview of her research has been published in the book *A Shadow of War: Archaeological Approaches to Uncovering the Darker Sides of Conflict from the 20th Century.* She is the author of "Sobibor and Other Nazi Extermination Sites: A Contextualisation of the Object," (in *Excavating Sobibor: Holocaust Archaeology Between Heritage, History and Memory,* ed. by Martjin Eickhoff, Erik Somers, and Jelke Take). A current research project deals with the contextualization of the find assemblages of different Nazi terror sites.

Ruth M. Van Dyke is a professor of anthropology at Binghamton University. She is the author or editor of six books, including *The Chaco Experience: Landscape and Ideology at the Center Place, Archaeologies of Memory,* and *The Greater Chaco Landscape: Ancestors, Scholarship, and Advocacy.*

INDEX

Cultural Heritage Studies

Edited by Katherine Hayes, University of Minnesota

www.ingramcontent.com/pod-product-compliance
Lightning Source LLC
Chambersburg PA
CBHW031414270326
41929CB00010BA/1448